# AROUND THE WORLD
# IN 2,000 PICTURES

*Trans-Canada DC-8*

*Grace Line Santa Rosa*

*Sabena Helicopter*

*Norwegian American Oslofjord*

*Alitalia DC-8 at Fiumicino*

*Swedish American Kungsholm*

*BOAC 707 at Idlewild*

*Italian Line Leonardo Da Vinci*

*Furness Ocean Monarch*

*Air France Caravelle*      *Cunard Queen Elizabeth*

# AROUND THE WORLD

# IN 2,000 PICTURES

"AROUND THE WORLD" AND "AROUND

THE U. S. A." NOW IN ONE VOLUME

## Edited by A. MILTON RUNYON
## and VILMA F. BERGANE

### 20 MAPS BY RAFAEL PALACIOS

## DOUBLEDAY & COMPANY, INC.
### Garden City, N.Y.

Lufthansa 707

Holland-America Rotterdam

Qantas 707

French Railroads Mistral

Pan American 707

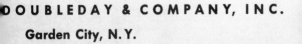

Incres Line Victoria

### ACKNOWLEDGMENTS

The editors wish to thank *The New York Times* and
the authors for permission to reprint the following
articles, copyright 1954 by *The New York Times:
New England,* by John H. Fenton; *The Midsouth,* by
Stacy V. Jones; *The South,* by John Popham; *The
Midwest,* by Richard J. H. Johnston; *The Plains
States,* by Seth S. King; *The Rocky Mountains,* by
Marshall Sprague; *The Southwest,* and *Southern Cali-
fornia,* by Gladwin Hill; *California — The Golden
Gate,* by Lawrence E. Davies; *The Northwest,* by
Richard L. Neuberger. All other rights in these articles
are specifically reserved to the authors.

# CONTENTS

# THE LURE OF WORLD TRAVEL
## by Richard Joseph

In the catalog of man's dreams, taking a trip around the world ranks with making a million dollars, being elected President of the United States or inheriting a South Sea island. It's the ultimate travel experience, and next to it even the most fabulous junket fades into insignificance.

Like so many dreams, a world-tour can become a reality for only a comparatively few people, even though you can now fly around the world for about two thousand dollars, and one airline already is promoting round-the-world flights for the two-week vacationist. Nevertheless the odds are still strongly against your visiting most of the places covered in the following pages.

That being the case, this book is a working substitute for a trip around the world. The well-over-a-thousand pictures which follow will give you many of the sights and evoke some of the sounds, smells, tastes and moods of those far-away places with the fabulous names. They cover all the free world outside the limits of the fifty U. S. states which can be reached conveniently by American pleasure travelers. You'll sense some of the space of the far Pacific, see the breeze rustling the leaves of the palm trees of Sumatra, smell the

*Mr. Joseph is Travel Editor of* Esquire Magazine *and author of* RICHARD JOSEPH'S GUIDE TO EUROPE AND THE MEDITERRANEAN, RICHARD JOSEPH'S WORLD WIDE MONEY CONVERTER AND TIPPING GUIDE, and RICHARD JOSEPH'S GUIDE TO THE PACIFIC.

delicate fragrance of jasmine tea handed you in a fragile cup by a geisha girl in Kyoto. You will feel the life pulsating through the pack-jammed sampans in Hong Kong harbor, absorb the peace of a Buddhist shrine in Thailand, understand the loneliness of Africa's vast open places, and come back to the world you know in the street scenes of western Europe.

The photographs are arranged in a number of tours, following the same itineraries a traveler would take in seeing the world in a series of different trips. And they've been chosen to give you the best possible idea of what you'd actually see on your world travels rather than dealing with impossibly remote spots or esoteric subjects available to the correspondent and professional photographer but not to the average pleasure traveler.

That's why you'll see many pictures of ordinary people the world

7

over, but none of political leaders or celebrities of any sort. The photos will reveal to you the usual life of the various countries of the world; they won't take you for a weekend at the country home of an Indian Maharajah or English Viscount, backstage at a rehearsal of the *Folies Bergère* or between the spokes of a wheel in a tractor factory.

The things you'll see in these pictures, in other words, are the things you'd really see on a tour of the world. And the pictures are the same sort of pictures that can be and frequently are taken by the average traveler (I've been able to contribute quite a few myself), although they've been carefully selected for subject interest and photographic excellence. The editors have screened out the fuzzy prints, and the shots of Grandma with the doorman of the Grande Hotel; nevertheless you'll recognize photos of some of the places you've been to as duplicates of some of the better pictures you've taken yourself.

That, for me, is one of the charms of the book, the identification the traveler will feel for many of the pictures he'll see. This volume really has a three-fold attraction: it will give the intending traveler a preview of some of the fantastic things he'll see in various parts of the globe, it will treat the man who has been there to some wonderfully nostalgic memories of what he's seen and experienced, and it will give the armchair traveler a knowledge of the world and an intimate feeling of having been to most of the colorful places on earth.

There's a proverb, allegedly ancient Chinese, to the effect that *"The world is a book, and he who stays at home reads only one page."* Read all the pages of this book, though, and you will have seen the world.

# GREAT BRITAIN AND IRELAND

Going by an English ship is perhaps the best introduction to Britain because you are surrounded by English tradition and atmosphere as soon as you step aboard. But there are plenty of delightful ways to get to England. Some ships put you off by tender at Plymouth, others dock at Liverpool, many at the great port of Southampton for the short train ride to London. If you're going to Ireland, take a ship that lands you at Cobh.

Flying across the Atlantic has its delights, too. You can go direct to Shannon or Dublin, for Ireland, to Glasgow for Scotland, to Manchester or London for England.

When you get there, hiring one of the easy-to-manage English cars is an excellent way to get about because the distances are so short. You'll readily get used to driving on the "wrong" side of the road, and you'll find many charming places for "tea" and for overnight stops. If you prefer, England is well covered by the British Railways network, and there are good bus lines. Most distances are too short for air travel, but the plane from London to Dublin avoids a possibly rough crossing of the 130-mile-wide Irish Sea. And the Channel Islands are most easily reached by plane from Gatwick airport.

The greatest appeal of England to many Americans is the great abundance of historic "things you've heard about" . . . Shakespeare's Stratford-on-Avon, the great mystery of Stonehenge, Westminster Abbey, the Houses of Parliament and Big Ben, the Tower of London, the Lake Country beloved of the poets, changing of the guard at Buckingham Palace, Peter Pan in Kensington Gardens, and Eros in Piccadilly. With the accession to the throne of young Elizabeth II, royalty has taken on new glamor. Theater is at its best in Lon-

don, and there is fine music, great collections of art. Golfers find historic links in Scotland. Cricket, soccer and horseracing are the great spectator sports.

England is but 500 miles long, and so narrow that it is nowhere possible to be as much as one hundred miles from the sea. The climate, affected by the Gulf Stream, is temperate. Visitors sometimes complain about excessive rainfall, but the abundant showers account for the rich green lawns, lush meadows, profuse flowers.

England's highest "mountain" is the 3210-foot pinnacle of Scafell Pike. Scotland does a bit better, with its Highland peak of Ben Nevis, at 4406 feet, and several others topping four thousand feet. The highest in Wales is the 3560-foot pinnacle of Snowdon. Ireland's Slieve Donard rises 2796 feet above sea level.

You'll find fascinating contrasts throughout the British Isles. Scotland's "Caledonia stern and wild" looks very different from the cozy fields and picturesque villages of England. Brick is the prevailing material for building in England; Scotland's buildings are mostly of solid stone. There are great differences in language — clipped, quick English talk, Scottish voices that are broad and rough, the rich, musical voices of Wales — probably greeting you in Welsh, the brogue of Ireland.

The photo tour of the British Isles, on the following pages, emphasizes the great cities of London, Liverpool, Edinburgh, Belfast, and Dublin, but it also takes you to the charming university towns of Oxford and Cambridge, and the walled city of Chester with its unique "Rows." You'll visit England's lovely Lake District, the hills and glens and lochs of Scotland, many interesting by-ways of Wales, the rugged seacoasts of Northern Ireland, and finally the varied scenic treasures of Ireland.

**Great Britain and Ireland**

*Atlantic Ocean*

*North Sea*

*Irish Sea*

*English Channel*

LONDON

HYDE PARK
GREEN PARK
ST. JAMES'S PARK
THAMES RIVER

1 TOWER BRIDGE
2 TOWER OF LONDON
3 BUCKINGHAM PALACE
4 PICCADILLY CIRCUS
5 TRAFALGAR SQUARE
6 BRITISH MUSEUM
7 ST. PAUL'S CATHEDRAL
8 WESTMINSTER ABBEY
9 HOUSES OF PARLIAMENT

SCOTLAND
Inverness
TROSSACHS
LOCH LOMOND
Glasgow  Edinburgh
GIANT'S CAUSEWAY

Londonderry
NORTHERN IRELAND
Belfast

Durham
LAKE DISTRICT
Windermere
York

IRELAND
Dublin
ARAN ISLANDS
SHANNON R.

ENGLAND
Llandudno  Liverpool
Rhyl  Chester
Caernarvon
WALES
Aberystwyth

Norwich
Ely
Cambridge
Colchester
Stratford-on-Avon
Oxford  London
COTSWOLD HILLS  THAMES R.
Salisbury  Canterbury
Brighton
Exeter
ISLE OF WIGHT

FRANCE

Scale of Miles
0  20  60  100

**LOVERS SIT BY THE THAMES, ON TOWER WALK, BESIDE THE BRIDGE.**

11

**Westminster Abbey** has been the setting for the coronation of English monarchs from the year 1066, which saw the crowning of Harold II, last of the Saxon kings, and William the Conqueror, down to the recent coronation of Elizabeth II. The Abbey, officially called *Collegiate Church* *of St. Peter in Westminster,* is one of the finest examples of Early English architecture in England. Poets' Corner (Longfellow is the only American poet included) is one of the high spots for visitors. Another is Henry VII's magnificent chapel. The third is the old Coronation Chair.

**Buckingham Palace** is residence of the Royal Family in London. When the Queen is there, the changing of guard ceremony takes place every other day at 10:30 a.m.

**The Houses of Parliament,** by the Thames, with Big Ben in the tower make the most celebrated landmark in England. Probably you've heard chimes of Big Ben by radio.

Photos: British Travel Association

13

**St. James's Palace** was built by Henry VIII in 1532. Changing of the guard ceremony takes place here when Queen is not in residence at Buckingham Palace.

**10 Downing Street** is the home of Prime Minister, equivalent of U.S. White House.

**Chelsea Arts Ball** at Royal Albert Hall, New Year's Eve, is England at its gayest.

**The Tower Bridge** spans the Thames just below the Tower of London. The great towers, joined by latticed footbridges, make it most impressive of the bridges.

**Tower of London,** guarded by the famous beefeaters, is a "must" for all visitors.

**Crown Jewels,** on display in the Tower, include the biggest diamond in existence.

**The Orb of England** and the Queen's Orb are among historic regalia in the display.

**St. Paul's Cathedral,** Renaissance master-piece of Sir Christopher Wren, stands on summit of Ludgate Hill, a landmark for miles. Visit the "whispering gallery."

**Hyde Park** has an area of 361 acres. Together with Kensington Gardens it makes a continuous park of more than 600 acres, favorite place for mass meetings.

**Crowds of workers** cross London Bridge on foot or by bus, on way to their shops and offices. Peak hour for the thousands of travelers is from 8:30 to 9:15 a.m.

Photos: British Travel Association; bottom, Henri Cartier-Bresson (Magnum)

**Trafalgar Square,** seen through terrace columns of the National Gallery, is a favorite site for political demonstrations. On south side towers Nelson Monument.

**Library in the House of Lords** contains works of legal and historical character.

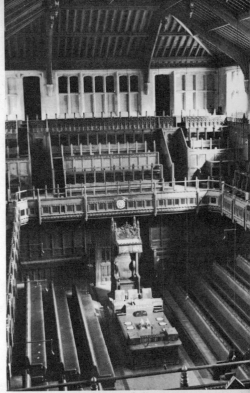

**Chamber of the House of Commons,** rebuilt in same style after 1941 bombing.

**The British Museum** is unrivaled for the variety of its exhibits, Elgin Marbles,

Rosetta Stone, one of four copies of the Magna Charta, four-million-book library.

# England LONDON

**Ceremony of Trooping the Color** is held at the Horse Guards Parade, Whitehall.

**When you've lost your car,** or your way, ask the policeman at Piccadilly Circus.

**Madame Tussaud's** Exhibition of Waxworks attracts many visitors including the

Pan American stewardess shown here looking at the tableau of Henry VIII.

Photos: William E. Reinhardt, Jr.; top right, Henri Cartier-Bresson (Magnum); bottom, British Travel Association

**Piccadilly Circus** is one of city's best-known features. It's a circle formed by the junction of five streets. The statue of Eros stands atop the central fountain.

Photo: British Travel Association

**Hampton Court Palace,** for over two centuries a royal residence, was started in 1514 by Cardinal Wolsey. Visit celebrated Maze in the gardens, the picture gallery.

**The Knights of the Garter Procession** enters St. George's Chapel, Windsor—a building of which it has been said, "Such perfection is scarcely of this world."

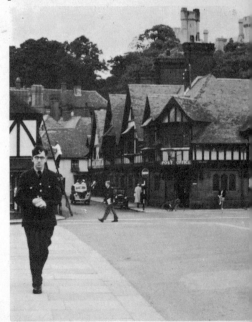

**Through Henry VIII's** gateway at Windsor Castle, we watch the royal guard.

**Arundel, Sussex,** is on a hillside below the twelfth-century Arundel Castle.

Photos: British Travel Association; bottom left,
A. Milton Runyon; bottom right, Charles Marschalek

**Oxford University** has 21 colleges for men, 4 for women. It dates back to 12th century. High Street is known to Oxford grads all over the world as "The High."

**Christ Church,** familiarly known as "the House," is the largest college in Oxford.

**Magdalen Tower,** bell-tower of Magdalen College, is setting of May Morning Hymn.

Photos: British Travel Association

**The "Backs"** are the lovely tree-shaded grounds on left bank of the River Cam.

**Cambridge University,** on the River Cam, is the other great seat of learning.

**St. John's College,** founded 1511, is one of the 20 colleges; 2 are for women.

**On way to Cambridge,** visit Audley End, palatial Jacobean Renaissance mansion.

**Boating,** or "punting," on the Cam is one of the delights of idyllic Cambridge.

**Stratford-on-Avon** was the birthplace, in 1564, of William Shakespeare. It at- tracts some 100,000 visitors a year, is near enough London for a day's visit.

**Shakespeare's birthplace** was originally part of a long row of terrace cottages.

**Anne Hathaway's cottage,** birthplace of Shakespeare's wife has thatched roof.

Photos: Richard Joseph; bottom, British Travel Association

**Shakespeare Memorial Theatre** is large, modern, seems out of keeping with the rest of Stratford, but is well suited to fine presentation of bard's great plays.

**This view** from Warwick Castle indicates charm of this medieval baronial castle.

**Tintern Abbey,** founded by Cistercians in 1131, is now romantic, roofless ruin.

**Canterbury,** one of most revered shrines, has been called "The Mother City of the Anglo-Saxon Race." Splendid cathedral begun in 1070, was completed in 1503

Canterbury was stormed by Julius Caesar. War bombings uncovered Roman ruins.

Visitors to Canterbury pass through the city gates, follow route of pilgrims of old.

Mermaid Row in Rye is peaceful English scene that attracts visitors and artists.

Knole, one of finest baronial mansions, has 365 rooms, is now open to visitors.

Oast houses, these odd conelike structures in Penshurst, are used for drying hops.

Dover Castle was built in 12th century by Henry II. Nearby is Roman lighthouse.

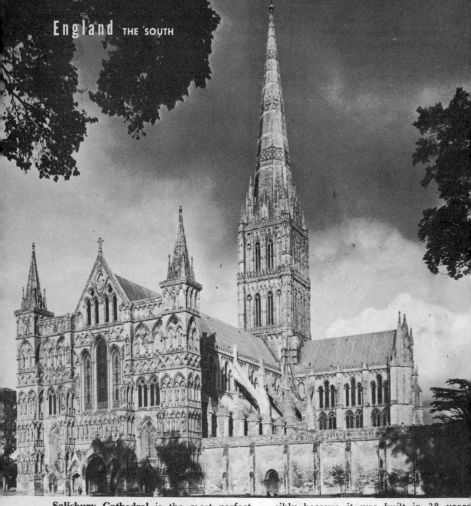

**Salisbury Cathedral** is the most perfect realization of pure English Gothic, possibly because it was built in 38 years with the 404-foot steeple added later

**Stonehenge**, a mass of stones set on end, is one of Britain's greatest curiosities.

**Druid ceremony** at dawn on Midsummer Day is one of the rituals held regularly

Photos: British Travel Association

**Brighton,** one hour by electric train from London, is England's largest and most famous seaside resort. Often crowded, it is referred to as "London by the Sea."

**Winchester,** with its red brick Georgian buildings, has true English personality.

**Once capital** of kingdom, Winchester is famous for its cathedral and its school.

**The Isle of Wight** is just off the south coast, below Southampton. The town of Ventnor, built on terraces above the sea, is one of the best-known health resorts.

Photos: Winchester by Richard Joseph; others by British Travel Association

**Exeter,** County town of Devon, has enough historic buildings to give you the feeling that it's one of the traditional centers of the lovely West of England.

**Ancient Guild Hall** in Exeter has pillared façade projecting over the sidewalk.

**Royal Clarence Hotel,** near Exeter Cathedral, has old-fashioned, quiet charm.

**Clovelly,** delightfully situated in a narrow rift in the cliffs of north Devon, descends in steps to a little cove. The picturesque houses have green trim.

**Menabilly** is home of Daphne du Maurier, author of *Jamaica Inn* and *Rebecca*.

**Chapel of Gyllyngdune,** in Falmouth, is said to be the smallest church in England.

**In typical country "pubs"** you'll find a darts game in progress most of the time.

English "pubs" have taken on many of the American "country store" qualities.

Photos: William E. Reinhardt, Jr.; center left, Doubleday; center right, Richard Joseph, bottom, Robert Capa (Magnum)

**Fifteenth-century George Inn,** Norton St. Philip, in Somerset, is called "the oldest licensed house in England." It's like hundreds of other country "pubs."

**Somerset's** lush fields make dairying a major industry. Its cheeses are famous.

**Broadway,** pretty village in Cotswold hills, is home of many artists, writers.

Photos: Richard Joseph

One of the show places of Hertfordshire s Hatfield House, Jacobean mansion built for Robert Cecil, Earl of Salisbury, Secretary of State to Queen Elizabeth.

The Norman town of Chepstow guards Vye River. This gate is part of old wall.

Wye Valley is one of the most beautiful corners of Britain, with Forest of Dean.

**Ely Cathedral** dominates the treeless fens for miles around. The striking West Tower, except for its octagonal top and turrets, is of Transition Norman period.

**In Tolleshunt D'Arcy** is home of Margery Allingham, famous for mystery novels.

**Norwich,** capital of Norfolk, is an ancient city with many beautiful houses.

Photos: British Travel Association; bottom left, A. Milton Runyon; bottom right, Richard Joseph

The Norfolk Broads, an area of shallow lagoons and placid streams, are near Norwich.

Colchester High Street was thoroughfare of the first Roman colony in Britain.

This gateway is all that's left of 11th-century Benedictine Abbey of St. John.

"Norwich Mercury" is said to be oldest English paper still using original name.

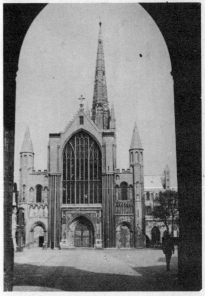

Norwich Cathedral is majestic structure, with graceful, tapering 313-ft. spire.

**York Minster** is largest of England's medieval cathedrals. Its chief glory is its stained glass, contained in 120 windows. Most famous are West and "Five Sisters."

**York** has maze of narrow streets with names like Shambles (above), Gillygate, Whip-ma-whop-ma-gate. The city walls with four gates, are mostly 14th century

**The Royal Scot,** British Railways' famous express, ascends Shap Fell, Westmoreland, the longest gradient and highest point on the run between London and Scotland.

**Hadrian's Wall,** seen here at Housesteads, was built by Romans in second century.

**Haworth, Yorkshire,** was the Vicarage home of the celebrated Brontë family.

**Durham Cathedral** contains coffin of St. Cuthbert, carried on famous wanderings.

**Harrowgate,** high on Yorkshire moors, in center of England, is a beautiful resort.

**The Anglican Cathedral** at Liverpool is one of the most modern churches, under construction since 1904. When completed, it will be the fourth largest in the world.

**Liverpool** has 6 miles of docks. Several of transatlantic ships land you there.

**The swashbuckling** John of Gaunt built one of the gateways in Lancaster Castle.

Photos: British Travel Association

**Chester,** with its well-preserved walls, is most medieval-looking town in England.

**Steps** give easy access to the walls, and you can walk along them for two miles.

**"The Rows"** are unique Chester feature: arcades, built high to avoid muddy roads.

They form continuous passage from shop to shop without going down to the street.

Photos: Richard Joseph

**Ullswater,** second in size, is said to be grandest of the English lakes in scenery.

**Buttermere** is one of the smaller lakes. There are 16 lakes, in 35 square miles.

**Windermere,** the largest lake, is ten miles long, so narrow it looks like a river.

Hugh Walpole set his Herries saga here; home also of Keats, Shelley, Wordsworth.

42

Photos: British Travel Association; bottom, Richard Joseph

**The hamlet of Seatoller** is one of the charming Cumberland villages that are best appreciated on a walking tour. Make your headquarters at a place like Keswick.

**Grasmere,** one of Lakeland's loveliest, was for 14 years the home of William Wordsworth. Visit Dove Cottage, where he lived, and the Wordsworth Museum.

**Eton boys:** You tell their standing by whether their collars are "turned down."

**At Epsom Downs,** the "Derby" and "Oaks" attract the fashionable crowds.

**Chimney sweep** of Lancaster might have stepped right out of a Dickens' novel.

**Oxford student** is one of 8,000 undergrads. There are 590 teachers, called fellows.

Photos: British Travel Association; top right, Richard Joseph

**DAILY CHANGING OF THE GUARD AT EDINBURGH CASTLE IS COLORFUL.**

# SCOTLAND MEANS HILLS AND HISTORY

When you talk of Scotland, some people think of Bobbie Burns, some think of Mary, Queen of Scots, and some of Ben Hogan's victory at Carnoustie. For Scotland is a land of great diversity, of great cities like Edinburgh and Glasgow, of hills and lochs, of poets and novelists and golfers, of unwavering national pride.

Photo: Richard Joseph

**From Scott Monument** in Princes Street, Sir Walter's statue looks across the city. The climb to the top is 287 steps, but you get a magnificent view on four sides.

**Princes Street** forms a valley down the middle of Edinburgh. On one side is old town, from great rock of Edinburgh castle to Holyroodhouse. Other side is new city.

Photos: British Travel Association

**At Holyrood Palace** tragic Mary, Queen of Scots, lived and ruled during 16th century. Old town between the castle and palace is called the Royal Mile.

**Behind the National Gallery** looms the great Castle Rock. From castle battlements you get a superb view of the city and the Forth River in the distance.

Photos: British Travel Association

# Scotland

**Glasgow** is the largest city in Scotland and the second largest in Great Britain.

**Biggest Glasgow industry** is shipbuilding John Brown's built Cunard's two *Queens*

**Loch Lomond,** 23 miles long, is "Queen of the Scottish Lochs." Trossachs tour takes you between Glasgow and Edinburgh by Loch Lomond, Loch Katrine.

Photos: Richard Joseph; top right, Maurice Greenberg (Black Star); bottom, British Travel Association

**Abbotsford** is Sir Walter Scott's estate, across from the tweed-milling town of Galashiels, south of Edinburgh. Scott lived in this baronial mansion till 1832.

**Loch Lomond steamer** heads north from Inversnaid, between bonnie, bonnie banks.

**The Forth Bridge,** near Edinburgh, a mile long, took seven years to build, in 1880's.

Photos: British Travel Association;
bottom left, Alleyne M. Runyon

49

# Scotland

**Dancing** is an important part of Scottish gatherings, where kilted males compete.

**Skirl of bagpipes** is a familiar sound. Reed wind instruments' origin is unknown.

**If you come** by ship direct to Scotland, tender takes you up Clyde to Glasgow.

**Bagpipe band** celebrates the arrival of *Britannic*. You won't forget eerie sound.

**CAERNARVON CASTLE WAS KEY FORTRESS IN THE WELSH CAMPAIGNS.**

# WALES IS LAND OF COAL, CONTRAST

If you read *How Green Was My Valley* by Richard Llewellyn, or saw the picture, you have some idea of this land of twisting roads, craggy mountains, of hard-working, song-loving people. You won't forget the beauty of Welsh choral singing when you've heard it in a country chapel. Song climax is annual Eisteddfod.

# Wales

**Llandudno** is a beach town on a peninsula at the northern tip of Wales. Planned a

**Elan Valley reservoir** at Aberystwyth .is in one of many green valleys of Wales.

**Aberystwyth** is west coast's big resort, with castle on rock jutting out to sea.

century ago, and laid out beautifully, it has mountains of Snowdonia as backdrop.

**Welsh children** turn out in their gayest costumes for Eisteddfod at Llangollen.

**Good place** for hiking is road from Barmouth to Dolgelley, where curfew rings.

**St. David's Cathedral,** Pembrokeshire, has none of Salisbury's lofty grace, but its low pitched roofs and square tower are in keeping with its bleak village. On the inside, the austerity changes to elaborate, almost Moorish ornamentation.

# NORTHERN IRELAND GAVE THE U.S. TEN PRESIDENTS

**CITY HALL LOOKS DOWN DONEGALL PLACE, BELFAST'S MAIN STREET.**

One reason why Northern Ireland will probably seem so familiar to you is that so many Ulster emigrants have come to the United States. Of the 33 men who have been Presidents, from George Washington to Dwight Eisenhower, at least ten are claimed to be of Ulster ancestry. Northern Ireland may be reached by boat or plane from Glasgow to Belfast, direct by plane from London. If you're coming up from Ireland, it's an easy trip by plane, train, bus or driving in your own car.

Photo: British Travel Association

55

# Northern Ireland

**Carrickfergus Castle** is one of the best preserved Norman castles in the world.

**There's wild country,** and farmlands with hedges dividing them into tiny tracts.

**Northern Ireland** Parliament Buildings are situated atop hillside at Stormont.

**Stormont Castle** houses Prime Minister and certain departments of government.

**Fair Head** is the most northerly point in County Antrim. Nearby is the interesting

Ballygalley Castle Hotel, a part of which dates back as far as the 17th century.

**The Giant's Causeway** is the greatest scenic attraction in Northern Ireland.

Legend says these great basalt rocks once formed causeway across sea to Scotland.

Photo: British Travel Association

# Northern Ireland

**Dunluce Castle** is near Portrush and Port Stewart which have wonderful beaches.

**Londonderry City** is 75 miles from Belfast. This is Shipquay Gate, Guild Hall.

**Bangor,** County Down, is historic town that has become a favorite sea resort.

**Belfast Castle** is one of city's many sights: Art Gallery, Museum, University.

**Because it has** a seacoast of 245 miles and many rivers, lakes and tideways, Northern Ireland has an abundance of boating, and some magnificent fishing.

58

# IRELAND INVITES YOU TO "COME BACK TO ERIN"

We mentioned the number of emigrants who had come from Northern Ireland to the U.S.A., and that's probably even more true of Ireland itself. As you walk down the street, you'll often think you recognize someone, because the second, third and fourth cousins in America look just like the folks back home. You'll find Ireland a peaceful land whose pastoral scenes, green fields and hills, and soft mists will calm your nerves.

Getting to Ireland can be fun. Maybe you'll land at Cobh from your transatlantic steamer, or touch down in your plane at Shannon Airport, busiest center of international air traffic in the world. Gayest trip is from London on the Irish Mail, leaving London at tea time. About 11 p.m. you board a trim little ship at Holyhead, and sleep until you arrive at Dun Laoghaire, a few minutes from Dublin, the next morning. Or you can fly from London to Dublin by Aer Lingus.

All in all, you'll find St. Patrick's Island one of the friendliest nations to visit, even if you don't win a Sweeps!

**O'CONNELL STREET SHOPPERS SET URBAN PACE UNIQUE IN IRELAND.**

Photo: Fogra Failte

**Ireland**

**The Custom House,** on the northern bank
of the River Liffey, between O'Connell
Bridge and the sea, was built in 179
from designs by James Gandon, Ireland'

most gifted architect. One of Dublin's finest public buildings, it ranks among the most beautiful in Europe. Burned in 1921, it has been completely restored.

Photo: Fogra Failte

**An Tostal** is Ireland's traditional festival, held each Spring. Here is a floral float passing the Presidential Dais and reviewing stand at the General Post Office

**Royal Dublin Society Horse Show** is a high spot of the Dublin social season.

**Arus Mhic Diarmuida** is the ultra-modern bus terminal of Ireland Transport Co

Photos: Fogra Failte

**County Sligo** combines wild seacoast with rolling plains, mountains like Benweeskin.

**Garravogue River** drains Lough Gill into sea. On its south bank is town of Sligo.

**Hunting to hounds** is a most popular sport. These are Meath foxhounds, from north of Dublin. Other noted packs are Duhallow hounds, Tipperary foxhounds.

Photos: Fogra Failte

# Ireland

**Ireland's fertile fields** and pastures occupy more than half nation's working people.

**Tipperary** plays Kilkenny in Hurling, a Irish national sport for 3,000 year

**"Lips that touch** the Blarney stone will have the gift of gab," according to the Irish myth. Famous stone is at Blarney Castle, is bussed by thousands annually

Photo: Fogra Failt

**Glandore,** fishing village on a small inlet of the Atlantic, in the southern part of County Cork, has a population of 82, is noted for its delightfully mild climate.

Photo: Fogra Failte

# Ireland

**This Aran girl** lives on Inishmore, one of 3 Aran Islands, 28 mi. west of Galway.

**Aran Islanders** are rugged; not as primitive as shown in movie, *Man of Aran*

**Glendalough,** County Wicklow, means Glen of the Two Lakes. Thackeray called it "sweet, wild and sad even in sunshine." Visit the 6th-century St. Kevin Monastery

66

Photos: Fogra Failt

# SCANDINAVIA

The Scandinavian countries are a geographical unit, joined by many ties of language, race and religion. And yet the several countries, Norway, Sweden, Finland, Denmark, and Iceland, have many differences that make for delightful variety.

The first prehistoric cities of Scandinavia were founded by tall, blond Vikings who were not converted to Christianity until the year 1000. Wonderful relics of their art are to be found in the museums of Oslo, Stockholm and Copenhagen.

Scandinavia is easily reached by air from the U.S., with some flights offering free stopover privilege at Iceland. The Swedish American Line and Norwegian America Line offer direct service from New York to Scandinavian ports. From England, there is frequent service by sea and by air, and the same applies if you come from France or from the Benelux area or Germany. The *North Express* runs from Paris to Germany. Denmark, Norway, and Sweden; and the *Scandinavian-Italian Express* provides service between Rome and Switzerland, Germany, Denmark, and Sweden.

Shopping is delightful in Scandinavia, for designers and craftsmen take great pride in their work. All the countries maintain permanent exhibits of arts and crafts, where you can examine them at leisure. In Copenhagen, for instance, there is Den Permanente, located in the Vesterport, near the central railroad station, where you'll see products of famous Danish manufacturers side by side with those of village craftsmen. There is the famous Danish silverware, of course, and Danish porcelain, flax linens, pewter, toys.

Robert Capa's photo of a typical Norwegian harbor scene starts our tour of Scandinavia. We visit Oslo, Bergen, Stavanger, Trondheim, the mountains, and Norway's spectacular fjords. Crossing the

**Clear-weather views from air are superb.**

border to Sweden, we explore Stockholm and its environs, the famous Gota Canal, and get as far north as Swedish Lapland.

Crossing the Gulf of Bothnia, we come to Helsinki, capital of Finland—the brave country with a unique record: It is the only European country, bordering on the U.S.S.R. at the start of World War II, that is not now a part of the Soviet Union or behind the Iron Curtain. We see both traditional buildings and some of Finland's eye-catching modern architecture; we visit several resorts, and Finnish Lapland.

Next we come to the friendly country of Denmark, with its memories of Hans Christian Andersen. A dozen photos bring Copenhagen to life, and then we visit Odense, Regensen, Ribe, Randers, Aarhus, and the "Elsinore Castle" of Hamlet. Our tour of Scandinavia ends in Iceland, once under Norwegian and then Danish rule, but officially declared the Republic of Iceland on June 17, 1944. We see the nation's only city, Reykjavik, and one of the steep waterfalls, Gullfoss, which occur frequently in the country's icy rivers.

Photo: Konstantin Kostich

Arctic Ocean

ICELAND

Reykjavik

Miles 0 50 100

Atlantic Ocean

LOFOTEN ISLANDS

U.S.S.R.

LAPLAND

Rovaniemi

SWEDEN

Gulf of Bothnia

FINLAND

Trondheim

Turku
Helsinki

Bergen

NORWAY

Oslo

Stockholm

Stavanger

GÖTA CANAL

Skagerrak

Kattegat

U.S.S.R.

DENMARK

Aarhus

JUTLAND
Ribe

Odense

FYN

Elsinore
Copenhagen

ZEALAND

Baltic Sea

GERMANY

POLAND

S

Scale of Miles
0 50 100 150 200

Scandinavia

In Henningsvaer Harbor, Lofoten Islands, nearly 1000 fishing boats moor for week end.

# RUGGED NORWAY HAS MIDNIGHT SUN

Norway is a long, rangy country, with terrific distances, but you'll find the magnificent scenery worth the travel. People everywhere are friendly, from the cosmopolitan residents of Oslo to the Lapps of Nordland, "Land of the Midnight Sun." The fjords, deep inlets from sea, are nation's most spectacular sight.

Photo: Robert Capa (Magnum)

**Across Oslo harbor,** you see the new City Hall, inaugurated in 1950 during the city's 900th birthday celebrations. Fjor is the city's beautiful, sheltered harbor

**Statue of Henrik Ibsen,** famous for his plays, stands before the National Theater.

**Oslo University,** founded 1811, has beauti ful buildings. Also visit Nobel Institute

Photos: Norwegian National Travel Offic

Oslo is modern in design, with planned business and residential neighborhoods.

"Karl Johans Gate" is the main business street, from station to Royal Palace.

Oslo's parks are famous. This is flower market, in the city. Holmenkollen, in hills

behind town, gives a magnificent view. Bygdoy Museum has the *Kon-Tiki* raft.

# Norway

**Geiranger Fjord** is noted for the Pulpit, a rock promontory, Bridal Veil Falls.

**Trondheim** is Norway's 3rd city, seapo and gateway to north. This is marke

**Bergen,** Norway's 2nd largest city, has miles of docks, old Hanseatic buildings

dating from early 16th century when th League dominated the commercial life

Photos: Norwegian National Travel Office
top right, Burton Holmes (Ewing Galloway

**Jotunheim Mountains,** in south central Norway, are popular for hiking. Legend says these majestic mountains, with 8,097 ft. peak, are home of "Jotuns," or giants.

**Norwegian children** might have stepped out of the pages of *"Leif the Lucky."*

**Chair lift** at Krokkleiva outside Oslo gives mountain climbing thrill easy way.

**Heddel Stav church,** Telemark, is one of thirty 700- to 900-year-old timber churches.

**Market place at Stavanger:** This 8th-century city is one of Norway's oldest.

Photos: Norwegian National Travel Office

Stockholm's many waterways and canals give it the title of "the Venice of the North." At top right is City Hall, most magnificent modern building in Europe.

# SWEDEN OFFERS A GAY VÄLKOMMEN!

Sweden has everything to attract the tourist: it's the land of smörgasbord and wonderful things to eat; it shares marvelous scenery and such natural phenomena as the midnight sun with its neighbor, Norway; and happy, vigorous Swedes like visitors, make them welcome.

Photo: Swedish National Travel Office

**Royal Dramatic Theater** saw debuts of Greta Garbo, Ingrid Bergman, others.

**Stockholm's new office buildings,** close to Concert Hall, herald new era in city's life.

**Impressive Grand Hotel** is located at the fashionable resort of Saltsjöbaden in the Stockholm archipelago, about one hour's trip from the center of the city.

# Sweden

**Fiddlers** of Dalarna Province preserve charming customs and manner of dress.

**St. Lucia's Day,** December 13, is cele- brated by girls wearing candle crowns.

**Lapland** extends across the northern end of Norway, Sweden, Finland, and north-

**Sofia Girls** demonstrate their grace and rhythm at Jubilee celebration in Town Hall gardens. Swedes love to keep fit.

**Stout fishing boats** put out into Baltic

Photos: Swedish National Travel Office

west extremity of USSR. Mount Akka, in Swedish Lapland, is one of the most beautiful mountains in the country, with parts of it covered by eternal snows.

from Karlshamn port. Sport fishing is good.

**Regattas** in the Stockholm archipelago demonstrate skillful boat-handling of Swedish sailors, "born" with the knowledge.

# Sweden

**Arsta Railway Bridge,** Stockholm, frames the modern Southern General Hospital.

**View of Skeppsbron docks** shows many boats that go to coastal points, Finland.

**The Old City,** also called "The City between the Bridges," is the oldest part of Stockholm. It retains much of its medieval character and has many notable building.

**The Kvikkjokk region** of Lapland, with many lakes, rivers, has rich vegetation.

**Gota Canal** offers charming steamer trip, 350 miles, Gothenburg to Stockholm.

**THIS IS PARLIAMENT IN HELSINKI, "WHITE CITY OF THE NORTH."**

# FINLAND IS MODERN AND CORDIAL

Finland is known for its ultra-modern architecture, sunlit nights, beautiful scenery. Its people are blond, blue-eyed, and hospitable. If you want a vacation in an off-the-beaten-track country that offers some of the best facilities for comfort, your answer is Finland, a democratic republic that is ripe for discovery.

**Helsinki Stadium,** site of 1952 Olympic Games, shows sport-mindedness of Finns.

Although city is over 400 years old, it has largely been rebuilt in 20th century.

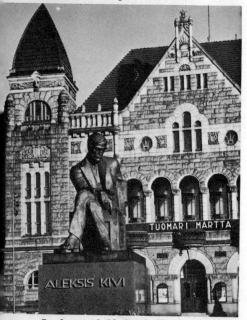

**In front of National Theater** is statue of Aleksis Kivi, 19th-century novelist.

**"Havis Amanda"** statue symbolizes "The Maid Helsinki rising from the waters."

**Rovaniemi,** capital of Finnish Lapland, is just south of the Arctic Circle. It is a winter-sports center and the trading and administrative center of that area.

**Pallastunturi Inn,** in Finnish Lapland, is good center for winter sports. There's skiing, hiking, hunting, salmon fishing. It's nearly 700 miles north of Helsinki.

**Reindeer** are frequent sight in Lapland; they pull a narrow sledge called *pulkka*.

**Lapp newlyweds** show colorful costumes, the men with white reindeer fur *peski*.

**Aulanko National Park** is top resort and recreation area. This is Hotel Aulanko.

**Olavinlinna Castle** is in East Finland's lake region at summer spa of Savonlinna.

**The Sauna,** famous Finnish steam bath, is fixture of every home and of many hotels.

**Vehoniemi Tourist Inn** is a delightful stopping place in south central Finland.

From here you can go by water bus through lake regions to Aulanko Park.

Photos: Finnish National Travel Office

**COPENHAGEN'S DANISH RENAISSANCE TOWN HALL WAS BUILT IN 1894.**

# OR FRIENDLINESS,
# OME TO DENMARK

Among the predominant characteristics of Denmark are friendliness, flowers and song. The nation consists of the peninsula of Jutland and some 500 islands, including the large ones of Fyn and Zealand, the island that contains the capital city of Copenhagen, often called with good reason "the Paris of Scandinavia."

83

# Denmark COPENHAGEN

**Gefion Fountain** is at beginning of Langelinie, delightful walk beside the sea.

**Statue of "The Little Mermaid"** is based on one of Andersen's noted fairy tales

**The Tivoli** is beautifully landscaped amusement park in the center of town,

where you can hear symphony, dance dine, attend famous pantomime theater

**The Banqueting Hall** in Christiansborg Castle is used by the King to receive in audience any of his subjects who have a problem or grievance to be discussed.

**Church of Our Savior** has an uncommon winding stairs on *outside* of the spire.

**Frederiksborg Palace,** in suburb of Copenhagen, now houses Historical Museum.

**Palace of Amalienborg** is the present royal residence, and the Changing of the Guard takes place there at noon daily, with waving flags, fanfare of trumpets.

**Silver** is Denmark's top shopping attraction; Georg Jensen is most famous name.

**Tivoli restaurants** are good places to try the celebrated Danish smørrebrød.

**At going-to-work time** and quitting time a bicycle avalanche sweeps the streets.

**As fresh hauls** are brought in, fisherwomen clean them at quayside market.

**The large sight-seeing motorboats** that ply the canals take visitors past many of the most interesting parts of the city. Christiansborg Castle tower is at left.

Photos: Danish National Travel Office; top right, Konstantin Ko-stich; center right, A. Milton Runyon

# Denmark

**Rosenholm Castle,** in charming Jutland setting, is one of beautiful old castles.

**Folk dances** are performed at open-air Museum at Lyngby, near Copenhagen.

**Archways** of Christiansborg Castle glow with the lights of a midwinter evening.

**Unobtrusive doorway** on a Copenhagen street opens to this lovely old courtyard.

**Professor Olsen** is one of the master designers of Royal Copenhagen Porcelain.

**Hans Christian Andersen's characters** live on in Royal Copenhagen figurines.

In this little house in Odense, great story teller Andersen lived as a child.

Autumn sunshine gives mystic quality to impressive towers of Rosenborg Castle.

Round Tower at Regensen, built by King Christian V, now serves as observatory.

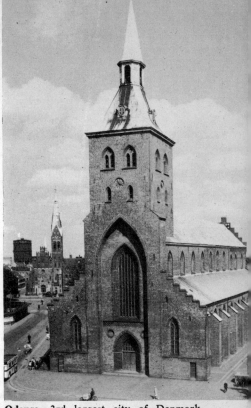

Odense, 3rd largest city of Denmark, has cathedral honoring Saint Canute.

Ribe is one of the fairytale towns of Denmark where storks nest on the roofs.

# Denmark

Old town of Randers was important commercial center back in the Middle Ages.

Aarhus, Denmark's second city, has Town Hall that's ultramodern in architecture

Probably the smallest Town Hall in the world is to be found in Aebeltoft, Jut-

land, a fairytale town that dates from the 14th century. Noted for fisheries.

Late autumn sunshine casts long shadows of strollers in Royal Square, Copenhagen.

The Jelling Runic Stone was erected in year 980 by King Harald the Bluetooth.

Ancient guns guard Kronborg Castle, the "Elsinore Castle" of the play, *Hamlet*.

**Children's Day celebration** is one of the many expressions of Danish gaiety.

**Kronborg Castle** at Elsinore is the annual setting for the "Hamlet Festival."

From heights of the ramparts you can see the not-far-distant coast of Sweden.

**Lovely Danish countryside** is best seen slowly, traveling by bicycle or car. In

small town you may come across peasants and fishermen in charming old costumes.

Photos: Konstantin Kostich; center, Danish National Travel Office

**Reykjavik,** capital of Iceland, is chief port of nation, commercial and fishing center. Unique hot-water supply system built 1945, utilizes natural hot spring

**Gullfoss** gets its name of "Golden Fall" from double rainbow seen in its spray.

# ICELAND IS ONE OF
# NEWER REPUBLICS

The first permanent settlement of Iceland was made in 874. The Althing, general assembly, was established in 930 and is the oldest legislative body in the world still in existence. After a referendum in 1944, the union with Denmark was ended and the new republic was proclaimed.

Average annual temperature at the capital ranges from 30° in January to 52° in July. Only about a quarter of the land is habitable, mainly the west, north and east coasts. Iceland is the westernmost state of Europe, 500 miles northwest of Scotland. It is completely "different," a magic, bewitching land

Photos: Ewing Galloway; bottom
Hans Malmben (Black Star

# EUROPE

Because we have reserved the southern part of Europe for the Mediterranean Cruise section, this part covers the three Benelux countries, France, Monaco, Germany, Austria, and Switzerland. To get to this part of the continent from the United States or Canada, you are faced with the same happy dilemma: which way to travel. If you are of the school of thought that believes in stepping at once into the land of your choice, you can do so by boarding one of the foreign-flag carriers. Transatlantic ships will land you at Hamburg or Bremen in Germany, Rotterdam in Holland, Cherbourg or Le Havre in France — or the Mediterranean ports of Marseilles or Cannes. Principal international airports for these countries are Amsterdam, Brussels, Paris, Nice, Geneva, Zurich and Frankfurt.

When you arrive on the continent, there are travel choices, too. You may want to hire a car, as so many people are now doing. The railroads have many de luxe trains with romantic names, *Golden Arrow, Blue Train, Mistral, Orient Express.* And the new TEE trains (Trans-Europ-Express) go by names like *Edelweiss, Helvetia, Rhein-Main, Paris-Ruhr,* and *Saphir.* Buses are becoming increasingly popular, with good services like Europabus.

Now turn the page for a picture preview, or postview, of your great journey. First we visit The Netherlands, the land of dikes and windmills, where more than half the population lives below the level of the sea. Next we come to Belgium with its architectural masterpieces such as Antwerp's Cathedral of Notre Dame, the *Grand' Place* of Brussels with its 14th century Town Hall, the Romanesque towers of the cathedral at Tournai. The last country in the Benelux group is little Luxembourg, about two-thirds the size of Long Island, a land of forested hills, farms and

**You travel in comfort on "Blue Train."**
meadows, medieval cities.

And now we are in Paris, perhaps the most beloved, most celebrated city in the world! The photos hint at the magic of its monuments, its cathedrals, its bistros, the quaint, winding streets, the grand boulevards, the fountains in the parks, the *joie de vivre.* We travel outside Paris, to Versailles, to Chartres and Fontainebleau. We visit Normandy and Brittany, the Chateau country, Alsace, and then go down to the Basque country and the fascinating Riviera, with a side-trip to the Monaco that's been made even more famous by Princess Grace.

Germany and Austria are next on our photographic visit. We see the busy cities, sprung to new life after the war, we watch the gaiety of a Mardi Gras celebration, wander through quaint villages, along terraced rivers and through the Black Forest, the towering Alps, and fertile, green valleys.

Finally we come to spectacular Switzerland, with its four official languages — German, French, Italian, and Romansh — and fourfold appeal to visitors: the Swiss Alps, the sparkling lake resorts, some of the world's best food and most comfortable hotels.

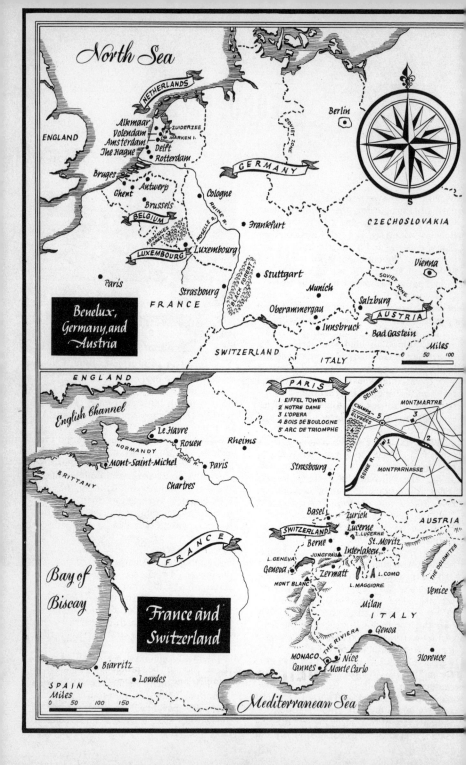

**AMSTERDAM HAS 1,000 CANALS, MOST GOING DIRECTLY THROUGH CITY.**

# HOLLAND MEANS WINDMILLS, TULIPS

The Netherlands is a compact country, about one and a half times the size of Massachusetts. Because a quarter of the land is below sea level, as much as 21 feet, it has to be protected by dikes, windmills and electric pumps. Holland has picturesque old towns, villages that cling to old customs, and modern cities.

**Glass-top passenger boat** traverses the Amstel River. Dam on this river, from which city gets its name, was constructe in 13th century. City has 400 bridge

**Kalverstraat,** with its many silversmiths, and Leidschestraat are shopping centers.

**Rijksmuseum** has fine Dutch and Flem ish paintings, Rembrandt's *Night Watc*

**Flower vendor** displays her blooms beside Amsterdam's ancient Powder Tower.

**Hotel L'Europe** has steps at its front door giving easy access to the canal.

**Royal Palace,** on Dam Square, is not the Queen's home, is used for state affairs.

Amsterdam is a world-famous center for the cutting and polishing of diamonds.

**Peace Palace at The Hague,** built 1913, now houses the International Court of Justice under the UN. The Hague is one of the most beautiful cities of Europe.

**Parliament Buildings:** The Hague is not the capital, but is seat of government.

**The Royal Family** arrives at "Hall of Knights" for the opening of Parliament.

Photos: Burton Holmes (Ewing Galloway); Netherlands National Tourist Office; Netherlands Information Service

**Delft,** five miles from The Hague, is
one of the most typical old Dutch towns.

**A center for ceramics,** Delft sends its
blue china and pottery all over world.

**Rotterdam,** principal Netherlands port,
is rising anew from 1940 devastation.

**On the lake at Sneek,** northern Holland,
many international regattas take place.

Photos: Netherlands National Tourist
Office; bottom right, Konstantin Kostich

# Netherlands

**Scheveningen,** fashionable sea resort near The Hague, has annual Music Festival.

**Kampen** is an ancient city with town hall many buildings dating to 14th century

**Breda** was site of treaty that gave New York and New Jersey colonies to British.

**In Alkmaar,** cheese market comes to life on Friday mornings, May to September.

**Cheeses come to Alkmaar** by barge, are unloaded by men with traditional garb.

# ELGIUM DISPLAYS MANY
# REASURES FOR VISITORS

**ANTWERP IS RIVALED ONLY BY ROTTERDAM AS TOP EUROPEAN PORT.**

Belgium is a tiny country, 175 miles at its greatest length, but it is a tremendous treasure house of Flemish painting and Renaissance architecture. Here, oil painting began at least as early as in Italy. Another of Belgium's great tourist attractions is its forty miles of fine beaches, with resorts like Spa, Ostend and Knokke-LeZoute. Still another magnet is green beauty of Ardennes forest.

Photo: Le Mont (Ewing Galloway)

**Fortress-like Steen** is one of the few traces left of medieval Antwerp. Parts date back to the 10th century; during 13th century the castle was a prison.

**Not all windmills** are in Holland. This impressive one is on the way to Ghent.

**Fountain of the Nymphs** stands in front of Antwerp's late Gothic guild houses.

**Cathedral of Notre Dame,** Antwerp's incomparable Gothic structure, was built in 14th and 15th centuries, has 400-ft. spire. Contains several Rubens paintings.

Photo: Ewing Galloway

103

**Center of Brussels** is *Grand' Place,* site of original 10th century settlement. Here are situated Town Hall (above), begun in 14th century, and medieval guildhalls.

**Arcade Cinquantenaire** opens on a park and connects two galleries, one containing military antiquities, the other an art collection with rare ivories, enamels.

**Brussels, capital of Belgium,** is center of country's banking and commercial life, and one of Europe's richest, most beautiful cities. Town square has flower stalls.

Photos: Ewing Galloway; bottom,
Pan American World Airways

**Ghent is main city** of East Flanders, has 10th century cathedral, old guildhalls.

**Bruges** (right) is Flemish for bridges; more than 50 cross the canals of this famed medieval town dating from the 7th century. Caxton learned printing here.

**The Citadel** rises atop a cliff in Dinant on the Meuse, with 13th century church in foreground. This resort town is noted for copper handicrafts, Montfat grottoes.

**The cathedral at Tournai** is one of the most notable in Belgium, with Romanesque towers, a Gothic choir. Contains famous paintings by Jordaens, Massys, etc.

Photos: Three Lions; bottom, Official Belgian Tourist Bureau

**VIANDEN CASTLE IS DATED 9TH CENTURY, HAS SOME ROMAN STONES.**

# TINY LUXEMBOURG HAS A BIG HEART

A little smaller in size than Rhode Island, Luxembourg is varied in topography. The rugged northern section is crossed by the Ardennes. The fertile south is a country of farms, meadowland, vineyards. The city of Luxembourg, capital of the Grand Duchy, was once a walled fortress. People are most cordial.

Photo: Ewing Galloway

# Luxembourg

**Luxembourg** is a completely "different" city, with deep gorges, great bridges, and with farms right in center of town. Industries are concentrated in suburbs

**Esch-sur-Sûre** is tiny town encircled by Sûre River, in the Luxembourg Ardennes.

**Clervaux,** situated on the Clerf River in the Ardennes, has 12th-century castle.

Photos: Ewing Galloway; Luxembourg National Tourist Office

# 350,000 AMERICANS SEE FRANCE YEARLY

**EIFFEL TOWER, TRADEMARK OF PARIS, REACHES 984 FEET INTO SKY.**

The one spot that most Americans going abroad head for is Paris, the city that "has everything for everyone." And the whole of France is a land of enormous variety: the quaint towns of Normandy and Brittany, the glorious sun-deck of the Riviera, the magnificent Chateau Country, winter sports in the French Alps. And everywhere, but everywhere, the food makes travelers pigs in clover.

Photo: Konstantin Kostich

**Notre Dame** overlooks the bookstalls on left bank of Seine, near Place St. Michel.

**In the salons of "haute couture"** buyers get their first look at the newest fashions.

**Cathedral of Notre Dame** has impressive location on tiny Île de la Cité in the Seine, the oldest part of Paris. You can climb the tower, see great 13-ton bell

Photos: A. L. Koolish; top right, Konstantin Kostich; bottom, TWA Trans World Airline

**Île St. Louis** is next to Île de la Cité; they're like two ships in the Seine, moored by bridges like Pont de la Tournelle (above). It's quiet, lonely here.

**The Panthéon** is the burial place of the patron saint of Paris, Saint Genevieve.

**The Madeleine church** is built like a Roman temple, with Corinthian colonnade.

**Magnificent Opera House** is the largest theater in the world, although it has fewer seats than the Châtelet or Milan's La Scala. Façade is lavishly decorated

**Sacré-Coeur,** on top of Montmartre, is oriental-looking church of white stone.

**Little streets in Montmartre,** full of cafés, tiny shops, lead to Sacré-Coeur

**Artist** paints in front of tiny 12th century church of St. Julien-le-Pauvre.

**Vendôme Column** has bronze bas-reliefs made from cannon Napoleon captured.

**Arc de Triomphe du Carrousel** is reduced copy of the Arch of Septimius Severus in

Rome. On top is a bronze chariot group. Building in background is the Louvre.

**Bois de Boulogne** is huge park on west side of Paris, with lakes and ponds, two race tracks—Auteuil and Longcham lovely drives and fine summer restauran

**Métro** is elaborate system of fourteen underground railways, with interchanges.

**Les Invalides,** founded as home for di abled soldiers, contains Napoleon's tom

**The Foreign Legion** parades down the ree-lined Champs-Elysées to celebrate July 14th, Bastille Day, or Fête Nationale. At top is the great *Arc de Triomphe*.

**Les Halles** are the great Paris produce markets, where you wind up a big night at four a.m. for a bowl of onion soup with the farmers and market workers.

**The Sorbonne**, the University of Paris, was started in 1253 as theological school.

**Gardens of the Palais-Royal** make quiet park near the fashionable shopping area.

Photos: French Government Tourist Office

**Auteuil,** in the Bois de Boulogne, has steeplechases, Longchamp has flat racing.

**Kiosks** for newspapers and magazines are a distinctive sight along Paris boulevards.

**Palais du Luxembourg,** once a royal residence, is noted for beautiful gardens.

**Marché aux Puces,** or "Flea Market," has art, antiques, bargains for skillful buyers.

**Arc de Triomphe** is the largest triumphal arch in the world, 160 feet high. Ride to top for magnificent view, since avenues radiate from arch in all directions.

**Beautiful Sainte-Chapelle** was built by St. Louis as shrine for Crown of Thorns.

**The Bourse** is the Paris stock exchange, housed in building like a Roman temple.

**Shops** line arcaded Rue de Rivoli. Rue de Castiglione leads to Place Vendôme.

**Comédie-Française** does plays of Molière, other greats, as well as modern drama.

**Folies Bergère** is probably best known music hall in the world, famous for the elaborateness of its shows, with some three hours of beauty, music and color.

**Imposing western façade** of great Palace of Versailles has 375 windows, many in Hall of Mirrors where World War I treaty was signed. Palace housed 10,000.

**10½-mile trip** to Versailles gardens is a popular Sunday outing for Parisians.

**Versailles fountains** play on certain Sundays, are sometimes lighted at night.

France

**Chartres Cathedral** is noted for stained glass, sculpture, and two lofty spires, 375 ft. and 350 ft. Ornate taller one is work of gifted artist Jehan de Beuce.

**Fontainebleau,** second in interest only to Versailles, has lovely forest nearby.

**La Malmaison** was scene of literary and artistic salon of Josephine Bonaparte.

**Etretat,** 15 miles from Le Havre, is resort with beach flanked by white cliffs.

**Port of Le Havre,** with 2 big breakwaters, accommodates liners big as *United States.*

**Honfleur,** picturesque seaport at mouth of Seine, has 15th century wooden church.

**Lisieux,** with shrine of St. Theresa, has become an important place of pilgrimage.

**Exquisite lace** is made in Chartres, Le Puy, Alençon, treasured everywhere.

**Vierville-sur-Mer** was "Omaha Beach" of 1944 American landings in Normandy.

Photos: French Government Tourist Office; bottom left, Richard Joseph

**Mont-Saint-Michel** is the great "citadel in the sea" connected with mainland by mile-long causeway. Abbey, founded in 708, is France's greatest tourist mecca

**Saint-Servan** (above) is part of resort area that includes Saint-Malo, Paramé.

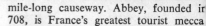

**Novelist Chateaubriand** spent his boyhood in this castle near Saint-Malo.

Photos: Konstantin Kostich; bottom, French Government Tourist Office

**Dinan,** with medieval walls, towers, is stopping place on way to Brittany coast.

**Douarnenez** is near tip of Brittany, picturesque fishing port for lobster, tuna.

**Thatched cottages** of Normandy are like their British cousins, even more homey.

**Concarneau** fishing boats go out into Bay of Biscay in search of sardines, tuna.

# France

**Rheims Cathedral,** begun 1211, century in building, is French national symbol.

**Grosse Horloge,** Renaissance clock tower, is feature of Rouen, port city on Seine.

**Champagne grapes,** grown on Île-de-France crest, are processed at Rheims.

**Hay wagons,** and signs advertising *apéritif* wines, are often seen on roads.

Photos: French Government Tourist Office; bottom left, Konstantin Kostich; bottom right, Richard Joseph

Chenonceaux was the home of Diane de Poitiers, mistress of Henry II. Unique feature is bridge over Cher river, built by Delorme for Catherine de' Medici.

Chambord, the great castle of François I, stands in the midst of 13,344 acre park. The roof is remarkable for its pinnacles, sculptured chimneys, spires, and capitals.

Chaumont, with its massive feudal towers, was chateau used by Catherine de' Medici.

Church at Saint-Cyr: Balzac and Anatole France lived in this village on Loire.

Photos: French Government Tourist Office

127

**Girls of Alsace** still wear long plaits, and the traditional big-bowed costumes.

**Strasbourg** is capital of Alsace, and one of the great artistic centers of Europe

**Château de Haut-Koenigsbourg,** on high Vosges peak, looks across to Germany.

**Colmar,** "Little Venice," is lovely town of ancient houses along the River Lauch.

Photos: French Government Tourist Office

**Chamonix** is leading summer and winter resort of the French Alps, dominated by fabulous 15,771-foot Mont Blanc. Photo shows shimmering icefield, *Mer de Glace.*

**Cable railway** carries skiers, tourists to great view from top of Mont Brévent.

**La Clusaz** is tiny winter sports resort on road between Chamonix, Annecy.

**Biarritz,** on Bay of Biscay, is one of France's most fashionable resorts. Its 7-mile beach, mild climate attracted Napoleon III, Empress Eugenie, other royalty

**Basilica at Lourdes** ranks next to Rome as leading Catholic place of pilgrimage.

**Thousands** come annually to be cured a grotto where St. Bernadette saw vision

**Salies-de-Béarn,** with charming homes, health resort just east of Biarritz.

**Cauterets,** with its hot sulphur springs, is spa and resort of central Pyrenees.

**Lake of Gaube,** near Cauterets, is fine spot for hiking amid scenic splendor.

**Basque game of pelote** is well attended at the village of Saint-Jean-Pied-de-Port.

**During Middle Ages,** Saint-Jean was end of much-traveled mountain pass to Spain.

**Dances** of the Basque country are vigorous, colorful as the costumes of dancers.

Photos: French Government Tourist Office

131

**Cannes** is headquarters for the British colony on the Côte d'Azur, and yachting center for the whole Riviera, with two fine beaches, two casinos, many hotels

**St. Jean** is an old fishing port at tip of lovely Cap Ferrat, abode of the wealthy.

**Walking** is a pleasure on Cap Ferrat, for autos are barred from many promenades

Photos: Konstantin Kostich; bottom left, French Government Tourist Office; bottom right, Richard Joseph

Cuisine at Nice is mixture of Parisian, Provincial and Italian—and wonderful!

**Nice,** Queen of the Riviera, is a major city as well as most fashionable resort.

**Menton** is at the very tip of the Riviera, with the Italian frontier at its edge.

Many habitués like it because the Alpes-Maritimes loom right over the beaches.

# MONACO IS 370 ACRES OF GAIETY

**Prince's Palace** is guarded, but there's no customs barrier at Monaco frontier.

Next to Vatican City, Monaco is the world's smallest state. It has a population of 20,000, but only about 2,000 are actually citizens or Monégasques. They are not allowed in the Casino, but they don't have to pay taxes because the Casino at Monte Carlo makes sufficient money to finance the whole principality. Monaco has been independent ever since the end of the Napoleonic Wars, in 1815.

**Monte Carlo Casino** is world famous, not only for its roulette wheels and other intricate forms of gambling, but also for a first-class theater and concert room.

134

**MUNICH IS FAMOUS FOR MARDI GRAS FESTIVITIES, COSTUME BALLS.**

# ROMANTIC GERMANY
# COMES TO NEW LIFE

West Germany, the German Federal Republic, has much to offer the tourist: its old medieval towns, gray with age, its majestic rivers and idyllic landscapes. While the people are throwing much of their energy into reconstruction, they have time for fun, and Germany now has some of the gayest night life in Europe. Frankfurt is good place for first stop.

Photo: Robert Copa (Magnum)

**Pension Anton Lang at Oberammergau:** Passion Play is performed every 10 years.

**Oberammergau Play** is now presented in modern theater, needs 1250 performers.

**Between Passion Plays,** the residents of Oberammergau carve religious figures.

**Garmisch-Partenkirchen,** site of Olympic winter games in 1936, is great ski resort.

**Ehrenfels Castle** is 13th century relic, amid terraced vineyards on Rhine river.

**Danube River** at Riedlingen (below): After the Volga, it's continent's longest.

**Lindau** is old town on an island in Lake Constance, with bridges to mainland.

**Kehlsteinhaus** at Berchtesgaden looks out over the beautiful Salzburg Alps.

Photos: German Tourist Information Office; top, Charles Marschalek

**Heidelberg,** on Neckar river, is noted for country's most famous university, and for Heidelberg Castle, imposing ruin built and rebuilt over past 700 years.

**Mainz,** one of Germany's great historical cities, celebrates Rose Monday Festival.

**The Black Forest** has modest ski lodges, plush resort centers like Baden-Baden.

**"Trinkhalle"** at **Baden-Baden** is lovely spot to imbibe healthful spring waters.

Photos: German Tourist Information Office

**Cologne at night:** majestic cathedral sustained only slight damage in the war. Begun in 1248, it was completed in 1880; contains relics of Wise Men of the East.

**Berlin's main street,** Kurfürstendamm, is again busy with shopping, entertainment. This is view of the restored boulevard as it looks from the Kempinski Hotel.

Photos: German Tourist Information Office

# AUSTRIA IS LAND OF ALPS, GREEN VALLEYS, AND MUSIC

Austria, the "heart of Europe," is famed for its towering Alps, its meadows and forests and villages, and its wealth of entertainment, climaxed by the Salzburg Music Festival. You'll enjoy seeing the gay Tyrolean costumes, flowered shawls and dirndls. You'll wander in fairy-tale villages like this one in the Tyrol.

**Kitzbühel** is a Tyrolean medieval town that is both winter and summer resort.

**Innsbruck's Maria Theresa Street** leads toward high peaks of the Eastern Alps.

The Graben, the "moat," is now principal shopping street in great city of Vienna.

Belvedere Palace was built for Prince Eugene who kept the Turks out of Europe.

Vienna's Opera House, one of world's renowned, is only one at street level.

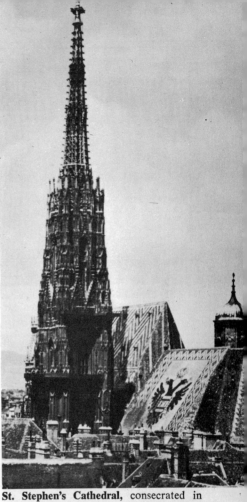

St. Stephen's Cathedral, consecrated in 1147, has slender 448-foot Gothic spire.

The famous "white horses of Vienna" give performance at Salzburg Festival.

# Austria

**How to climb an ice wall** is taught at the High Alpine School at Heiligenblut.

**Church at St. Wolfgang** contains Pacher altar, world's most valuable wood carving.

**Zell am See,** because of conjunction of air currents, is ideal place for gliding.

**At Salzburg Festival,** Hofmannsthal's "Jedermann" is staged on the domplatz.

**Peasant festival at Schwaz:** This is a typical feature of the Austrian scene.


142

Photos: Austrian State Tourist Department; bottom left, Pan American World Airways

# SWITZERLAND MEANS MOUNTAINS AND WATCHES AND CHOCOLATES

**JUNGFRAU'S MIGHTY 13,650-FT. PEAK WAS FIRST CLIMBED IN 1811.**

In winter, Switzerland is unquestionably the winter sports capital of the world, and the glistening snow brings bright new beauty to its tremendous mountains. In summer, the sparkling lake resorts are at their best. Throughout the year, the country is one of boundless hospitality with some of the best food and the most comfortable hotels in the world. If you like creature comforts, this is for you!

Photo: A. L. Koolish

# Switzerland

**League of Nations buildings** at Geneva symbolize Switzerland as great neutral.

**This is a typical holiday home** in Swiss chalet style, at Villars-sur-Ollon, Vaud.

**Calvin Memorial** in Geneva's *Promenade des Bastions* hails freedom of religion.

**The Lake of Geneva** is enlivened by many trim excursion steamers which take you from Geneva, at west end of lake, to Lausanne. Vevey, Montreux, other points.

**Castle of Chillon,** near Montreux on Lake Geneva, is one of the best preserved medieval castles in Europe—the scene of Byron's poem, "The Prisoner of Chillon."

**Montreux** itself is a charming town, huddled between the lake and the Alpine peak of Rochers de Naye, 6,700 feet. This is chief resort area of French Switzerland.

Photos: TWA Trans World Airline; bottom, Konstantin Kostich

# Switzerland

**Open air train** takes passengers up the scenic slopes of Rigi, near Lucerne.

**Lucerne** is gateway to "Land of William Tell." This is Hofkirche, founded in 735.

**Older parts of Lucerne,** with charming houses like this, are on right bank of

the Reuss. Vacation capital of Switzerland, Lucerne has magnificent scenery.

**'iew from Jungfraujoch** is magnificent. his is the highest point in Europe that is reached by rail—over 11,000 feet. Innumerable summits are seen all around.

**)utdoor shopping in Lugano:** this ancient own in the south is Italian in character.

**Lido Beach at Lugano** offers fine food, amidst gorgeous lake and mountain views.

Photos: A. L. Koolish; bottom,
wiss National Travel Office

**The noble Grossmünster church** and the Helmhaus museum are cherished land- marks of Zurich, largest city in Switzer- land, on Lake of Zurich, Limmat river

**Basel,** at French and German borders on Rhine, has market that's open every day.

**Basel's** new Industries Fair Building has giant clock with 12-ft. sweep second hand.

Photos: Swiss National Travel Office

**Houses of Parliament in Berne,** capital of Switzerland. With its arcades on the older streets, and its many fountains, Berne's medieval air attracts visitors.

**Visitors** to library of St. Gall's Abbey put on slippers to protect ancient floors.

**Clock Tower** is Berne's traditional landmark and the bear is the city's mascot.

# Switzerland

**Davos,** in 5,000-foot high valley, is first-rank place for skating and skiing.

**Sports train** of Gornergrat railway at Zermatt climbs toward the Matterhorn

**Cresta Toboggan Run,** at St. Moritz, is ¾ mile long, with a drop of 500 feet.

**Laboratory for Horological Research** at Neuchâtel is pride of the watch industry.

**Travelers** in Zurich candy shop stock up on the world-famous Swiss chocolates.

# THE MEDITERRANEAN

ost people are anxious to visit the 'adle of Western civilization" that the editerranean area represents, with such its of early culture and religious development as Rome, Athens, Venice, Jerusem and other ancient cities.

There are many pleasant ways to get to e Mediterranean. Several of the major lines fly direct to Rome from U.S. ies. And of course Rome is one of the ijor terminals of lines from Northern rope. Other principal airports on the editerranean are Nice, Barcelona, hens, Istanbul, Beirut, Tel Aviv, and iro. By ship, you can sail to Lisbon, braltar, Cannes, Genoa, and Naples, d there are many special cruises of the editerranean.

However you go, you'll find the Mediranean area warm and sunny. The mate has become so famous that other gions around the world often advertise eir "Mediterranean-like climate." And u are always surrounded by history: om the days of the Phoenicians, through e glories of Carthage, Greece and Rome, wn to the present day importance of e great shipping lanes between the ports Europe and Asia.

Our Mediterranean photo-tour starts th the westernmost country, Portugal. is just a little larger than the state of aine, but it has nearly ten times as many ople. We visit Lisbon and nearby Sintra, storil, and the fishing village of Nazaré. nen we go on to the Portuguese islands, adeira and the Azores. The neighboring untry of Spain is next on the itinerary, th a dozen views of Madrid at work d play, and side-trips to Toledo, Sego-a, Grenada, Málaga, Seville, and then n to Barcelona, the Costa Brava, and the land of Majorca.

We cross the sea to Tunisia, Algeria, and Morocco, before coming to the paradise that is the goal of so many travelers — Italy. Here we see the glorious ruins of Rome, the modern city, and the Vatican, before going on to beautiful Florence, wondrous Venice, the Dolomites, the great industrial city of Milan, the Lake District, Genoa, Naples and the isle of Capri, and the fascinating island of Sicily.

Now we come to Athens, for more than a thousand years the cultural center of the Western world. We see the Parthenon and other ancient structures built on the Acropolis during the Golden Age of Pericles; and we see the Academy of Athens and proud buildings of the modern metropolis. A view of Corfu hints at the beauties of the Greek Islands.

After a brief look at Yugoslavia, on the Adriatic, we spend some time in Israel, ancient "Land of the Bible." Visits to Turkey and to Lebanon bring to an end our tour of the shimmering blue Mediterranean.

**Gibraltar is seen from "Independence."**

oto: American Export Lines

The Mediterranean

Atlantic Ocean

Mediterranean Sea

ENGLAND

GERMANY

POLAND

CZECHOSLOVAKIA

AUSTRIA

HUNGARY

RUMANIA

BULGARIA

GREECE

TURKEY

FRANCE

ITALY

YUGOSLAVIA

ADRIATIC SEA

Black Sea

Istanbul

Ankara

Athens

SYRIA

LEBANON

Beirut

ISRAEL

EGYPT

SUEZ CANAL

PORTUGAL

SPAIN

Coimbra

Lisbon

Segovia

Madrid

Toledo

Seville

Granada

Malaga

Casablanca

MOROCCO

ALGERIA

Algiers

TUNISIA

Tunis

LIBYA

Barcelona

L. MAGGIORE

L. COMO

DOLOMITES

Milan

Venice

Florence

Genoa

Rome

Naples

Capri

Sorrento

Pompeii

Taormina

MT. ETNA

SICILY

Palermo

Syracuse

Belgrade

Dubrovnik

Miles
0  100  200  300

SYRIA

Haifa

Tel Aviv

Jerusalem

ISRAEL

JORDAN

EGYPT

MILES
0    50

ROME

TIBER R

COLOSSEUM

VATICAN CITY

ST. PETER'S

1 Mile

# PORTUGAL INVITES YOU TO ITS SUNNY COAST

Portugal offers much charm for visitors who want to get off beaten pathways. Its principal cities have modern hotels and there are "tourist inns" in the smaller places. Main playland of the country is along the coast, the Portuguese Riviera, with resorts like Estoril and Cascais. Lisbon is one of the great international capitals of the world, with a "different" atmosphere that stems from its glamorous past when Portugal ruled half the New World. Monument above is in memory of the Marques de Pombal who rebuilt Lisbon after the 1755 earthquake.

Photo: TWA Trans World Airline

153

# Portugal

**Rossio Square** is geographical center of Lisbon. It has flower market, statue of Peter the 4th, and is flanked by national theater and the central railroad station.

**Castle of St. George** was site of famous battle that repulsed the Moors in 1147.

**Alfama district,** crowded and colorful, is clustered about 12th century cathedral.

**Sintra,** 14 miles northwest of Lisbon, has the Palace of Pena perched high on a hill above the town, most fascinating of the country's magnificent old royal palaces.

**Fishing** is major occupation in the many harbors of Portugal. These gaily painted boats are at Lisbon. Some fishermen use nets that are floated out from the shore.

Photos: TWA Trans World Airline

# Portugal

**Basilica of Shrine of Our Lady** at Fátima attracts almost as many as Lourdes.

**Coimbra** is Portugal's university city. "S Velha" is a 12th century Roman edifice

**Estoril** is fabulous seaside resort, just 15 miles from Lisbon, with magnificent

beach, flower gardens, casino, fine hotels bridle paths by the sea and up into hills

**Oporto**, second city of Portugal, is famous for port wine. This is cathedral.

**Nazaré** is typical fishing village where men wear bright plaids and stocking caps.

156

Photos: Casa de Portugal; top left, center, TWA Trans World Airline

**Madeira,** Portuguese island 625 miles to southwest of Lisbon, is known as "Pearl of the Atlantic." S.S. *Independence* is shown in beautiful harbor of Funchal.

**Wood-sled** transportation indicates the primitiveness of life on Madeira island.

**Santa Maria** is one of the 9 main Azores islands, 1200 miles to west of Lisbon.

# SPAIN IS LAND OF GREAT TRADITIONS

Spanish civilization dates back to the stone age. The Basques may be descended from Cro-Magnon man whose art has been found in caves at Altamira. The history of Spain is long and involved, but it reached a great climax after Columbus' discovery of America sparked enormous expansion of the empire which came to include almost all of the Americas and around the world to the Philippines. The Spain of today is a land of color, music and gaiety, with many reminders of past glories. Madrid (Plaza Mayor above) is Spain's capital and geographical center.

**Castellana Hilton Hotel** is newest and most luxurious in the gay city of Madrid.

**Madrid's newer sections** with spacious streets contrast with the old quarters.

**With over a million** population, Madrid has subway, other modern transportation.

**Calle de Alcalá** is one of several wide tree-lined boulevards in modern Madrid.

Prado Museum is one of world's greatest, with works of Velázquez, other masters.

Even in busy Madrid, one can see farm carts lumbering slowly along to market

Puerta del Sol, once one of gates of old ramparts of Madrid leveled 4 centuries ago, has undergone a recent face-lifting and become principal square of the city

Throne Room is one of many impressive parlors in the sumptuous Royal Palace.

Palace, built on the site of old alcazar houses many of Spain's treasures of art

Photos: Spanish State Tourist Office; top left, TWA Trans World Airline; top right, Charles Marschalek

160

**Outstanding feature of Madrid** is the great number of broad squares and noble avenues. Here the horses of the Cibeles Fountain head for the Calle de Alcalá.

**Rose gardens** are a feature of beautiful Retiro Park, with its lovely trees, lake.

**Concert at Retiro Park** is at other end of entertainment scale from 2 bull rings.

**San Juan de los Reyes,** in Toledo, was built by Ferdinand and Isabella.

**Santo Tomé church** houses the painting by El Greco, *The Burial of Count Orgaz*

**Toledo's greatest glory** is its splendid cathedral, a combination of five styles.

**Steep cobbled streets** of Toledo remind one of Moorish towns of North Africa.

Photos: TWA Trans World Airline; bottom right, Richard Joseph

**mposing walls** of Toledo include the Bisagra Gate (above) and the Mudejar Gate. Most noteworthy secular building is the alcazar, palace of King Charles V.

**Many-turreted alcazar,** in Segovia, was site of crowning of Queen Isabella I.

**Lofty Roman aqueduct,** with 170 arches, is still used to supply water to Segovia.

**Grapes,** for home use, and olives for ex
port, are Spain's main industrial crops

**Granada's Alhambra,** home of Moorish
kings, is the finest Moorish art in Spain.

**Granada gypsies** perform a gay dance
for tourists before one of their houses.

**Málaga,** noted for sweet Malaga wine, is
famed winter resort on the Mediterranean.

It is one of the oldest cities of Spain,
said to have been founded by Phoenicians.

Photos: Virginia Black; Richard Joseph; Pan American World Airways; Spanish State Tourist Office

164

**Salon Arabe** shows exquisite decorations of the alcazar, Moorish palace in Seville.

**Lofty Giralda Tower,** over 300 feet high, is part of beautiful cathedral of Seville.

**Typical Majorcan dress** is worn by this woman climbing a "street" in Pollensa.

**Spanish mantillas** come into their own at the Seville Fair which follows Holy Week.

# Spain

**Fight** over design prevented completion of Barcelona's Church of the Holy Family.

**Costa Brava** (rugged coast) is section between the French Riviera and Barcelona.

**Battle-scarred gates** lead to Valencia, Spain's third city, near Mediterranean.

Photos: Pan American World Airways; bottom left, Spanish State Tourist Office

**Spain is noted** for its many fiestas at different seasons, this one at Santander.

**Bullfight at El Espinar,** near Barcelona, (below) is one of 500 a year in Spain.

**Santander** is surrounded by the Picos de Europa, mountains that rise to 8800 feet.

**Santiago de Compostela,** at Spain's northwest tip, is a pilgrim city of world renown.

Photos: Spanish State Tourist Office

# Spain

**Country homes** in Majorca feature cos chimney corner seats by the kitchen fire

**Mountain village** of Valldemosa is on the Spanish island of Majorca, in Balearics.

**Canary Islands** are Spanish possession off northwest Africa. This is Santa Cruz

**Old houses at Sóller,** on Majorca, are reflected in waters on the picturesque harbor. The town is surrounded by orang trees; its port ships oranges and wine

# TUNISIA IS SITE OF ANCIENT CARTHAGE

700,000 people lived in Carthage before the time of Christ; now it's a desolate plain. When you visit Tunisia, in North Africa, you'll feel that ancient history peers over your 20th century shoulder.

**Tunis** is capital of Tunisia and a mecca for tourists looking for the unusual.

**Old Moslem quarter** of Tunis is a maze of crooked streets, extensive bazaars.

**In the tree-lined square** which runs from cathedral to port are many sidewalk cafés.

**Newly excavated ruins** of Carthage baths bring back memories of high school Latin.

Photos: TWA Trans World Airline

# ALGERIA IS LAND OF MYSTERY

Once the home of the Barbary pirates, Algeria has long been a land of strife and mystery. The narrow region along the Mediterranean is fertile, but the Sahara desert covers seven eighths of Algeria.

**Algiers** is the capital of Algeria and chief Mediterranean port, stretching along the bay for ten miles, its white houses gleaming brilliantly in the strong tropical sun.

**Famous "Ouled-Naïl" dancers** perform at tiny Bou-Saâda, 125 miles from Algiers.

**Dancers** take their name from Ouled-Naïl mountains, on edge of the Sahara desert.

**Cathedral** on Place Malakoff is one of the many impressive buildings in Algiers.

**Hammam-Meskoutine** is noted spa with hot springs in the Constantine mountains.

**Casbah section** of old Algiers has real labyrinth of narrow terraced streets.

**Rommel Gorge from above:** Atlas mountains cut off desert interior from the sea.

**Roman ruins at Djemila** include arch of triumph, a forum, 3rd century temple.

Photos: TWA Trans World Airline

# ANCIENT, MODERN MIX IN MOROCCO

Morocco extends along the Atlantic and Mediterranean at the northwest corner of Africa. The Arabic name for the country means "the farthest west." The dry, rocky Atlas Mountains cover nearly all Morocco.

**Casablanca,** the largest city of Morocco, was the setting for the history-making conference between President Roosevelt and Prime Minister Churchill in 1943.

**Modern-looking Anfa Hotel,** on a green bluff outside the city, was meeting site.

**Modern Casablanca** forms a semicircle around old city. This is the Post Office.

**THE COLOSSEUM IS BEST KNOWN SYMBOL OF MIGHT OF ANCIENT ROME.**

# SUNNY ITALY IS A PARADISE ON EARTH

The surrounding sea and the protecting Alps give Italy a wonderfully balanced climate in both winter and summer. The scenery has great variety: lovely beaches, beautiful lake resorts, magnificent Alps and Apennines and Dolomites. Lovers of culture, history find incomparable wealth in Italian art and archeology.

Photo: TWA Trans World Airline

173

**The Colosseum** had room for 50,000. Cross commemorates the early Christian martyrs who died in the amphitheater, victims of lions, sport of early Romans.

**Forum Romanum** was the center of economic, political and religious life of ancient Rome. This is site of Castor's Temple and temple of the vestal virgins.

**The Tiber River** winds through Rome much as the Seine through Paris, the Thames through London. This is Sant' Angelo bridge, with dome of St. Peter's.

**Vatican Library** is one of world's most beautiful. Contains over half a million books, and many rare manuscripts like 4th century Codex Vaticanus of Bible.

Photos: Konstantin Kostich; bottom, Italian State Tourist Office

**St. Peter's,** covering an area of 163,728 square feet, is largest, most majestic of Christian churches. Colonnades are by Bernini; great dome by Michelangelo.

**Papal Fountain** has insignia of the Chigi, same shape as crown worn by Pope Pius.

**Swiss Guards** have served at the Holy See as attendants of the Pope since 1505.

**Castel Sant'Angelo,** approached by the celebrated Sant'Angelo bridge over the Tiber, was built at command of Emperor Hadrian as mausoleum for Roman rulers

**Formal gardens** of Castel Gandolfo: This is country residence of the Pope, south of Rome on the Appian Way, and by the Lateran treaty now part of Vatican City

**Claudian Aqueduct,** with its series of superb arches, was built in year 52 A.D.

**Villa d'Este,** with fountains, terraced gardens, is beauty spot at nearby Tivoli.

**Leonardo da Vinci International Airport,** at Fiumicino, serves jet flights for Rome.

**Tivoli,** viewed from Villa d'Este: town is noted for waterfalls, Hadrian's villa.

Photos: Konstantin Kostich; top
left, TWA Trans World Airline

**Florence** was "cradle of the Italian Renaissance." Uffizi Palace, in background, has one of world's richest collections of paintings and 1,500,000 volume library.

Photo: Konstantin Kostich

**Ponte Vecchio,** across the Arno, contains many tiny shops. Gallery across top, that connected Uffizi Palace (tower at left) with Pitti Palace, was partly destroyed.

**Beautiful Boboli gardens** are on grounds of Pitti Palace, once residence of the great Medici family, Florentine statesmen, rulers, and patrons of the arts.

Photos: TWA Trans World Airline;
bottom, Italian State Tourist Office

**The mystic quality** of Venice expresses itself in this photo of gondolas before San Marco square, with Santa Maria della Salute seen through early evening haze.

**Venice** is intricate network of canals, big and small, with countless bridges.

**Bridge of Sighs** was passage for prisoners from Ducal Palace to airless cells.

Photos: A. Milton Runyon;
bottom left, Richard Joseph

**Rialto Bridge** over the Grand Canal has two rows of shops, twelve on each side.

**Ca' d'Oro**, the Golden House, is splendid home of 15th century Venetian patriarch.

**Cathedral of San Marco**, dedicated in 830 to patron saint of Venice, is most ornate.

**Grand Canal,** 2 miles long, is the chief artery of Venice, winding in an S-curve from the Piazza San Marco to the railroad station. Width averages 228 feet.

**At top of cable railway** at Ortisei, you can have refreshments while enjoying the magnificent panorama. Town is known for carving of toys, religious articles.

**Wild flowers** add to beauty of Dolomites near principal resort, Cortina d'Ampezzo.

**Dolomite Alps** of northern Italy are known for vivid sunrise, sunset colors.

**In driving through Dolomites,** you often come on wayside shrines on roads that reach almost 9,000 feet. Highest peak is Marmolada, towering up 10,964 feet.

**Cortina d'Ampezzo** is both a summer and winter resort, in center of Dolomites, one of Europe's finest mountain areas. Brenner Pass is 45 miles to northwest.

Photo: Konstantin Kostich; bottom, Italian State Tourist Office

**Milan cathedral** is elaborately decorated with over 100 pinnacles, 3,000 statues.

An elevator takes you to the roof where you can see white marble figures close by.

Photo: Konstantin Kostich

Opposite Milan cathedral is the Galleria Vittorio Emanuele where all Milan meets.

Castello Sforzesco was once a barracks, now interesting archeological museum.

Milan, chief industrial center of Italy, has world's grandest railroad station.

Convent with Leonardo's *Last Supper* is next to Santa Maria delle Grazie church.

La Scala Opera House, with its red and gold auditorium, is world's most noted.

Leonardo da Vinci—painter, sculptor, architect and engineer—faces La Scala.

Photos: A. Milton Runyon; top right, center right, TWA Trans World Airline; bottom, Charles Marschalek

**Bellagio** is on tip of promontory that divides beautiful Lake Como into its two southern arms. This popular resort has many villas, gardens, ancient church.

**Lake Como,** Italy's 3rd largest, is in Lombardy, 25 miles to north of Milan.

**Lake steamers** call at resorts of Como, Bellagio, Lecco, Tremezzo, and others.

Photos: Italian State Tourist Office; bottom, Konstantin Kostich

**Lake Garda** has wonderfully clear blue waters, many lovely white villages. This is Riva, at northwest extremity of the lake, with palace built by the Venetians.

**Lake Maggiore** contains famous Borromean Islands. This is view from Isola Bella, site of 1934 conference at which Germany denounced the Versailles treaty.

Photos: Konstantin Kostich; bottom, Charles Marschalek

**Genoa,** port city at center of the Italian Riviera, rises from waterfront to height of over 1,000 feet in surrounding hills. Municipal palace has letters of Columbus.

**Maritime Station** at Genoa is home port of Italian Line ships and port of call of many others. Genoa rivals Marseilles as chief seaport of the Mediterranean.

Photos: Konstantin Kostich; bottom, Italian State Tourist Office

taly

**Cathedral at Orvieto** is noted for its gleaming façade, miracle of fine carving.

**The 12th century church** of St. Francis of Assisi is monument to his gentle spirit.

**Pisa's graceful Leaning Tower** is 180 ft. high, and 14 ft. out of perpendicular.

**Lerici** is resort on Gulf of Spezia, one of largest, safest Mediterranean harbors.

Nearby is a 12th century Pisan castle, which is now used as marine observatory.

**Greatest spectacle in Naples** is lovely view across the bay to no-longer-smoking Vesuvius. Many parts of the city have grown up into the surrounding hills and are reached by funiculars. Neapolitans are famous for songs like *Santa Lucia*.

**Caruso** was hissed at his debut at San Carlo Opera House. Though he was often urged to return after he made his fame international, he would never come back.

**Castel dell'Ovo** (Castle of the Egg) is on its own tiny island opposite the Via Parthenope where the principal hotels of Naples are located. The medieval castle was begun by the Norman King William I, completed and modified by his successors.

# Italy CAPRI

**Umberto I Square** is the center of lovely Capri.

**Marina Piccola** looks out to great Faraglioni rocks.

**The island of Capri,** in the Bay of Naples, attracts thousands of visitors with its climate and scenery.

**Visitors arrive** at Capri by small steamers from Naples, a distance of 20 miles.

**Blue Grotto** gets its name from dazzling blue light produced by the bright sun.

The island covers about four square miles; 1920-ft. Mount Solaro is its highest point.

**Funicular railway** links Marina Grande with town of Capri, 456 feet higher up.

**Pompeii** was buried by the eruption of Vesuvius in 79 A.D. This is the Forum.

**Temple of Apollo** is one of ruins foun by excavations that were begun in 176?

**Lava-paved streets** of Pompeii were used by chariots of city's 20,000 residents.

**Well-preserved homes** are chief source of information about ancient domestic life.

**Sorrento** is charmingly situated amid orange and lemon groves on mountainous peninsula south of Bay of Naples. *Come Back to Sorrento* is more than a song.

**Most dramatic road** in Italy is the one from Sorrento to Amalfi, along rugged coast and over the hills that rise to a 4,734 foot height in Monte Sant'Angelo.

Photos: Konstantin Kostich

# Italy SICILY

**Sicily** is known as "Island of the Sun" and brightness penetrates narrow alleys

**From Taormina,** you can see Sicily's Mt. Etna, highest active volcano in Europe.

**Greek Theater** of Syracuse is largest most beautiful of all the Hellenic ruins

**Palermo at night:** With over 500,000 inhabitants, it is one of Italy's largest and most aristocratic cities. Buildings range from Norman-Arab to 20th century.

TEMPLE OF JUPITER DATES FROM DAYS OF ROMAN RULE IN ATHENS.

# THE MAJESTY OF GREECE LIVES ON

Whether or not you've read the works of Plato and Aristotle, you'll want to know something of the great civilization that reached its peak more than four centuries before Christ. A visit to the Acropolis time-machines you back through the centuries. And you'll find modern Athens a bright and busy city of 1¼ million.

**Academy of Athens,** University of Athens and National Library are proud buildings of modern Athens. The city is politica economic and cultural center of Greece

**Your imagination** can place thousands of listeners in the vast Temple of Music.

**Palace guard** reminds you that in 1946 a plebiscite called for return of monarch

Photos: Royal Greek Embassy Information Service; bottom left, S. A Booth; bottom right, Richard Joseph

**The Acropolis** rises proudly on 180-foot hill above the Attic plain. The Parthenon and many large buildings were built in Golden Age of Pericles, 2400 years ago.

**Picturesque Corfu,** second largest of the Ionian islands, was Homer's "Scheria."

**The Caryatids** have carried Erechtheum roof on their heads about 24 centuries.

# YUGOSLAVIA OFFERS SCENIC ADVENTURE

Yugoslavia is now a member of European Travel Commission and is inviting tourists to enjoy its good food and superb scenery of places like Dubrovnik and the Dalmatian Island of Rab in the Adriatic.

**Parliament in Belgrade:** Strategic site of capital makes it "key to Balkans."

**Budva** is port city on Adriatic, with an Orthodox Eastern cathedral, built 1418.

**Dubrovnik,** walled city on south coast, was called Arragosa, the root of *argosy*.

**Jajce** is medieval town on Vrbas river, with ruined castle and lovely waterfall.

Photos: Konstantin Kostich

**In Nazareth,** in the hills of Galilee, in Israel, are the narrow, winding cobblestone streets where Jesus himself walked. A visit brings to mind the days of 2,000 years ago.

# PAST AND PRESENT MEET IN ISRAEL

Modern Israel has much to offer visitors who are politically and socially aware of the ferment of our times. And as the ancient "Land of the Bible" it attracts pilgrims to Jerusalem, the River Jordan, Nazareth, Tiberias on the Sea of Galilee, and Mount Zion. New roads, hotels make it easy to visit old and new Israel.

# Israel

**Sunset over Jerusalem:** View shows the great no man's land between the old city and the new. On left is King David hotel. Buildings at right are in Arab sector.

**Haifa,** seen from Mt. Carmel, is principal seaport of Israel and industrial center.

**The Sheraton-Tel Aviv,** on the Mediterranean, is first Israel hotel run by U.S. chain.

204

Photos: Robert Capa (Magnum); Israel Government Tourist Office: Sheraton Hotels

**Dome of the Rock** mosque in Jerusalem, Jordan, is on the site of the temple where Jesus turned out the money changers, destroyed in A.D. 100's.

**From Mount of Olives** you see whole of Jerusalem spread out before you, and much of it seems as it might have been 2000 years ago, behind the ancient wall.

# JORDAN'S CITIES ARE FAMED BIBLICAL NAMES

Most of the people of Jordan live in ancient towns and cities close to the Dead Sea. Many of these communities, such as Old Jerusalem, Jericho, and Bethlehem are famous in Bible stories.

**SIRKECI SQUARE IN ISTANBUL IS THE BUSY CENTER OF A BUSY CITY.**

# TURKEY IS LINK
# BETWEEN EAST, WEST

Turkey is an ancient land that used to join Europe, Africa and Asia in its empire. Istanbul, once Constantinople, is partly in Europe, partly in Asia. It is the terminus of the famed Orient Express, scene of many motion picture spy thrillers. The Golden Horn, an inlet of the Bosporus, forms the excellent, well-sheltered harbor.

**Istanbul Hilton** is situated on elevation with spectacular view across the Bosporus.

**These old Roman ruins** are near Smyrna, port long known for its export of figs.

**Bosporus Strait** connects the Sea of Marmara and the Black Sea, separating European and Asian Turkey. The tower is part of Rumeli Hisar fortifications.

**From dock** near the Yeni (New) Mosque, ferry boats leave for Bosporus crossing.

**International commuters** read the news on daily trip between Europe and Asia.

Photos: Turkish Information Office

**BEIRUT, MAIN PORT FOR LEVANT STATES, IS CAPITAL OF LEBANON.**

## LEBANON HAS ANCIENT LURE

Lebanon is a tiny country, just 120 miles long and 35 wide, proclaimed an independent nation in 1941. Beirut, the capital, was a flourishing Phoenician city some 3000 years ago. Today it is trade and transportation center for both Oriental and Western Worlds, the gateway for travelers to Jordan and to Israel.

# ROUND-THE-WORLD CRUISE

**"President Cleveland" at Hong Kong.**

A Round-the-World Cruises is the most glamorous of voyages: it is the sort of trip that's offered as the grand prize in a contest, the kind that wealthy travelers with plenty of time take aboard a luxury liner, or that more and more people are now making by air, or a combination of air and sea. Each year a few lucky souls embark on conducted tours around the world, taking about three months, and costing some five thousand dollars and up, apiece. But many more are taking the more modest passenger ships, and passenger-carrying freighters, and exploring the growing number of airline routes to fascinating off-the-beaten track places.

Our round-the-world photo tour hops first to Japan with its abundance of natural beauties . . . cone-shaped mountains like Fujiyama, crystal-clear rivers, the white sands and green pine trees of the Inland Sea. We see something of the great city of Tokyo, the shrines of Kamakura, Nara, Nikko, and especially Kyoto, where the temple grounds show off to great advantage the highly-developed art of Japanese gardening.

Photo: American President Lines

Pausing briefly in Hong Kong, the exotic city which John C. Caldwell describes as "China, with a British accent," we visit Manila, in the Philippines, and then go on to romantic, mysterious Thailand. In Bangkok, four hundred multi-colored temples glitter side by side with the whiteness of many modern buildings. And we see the graceful Siamese dancers enacting the timeless lives of their gods.

We pay brief visits to crowded Java, where eighty million people live in an area the size of New York state; to Bali, the beautiful little island famous for its colorful textiles and friendly, handsome people; to Sumatra, with its rich natural resources.

By way of Burma, the "Happy Land," exciting Singapore, and Ceylon, we come to the great realm of India with its 400 million citizens, a seventh of the human race. We see something of the stupendous mountain wall, the Himalayas, that run along the entire northern boundary. We visit the great cities, Calcutta, New Delhi, Agra with its jewel-in-marble, the Taj Mahal, and Srinagar in the lovely Kashmir Valley. A brief visit to Pakistan, and then we go on to Egypt, realm of the camel, the Sphinx, the Pyramids and the mighty Nile.

Many round-the-world travelers complete their trip by way of the Mediterranean, but since we've already covered those lands, we choose to continue our journey down the east coast of Africa, visiting the countries of British East Africa, the Federation of Rhodesia and Nyasaland, and ending our journey in South Africa. On our way we see something of the jungles of Kenya, home of the lioness heroine of *Born Free,* the lands explored by Cecil Rhodes and David Livingston, the great Kimberly diamond mine.

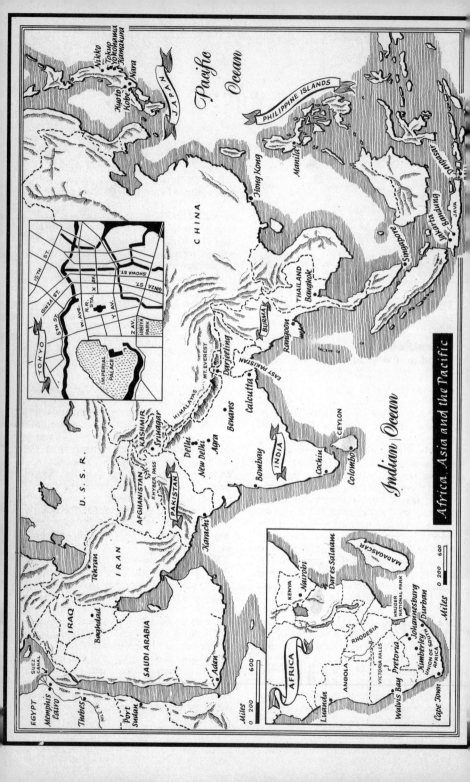

Africa, Asia and the Pacific

**NEARLY 50,000 CLIMB PERFECT CONE OF FUJIYAMA EVERY SUMMER.**

# JAPAN IS LAND OF EXQUISITE BEAUTY

The four islands of Japan offer scenery of every conceivable type: forests, lakes, mountains, swift rivers, hot springs, and miles of rice paddies. The charming gardens feature foliage rather than blooms. The cities offer Western comforts, but are filled with gaudy color. Buddhist temples, Shinto shrines are everywhere.

Photo: Japan Travel Bureau

**Tokyo,** capital of Japan, is on the shore of the Bay of Tokyo; it is traversed by several streams. In upper left, surrounded by moat, is Imperial Palace and grounds.

**Ginza Street,** brilliantly lit at night, is Tokyo's fashionable shopping district.

**Tokyo department stores** have roof playgrounds to keep children happy and busy.

**Hachiman Shinto Shrine,** at Kamakura, was built 1063, features long stairway.

Kamakura is beach resort on Sagami Bay, about an hour from Tokyo by train, car.

**Great bronze Buddha** of Kamakura stands 42 ft. high and dates from the year 1252.

**The Kabuki-za** in Tokyo is the best-known theater where classical drama is done.

**Stepping stones** in Heian Shrine's garden are set crooked, so devils will fall off.

**A Kyoto craftsman** weaves the fascinating patterns of lovely Japanese silk scarves.

**Kyoto** has some 3,000 Buddhist temples and Shinto shrines. One of most beautiful is Heian shrine, originally built in 794. This is one of Kyoto's several festivals.

Photos: Ewing Galloway; Peggy Mann; Japan Travel Bureau

**Nikko,** about 90 miles north of Tokyo, is summer resort in the Japanese Alps. It has 141,000-acre Nikko National Park. This is Shinto ceremony at Ieyasu Tomb.

**Japanese girl guide:** Customs of the land are explained in a charming, gay manner.

**Nara's** great 13-foot bell is in world's largest wooden building, Daibutsu-Den.

# HONG KONG IS BUSIEST PORT OF FAR EAST

**Typical** of the British Crown Colony of Hong Kong are streets so steep that they have to be terraced into steps. 28,000 British soldiers guard 2 million people.

**From top of Victoria Peak** you get view of tall buildings of Hong Kong and its harbor beyond. The cable railway trip up 1800-foot peak is a tourist favorite.

**White pagoda** is on estate of Aw Boon Haw, fabulous owner of "Tiger Balm."

**Fishing junks** tie up at port of Aberdeen, on either side of island from Hong Kong.

**Hong Kong** is one of the world's few free ports, where all goods are without duty.

Many Chinese articles are made here by factories moved from Shanghai, Canton.

Photo: Henri Cartier-Bresson (Magnum)

# THERE ARE 7,000 PHILIPPINE ISLANDS

The Republic of the Philippines, given full independence on July 4, 1946, has some 7,110 islands, with over 4,500 of the smaller ones still unnamed. Discovered by Magellan in 1521, the Philippines for more than 300 years were part of Spain's vast empire, were ceded to the U.S. in 1898. Today, the new democracy has up-to-date facilities for tourists, welcomes them to its friendly, charming resorts.

**Legaspi Landing, Manila Hotel:** Damaged by war, the hotel is now fully restored.

**Escolta Boulevard** is one of the shopping streets of Manila, Philippines' big city.

Photos: Ewing Galloway

**Rice terraces on Luzon** (below) date back 1500 years, are still cultivated today.

**University of Manila,** badly bombed in war, has world's largest sun dial in garden.

**Malacañan Palace** in Manila is official residence of President of the Philippines.

**Temple of Dawn,** in Bangkok, called *Wat Arun,* has 245-foot tower which gives a magnificent view of city from the top. It is surrounded by four smaller towers.

**CLASSICAL DANCING IS ONE OF THE GLORIES OF SIAM'S HERITAGE.**

# THAILAND IS A NATION OF TEMPLES

There are few more entrancing sights in the world than the many temples of Siam, the country that's been known officially as Thailand since 1949. Bangkok, capital city, has many canals. Houses are often of teakwood, roofed with red tile. It is colorful city of almost a million people.

**Wat Phra Keo** ("wat" means monastery or temple) is the most famous and wonderful of all. It has the great Emerald Buddha, wrought from a single piece of jaspar.

**Wat Benchamaborpitr** (Temple of the Fifth Sovereign) is built of Italian marble, Chinese tile, a combination of old Thai style with foreign materials, new methods.

Photos: TWA Trans World Airline

# JAKARTA, JAVA, IS INDONESIA CAPITAL

The Republic of Indonesia achieved its independence as recently as August 17, 1945. The island of Java, fourth largest of the Indonesia group, is most important industrially, culturally, and politically.

**Bandung** is favorite vacation spot, 75 miles southeast of Jakarta, and with much more comfortable climate. This is Savoy-Homann Hotel, every room with balcony.

**Java** is noted for colorful and intricate batik, producing magnificent designs.

**Native "taxis"** wait for travelers coming from Jakarta's Tugu railway station.

# BALI IS SYMBOL OF THE FAR-AWAY

If you were asked to name the most exotic, far-away-from-it-all place you could think of, you might very well say "Bali"—the Indonesian island of batik, dancing girls, and good leisurely living.

**Weaving** is occupation of many Balinese women; they do colorful batik dye work.

**Striking batik designs** are used on the costumes used for the ceremonial dances.

**Bali's predominant religion** is Hinduism which spread to island in 7th century.

**Women of Denpasar** demonstrate the grace of carriage for which Balinese are known. Many go in for ritual dancing, wearing colorful costumes headdresses.

Photos: Richard Joseph

223

**SUMATRA HAS MANY MOUNTAIN LAKES, LARGEST BEING LAKE TOBA.**

# SUMATRA COMPLETES INDONESIAN PICTURE

Sumatra is the second largest island of Indonesia. Jaya, Bali and Sumatra are the most important parts of the Indonesia group in terms of cultural development. There are major oil fields in Sumatra, and coal mines. The important cities of the island are Palembang, Medan, Padang.

Photo: Republic of Indonesia Information Office

# RANGOON MEANS "END OF STRIFE"

Originally a fishing village, Rangoon was won by King Alaungpaya, given its name to signalize his victory, and developed as the capital of Burma. Badly hit in World War II, it's now re-building.

**The Independence Monument,** Rangoon: Burma achieved independence in 1948.

**Shwe Dagon Pagoda,** 2 miles from center of Rangoon, is Buddha's greatest shrine.

**Downtown Rangoon** is dominated by the Sule Pagoda which enshrines a Hair of

Buddha and other Relics from India. At the right is the City Hall of Rangoon.

**Singapore** has regular taxis, but a more original way of getting about is in one of these "trishaws"—three-wheeled bicycles powered by sun-hatted drivers.

**ANDERSON BRIDGE CROSSES SINGAPORE RIVER BY THE POST OFFICE.**

# SINGAPORE IS GATE TO THE FAR EAST

The British Colony of Singapore is the main port of call on route from Europe to the Far East; midway between India and China. Its famous Raffles Hotel has long been a symbol of the romance of world trade, and the Singapore sling a symbol of relaxation after work or play.

Photos: Horace Bristol (Black Star); bottom, Deane Dickason (Ewing Galloway)

**Great Southern Hotel,** Chinese-operated, has casement windows for maximum ventilation in the hot months. Beside hotel at left is Palace Theater, also Chinese.

**Sultan Mohammed Mosque** is on North Bridge Road, near Arab Street. One of the most beautiful sights in Singapore is the botanical garden with its monkey-jungle.

**Clock-tower lighthouse** is landmark in busy downtown Colombo, surrounded by a great variety of vehicles: native ox-carts, jinrickshas, modern motor cars.

**PANORAMIC VIEW SHOWS HARBOR OF COLOMBO, CEYLON'S CAPITAL.**

# MUCH OF WORLD'S TEA COMES FROM CEYLON

Since 1948 Ceylon has been a dominion of the British Commonwealth. The capital city of Colombo has had many changes since World War I and is now one of the world's cleanest and most modern cities. Ceylon raises rice, coconuts, rubber, tea.

Photos: Deane Dickason (Ewing Galloway); bottom, Ewing Galloway

**Golden Buddha in temple at Colombo:** Outside of town about 6 miles is the Temple of Kelaniya, very sacred because of a visit made to this spot by the Buddha.

**The Perahera** is an annual pageant held in Kandy during the month of August.

**Mount Lavinia Hotel,** overlooking ocean, is only eight miles outside of Colombo.

# INDIA IS LAND OF MYRIAD WONDERS

The Republic of India (a sovereign state since January 1950) boasts the famous Taj Mahal, sacred Ganges River, the great cities of Bombay, Calcutta, New Delhi, and the fabulous pink city of Jaipur.

**The 20 ornate Jain temples** in Calcutta are one of the city's great sights. Jainism is an offshoot of Hinduism, one belief being that it's wrong to kill, even insects.

Photo: TWA Trans World Airline

**The Holy Ghat** is bathing place in the Hooghly River (one of the many mouths of the Ganges) in Calcutta. Native "bum" boats provide transportation on river.

**Calcutta's parks and gardens**—Botanical, Zoological, Eden—have much of interest.

**Belur Temple,** eight miles from Calcutta, is center of Shri Ramakrishna Mission.

**The Taj Mahal,** made entirely of white marble, is a world famed masterpiece. It was built 1630–48, at Agra, by Shah Jehan as memorial to his beloved wife.

**Panch Mahal** is one of ornate buildings at fabulous deserted city of Fatehpur Sikri, about 20 miles from Agra. City was abandoned because of lack of water.

Photos: Deane Dickason (Ewing Galloway); bottom, Richard Joseph

**New Delhi,** seat of the government of the Republic of India, is a magnificent city.

Picturesque old buildings mingle with modern ones. This is President's house.

**Group of round-the-world tourists** finds elephant ride the oddest transportation.

**Ten thousand Moslems** pray before great Mosque of Delhi on a Friday morning.

**Sikh taxi drivers** of Calcutta don't look like their New York or Chicago brethren.

**Jantar Mantar** is early 18th-century observatory constructed by a Rajput King.

**View of the Himalayas** (which in Sanskrit means "abode of snow") from Sandakphu. Conquest of Everest and Annapurna has drawn world interest in this great range.

**The Bathing Ghats** and temples on bank of the Ganges River are visited by tens of thousands each year. Hindus come to the sacred river as Moslems go to Mecca.

Photos: Ewing Galloway

# VALE OF KASHMIR IS A GARDEN SPOT

Kashmir is one of the loveliest countries of the East, traversed by lofty ranges of the Himalayas, with lakes, rivers, forests. It is noted for its rich agriculture and its manufactures, especially Cashmeres.

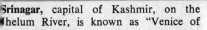

**Srinagar,** capital of Kashmir, on the Jhelum River, is known as "Venice of the East," intersected with canals and waterways, with boats as transportation.

**Dal Lake,** on outskirts of Srinagar, has several Moghul Gardens, visited by boat.

**A shikara,** a sort of Kashmiri gondola, takes you about in canalled Srinagar.

**Hyderabad,** one of main cities of Western Pakistan, has its own style of air-condi- tioning: wind scoops on most of th buildings take in air, force it downward

# PAKISTAN IS DIVIDED INTO TWO REGIONS

Pakistan, once a province of India, was made an independent state in 1947, as a homeland for Indian Moslems. The two parts of the nation are separated by 900 miles of Indian territory. The larger part is West Pakistan, with Karachi as its capital. East Pakistan, one-sixth as large, has as its regional capital, Dacca

**Balconies** are characteristic of houses in Karachi While auto traffic grows, the victorias still thrive

**Human-headed Sphinx** guards 3 Pyramids of Giza. At left is Pyramid of Khafra.

Near Great Pyramid, Kamal el-Malakh made his discovery of the Cheops bark.

**"Look, no hands!"** say camel-mounted nomads, eager for a piaster or two.

# EGYPT IS ANCIENT LAND OF THE NILE

The origin of Egypt's hoary culture is not revealed even in the many writings that have come down to us in all sorts of early forms. Some findings of the Ancient Kingdom date as far back as 3400 B.C., and the greatest creative period was from about 1580 to 945 B.C. Today you can ride in air-conditioned trains, stay in comfort at the Semiramis Hotel on the Nile (which has taken the place of burned-down Shepheard's), or at Mena House in shadow of pyramids.

**The great Citadel** in Cairo was built about 1179 by Saladin. It contains the beautiful Mosque of Mohammed Ali, with its alabaster walls, myriad lamps.

**Cairo bazaars** offer brass goods, marble and alabaster, gold and silver inlays.

**Nile boat** is shown opposite Cataract hotel at Aswan, site of irrigation dam.

Photos: TWA Trans World Airline, bottom right, Egyptian State Tourist Office

**Egyptian women of Luxor,** the ancient city of Thebes, use their heads to help their hands when there are burdens to carry. Tomb of Tut-ankh-amen is here.

**Egyptian wall paintings,** still remarkably bright, decorate wall of King Tut's tomb.

**Alabaster Sphinx** is one of sights at Memphis, capital of the Old Kingdom.

**Temple of Luxor,** built 1400 B.C., has huge pillars over fifty feet in height.

# ADVENTURE CALLS IN EAST AFRICA

Whether your name is Hemingway or Ruark or Smith, you'll find East Africa a land of great variety, abundant wild life, and amazing flora. It has the highest mountain on the continent, the Kibo peak of Kilimanjaro, only three degrees south of the equator. And it has Africa's largest lake, Victoria, stretching across the borders of Uganda, Tanganyika and Kenya.

**Uganda woman and child:** The Baganda are a very advanced, progressive people.

**Newly initiated Masai warriors:** They come from independent fighting tribe.

**Dar es Salaam,** meaning "Haven of Peace," is the capital of Tanganyika Terri-tory. This harbor, almost landlocked, handles over half of territory's exports.

**Two full-maned lions** seek the shade of a tree on Serengeti Plains, Tanganyika.

**Arab dhows** have traded with the East African coast for at least ten centuries.

**Elephants and other big game** abound in the Amboseli Game Reserve lying below Africa's highest mountain—the snow-capped dome of Kilimanjaro, 19,340 ft.

**Mt. Kenya** is 17,056 ft. high. Some of Kenya tribes think it residence of gods.

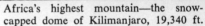

**Kilindini harbor** on Mombasa Island is the gateway to both Kenya and Uganda.

**VICTORIA FALLS SURPASSES NIAGARA IN BOTH WIDTH AND HEIGHT.**

# DAVID LIVINGSTONE
# EXPLORED RHODESIA

Explorer-missionary David Livingstone was the first white man to enter the region now included in the Federation of Rhodesia and Nyasaland. And the development of mineral resources by Cecil Rhodes led to the naming of Northern Rhodesia and Southern Rhodesia after him. Greatest natural feature of the area is Victoria Falls, 256 feet to 354 feet in height.

# OUTH AFRICA IS AND OF CONTRASTS

Union of South Africa, covering the broad southern tip of the continent, has busy cities like Johannesburg and Cape Town, fabulous gold mines, the great Kruger National Park, endless stretches of veld.

**ohannesburg's** busy Commissioner Street hows mushroom growth of gold center.

**Drakensberg mountains** tower above tourist hostel in Natal National Park.

**Pretoria** is the Union's administrative capital, though the legislature convenes

at Cape Town. Winston Churchill escaped from prison here during Boer War, 1899

# Union of South Africa

**Durban** is magnificently located on Natal Bay of the Indian Ocean. Marine Parade has many fine hotels. There is wonderfu surf, lake fishing, with unique ski-boats

**Visit to Kruger National Park** is thrilling. You stay in thatched cottages, cook meals outdoors if you like. You driv right by lions, zebras, leopards, hippos

244

**Kimberley diamond mine** reached 1,200 feet as open mine; shafts were carried to 4,000 feet. This mine was abandoned in 1915, but area is still diamond center.

**In Durban,** you see Zulus in gay costume and headdress drawing rickshas in street.

**All these diamonds** came from one day's output of Wesselton, Dutoitspan mines.

Photos: Pan American World Airways; bottom right, South African Tourist Corporation

# Union of South Africa

**Cape Town,** legislative capital of the Union, has many impressive buildings.

Flower Market is in front of City Hall, with Table Mountain in background.

**Aerial cableway** to top of Table Mountain, 3,500 feet, gives view of both

Atlantic and Indian Oceans. Cape Town has lovely harbor, is compared to Naples.

Photos: Pan American World Airways

# BERMUDA AND THE CARIBBEAN

The many islands, large and small, off the southeast coast of the United States have become most popular for both winter and summer vacations, because they give you "a trip abroad" with minimum time and any sort of expenditure you wish to make.

There are dozens of cruises through the Caribbean, especially from December through March, many of them by transatlantic liners put on the job of earning dollars for their owners during the time when travel to the European ports is slack. Taking such a ship is a good way to "try out" a trip abroad and see how it appeals to you.

There are also regularly scheduled trips throughout the year by vessels from New York to Bermuda and to Nassau, and from Miami and New Orleans to the Caribbean.

By air, almost any point in the West Indies is reached in a few hours. A network of air routes will take you any particular place, or a combination of places, quickly and pleasantly.

Variety is certainly offered by the enchanting isles of the West Indies. If you want gaiety, bustle and lots of entertainment, choose San Juan or Kingston. For quietude in the dignity of British colonial atmosphere, you'll like Nassau and Bermuda and Montego Bay. For the real "far, far away from it all" effect, you'll want one of the Virgin Islands, or Antigua, St. Lucia or one of the other isles of the Lesser Antilles. One of the best things to do is to make a sort of survey trip the first time, by cruise ship or by air, and "sample" several places on one trip. Cruise itineraries and air excursions often enable you to visit several of the islands at no greater cost than visiting one. Then you can pick the spot you like best for next time.

Our photo-cruise on the next pages starts with Bermuda, which is a good

Photo: Furness Bermuda Line

**"Ocean Monarch" docks at St. George's.**

thousand miles north of the Caribbean, but still shares the sub-tropical climate, thanks to the warm Gulf Stream. We skip quickly over Cuba, until happier times return there, and visit Nassau and other spots in the lovely Bahamas.

Our next stop is the lush green island of Jamaica, rimmed with its many fine beaches, over which hang leaning palms and mangroves. We visit the city of Kingston and the resorts of Montego Bay, Ocho Ríos and the others. Then we continue to Haiti, the famed republic of Christophe and his awesome fortress, the Citadelle. Pausing briefly in the Dominican Republic, we come to Puerto Rico, a commonwealth of the United States. Its lovely north shore, where San Juan and most of the resort hotels are located, is warmed by bright sunshine but cooled by gently puffing trade winds.

Stretching in a long arc, like giant stepping-stones between Puerto Rico and Venezuela, lie the sunny islands of the Lesser Antilles. Our tour includes Martinique, birthplace of Napoleon's Josephine; Guadeloupe; Antigua, where Lord Nelson was once stationed; the U.S. Virgin Islands; Trinidad, home of the Calypso songs; Tobago, Barbados, Grenada and St. Lucia. Finally we come to the Netherlands West Indies and the Fascinating Dutch island of Curaçao.

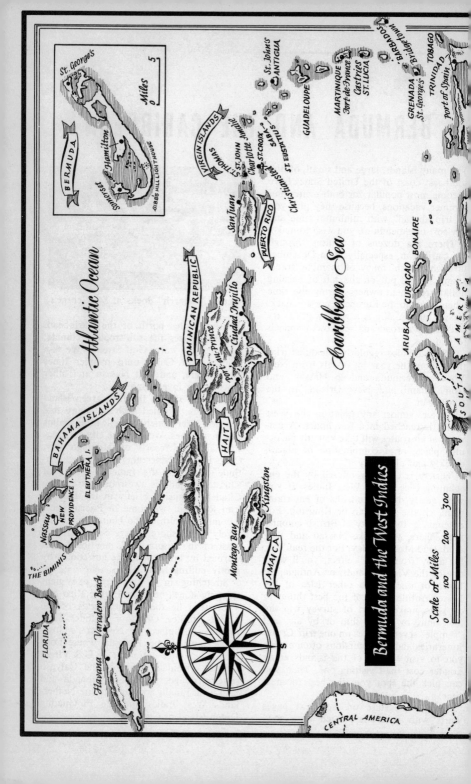

Bermuda and the West Indies

**FARAWAY COTTAGE COLONY, WARWICK PARISH, IS ONE OF NEWEST.**

# LOVELY BERMUDA HAS PEACE, QUIET

"Tranquil and contenting" were Mark Twain's words for Bermuda, and thousands of visitors have found it so, even when horses and carriages have given way to motorbikes and small English autos. Gulf Stream protection prevents extremes of temperature. Easter lilies, oleander combine with pink sands and blue-green sea waters for real beauty.

Photo: Bermuda News Bureau

# Bermuda

**Hamilton Harbor** is the home of Royal Bermuda Yacht Club, famous for racing of 14 ft. dinghies carrying 400 feet of canvas. Ferries run across busy harbor.

**Surreys and drays** have largely been replaced by Austins and Morris Minors.

**Bicycles and Velos**—bikes with motors on front wheel—are favorite transportation.

**Fields of Easter lilies** are a lovely sight in the spring. They're shipped everywhere.

**Bermuda homes** are built of native stone, in white, or in pastel pink, blue, purple.

**Grape Bay** has one of the many secluded beaches. The sands, eroded from coral rock, are often pink in color. The water sparkles in brilliant greens and blues.

Photos: Bermuda News Bureau;
top right, Lester L. Baker

**Par-le-Ville Gardens,** on Queen Street next to library, make a pleasant place to rest after a trip to Hamilton's many shops where you get fine British woolens.

**Front Street,** Hamilton, usually bustling, is very peaceful when shops are closed.

**Crystal Caves,** Leamington Caves offer stalactites and stalagmites, and souvenirs.

**SWIZZLE INN IS FAVORITE STOP.**

**WORLD'S TINIEST DRAW BRIDGE.**

Photos: Bermuda News Bureau; two at bottom, Richard Joseph

**Bermuda Cathedral** stands at a high point, is one of islands' many churches.

**The Devil's Hole,** a natural aquarium, is place where you can fish without hooks.

**Gibb's Hill Light House** affords a view from its top of many of the 150 islands.

**This "Moon Gate"** is one of several, an odd design said to be copied from China.

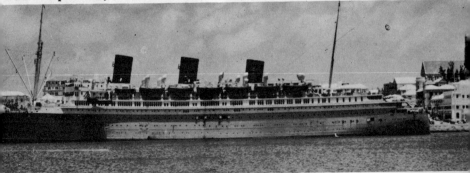

**S.S. QUEEN OF BERMUDA DOCKS RIGHT AT FRONT STREET, HAMILTON**

Photos: Bermuda News Bureau; top right, center left, A. Milton Runyon

**The Reefs Beach Club** is a picturesque cabana colony built on the rugged coral cliffs of the south shore overlooking Christian Bay, near Gibb's Hill Light.

Photo: A. Milton Runyon

**Inverurie Hotel,** on Hamilton Harbor, is one of the old stand-bys, recently modern-ized with balcony suites shown at the right. It's just ten minutes by ferry to Hamilton.

**The Ledgelets** is charming cottage colony on landscaped hillside in Sandys Parish. Guests have the use of a private white sand beach and small boats at Ely's Harbor.

**Palmetto Bay Colony** consists of a lovely old Bermuda house and modern cottages in a tropical setting on Harrington Sound. These guest houses are typical of Bermuda.

Photos: Bermuda News Bureau

# CUBA'S HEART WAS YOUNG AND GAY

Before the days of Castro, Cuba was always one of the most popular islands for U.S. visitors, and we hope that the happy days will come again when planes and ships can land tourists in Havana for the most exotic night life outside of Paris.

**San Francisco dock,** in Havana harbor, was principal landing point for tenders from ships anchored in the roadstead. It was just short walk to famed Sloppy Joe's.

**The National Capitol** dominates center of the metropolis, founded by Velasquez.

**Nacional de Cuba** is most famous hotel in the capital. New pool offers lush living.

256

Photos: A. L. Koolish; bottom left, Cuban Tourist Commission; right, Kirkeby Hotels

**San Cristobal,** known as the Columbus Cathedral, is over two hundred years old.

**Morro Castle,** at the entrance to Havana harbor, was built in the late 16th century.

**Paseo de Marti** (formerly "The Prado") runs from the center of Havana to the sea wall. Treelined, it reminds you of the Champs-Elysées, with its sidewalk cafés.

Photos: A. Milton Runyon; A. L. Koolish; Pan American World Airways

# NASSAU IS PART OF THE ENCHANTING BAHAMAS

**THE BRITISH COLONIAL HOTEL OFFERS TWO BEACHES, WATER-SKIING.**

You'll find Nassau the most dignified of the British islands, peaceful, bucolic. The beaches are magnificent, and the climate almost always warm and sunny. The Bahamas are one of the world's greatest sportfishing grounds, abounding in tuna, sailfish, barracuda, bonito, wahoo, and dolphin. Altogether there are some 700 islands in the Bahamas, and 2000 keys and reefs of coral sand and rock. They stretch a distance of about 800 miles, from southeast of·Florida, cover 4400 square miles.

Photo: A. Milton Runyon

**At the Straw Market,** in Rawson Square, you can buy straw hats, bags, table mats which are woven right before your eyes, and decorated with gaily colored shells.

**Christ Church** was designated as the Cathedral by Queen Victoria in 1861.

**The British Colonial** is Nassau's second largest hotel, with two beaches, pool.

**Paradise Beach** is as famous as Waikiki. Surf temperature averages 70°, even in winter. Palm trees and sun-shelters add to its charm. Note cruise ships at anchor.

**Prince George Dock** is the place you get boat for short trip to Paradise Beach.

**Horse and carriage** await visitors at Royal Victoria Hotel's tropical gardens.

Photos: Nassau Development Board — Frederic Maura

**Royal Victoria Hotel's** new garden pool is surrounded by luxuriant trees, plants.

**Bay Street** is famed for shops offering British textiles, gloves, leather goods.

**Queen's Staircase** is 65-step man-made canyon, carved out of the solid coral rock.

**Salt-water angling** in Nassau is action-packed, for big game fisherman, amateur.

**This octagonal building** was once a jail; in 1879 it was converted into a library.

**Fort Montagu Beach Hotel,** seen from Fort Montagu, is Nassau's third largest.

# Bahamas

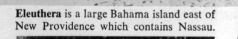

Eleuthera is a large Bahama island east of New Providence which contains Nassau.

Governor's Harbor has miles of beaches and town with name of French Leave.

Walker Cay is one of 700 Bahama islets. Columbus made his first landfall on one.

Bimini is the Bahama island closest to the U.S., noted for its big game fishing.

262

# SUMMER NEVER LEAVES JAMAICA

Largest British island in the West Indies, Jamaica offers beautiful mountain scenery, lovely beaches and good year 'round climate. Daytime temperatures are in the upper 70's all year, and trade winds make for cool nights.

Jamaica has five different resort areas: The first is the capital city of Kingston and suburban St. Andrews. At the eastern tip is Port Antonio and the northeast coast. Central Jamaica has Ocho Rios. Further west is Mandeville, its mountains and the south coast. And on the northwest coast is the famous Montego Bay.

Part of the Greater Antilles, Jamaica is about 148 miles long, and 52 miles wide at its widest point. It's like a turtle in shape, with the ridges of the east-west mountains forming the turtle's back. Blue Mountain Peak, the highest point, reaches 7520 feet above sea level. Many good harbors cut into the coast.

**Jamaican woman** plaits hat from young leaves of the light jipijapa palm.

**Noel Coward,** English author and playwright, makes his island home at "Blue Harbour."

Photos: Jamaica Tourist
Trade Development Board

# Jamaica

**Native markets** in Kingston offer fresh tropical fruits; shops have English goods.

**With razor sharp machete,** this cutter is about to start on a field of sugar cane.

**Flame blowers** provide entertainment at night for visitors at Hotel Casa Blanca.

**WATER SKIIERS SKIM PAST TOWER ISLE, JAMAICA'S $2,000,000 RESORT.**

Photos: Jamaica Tourist Trade Development Board; center right, Gerald Murison, bottom, Pierre Chong

**Fort Charles,** 1656, and Palisadoes airport are on long peninsula that encloses harbor.

**The south coast** has many lakes where fishing is fun, and even washing clothes!

**Doctor's Cave beach** at Montego Bay is one of the finest in the entire Caribbean. It has fine white coral sand and sea water so clear that a boat floating on its surface seems to be floating in mid-air! Bathing is a constant delight, with no rough surf.

**From near Berrydale,** on the northeast coast, a 2½ mile sinuously curving stretch of gentle rapids on the Rio Grande is the route of the unique sport of river-rafting."

**Montego Bay,** with fashionable Sunset Lodge and Casa Blanca Hotel, is today the Cannes of Jamaica, even though only 35 years ago it was just a fishing village.

Photos: Vilma F. Bergane; bottom, Jamaica Tourist Trade Development Board

# HAITI IS A 'MAGIC ISLAND"

To appreciate Haiti, you'll want to know something of its strange history, of Toussaint L'Ouverture, of Dessalines, of Henri Christophe, Haiti's Black Napoleon who built the fabulous *Citadelle*. Read John Vandercook's *Black Majesty,* or William Seabrook's *The Magic Island,* or Kenneth Roberts' novel of Haiti, *Lydia Bailey.*

Haiti lies in the western part of the island of Hispaniola in the West Indies, with the Dominican Republic occupying the rest of the island. The official language is French, but most people speak a French patois called Creole, a mixture of Indian, French, Spanish.

**Ubiquitous** small boys, usually less well dressed, pose for your photos.

**At Centre d'Art,** in Port-au-Prince, see work of many Haitian painters.

**The Citadelle** was built by Henri Christophe to stop French invasion that never came.

Photos: Pan American World Airways, top left, Jerry Hardy

TRUJILLO PEACE MONUMENT IS AT SANTIAGO DE LOS CABALLEROS.

# THE DOMINICAN REPUBLIC
# COMBINES OLD AND NEW

Founded 1496 by Bartholomew Columbus, Ciudad Trujillo (formerly Santo Domingo) is the oldest permanent European settlement in the New World. Dominican Republic occupies eastern part of Hispaniola Island, Haiti western.

Photo: Dominican Republic Information Center

# "SWITZERLAND OF THE AMERICAS" — PUERTO RICO

A commonwealth of the United States, yet distinctly foreign in its atmosphere, 100-mile-long Puerto Rico offers mountain scenery to rival French and Swiss Alps, beautiful beaches, and pleasant climate. Winter temperatures average 74.5° and summer, 80°, a difference of only 5.5°. San Juan and most of the major hotels are located on the northern shore of the island which gets full benefit of the gently puffing trade winds, even in the summer time.

**Fabulous Caribe Hilton, with its New Garden Wing, Is Located Right on the Ocean.**

Photo: Hilton Hotels International

**Porta Coeli,** "gate of heaven," one of the oldest churches in the western hemisphere.

**Flower market** offers a profusion of exotic blooms from tropical gardens.

**Luquillo Beach** is a mile-long crescent, fringed with palms, near El Yunque forest.

**University of Puerto Rico** has many students and professors from U.S.A.

Photos: Hamilton Wright

**El Morro,** built in 1539 with ship ballast, guards entrance to San Juan harbor.

**Dorado Beach Hotel,** 20 miles west of San Juan, has two crescent beaches, golf course.

**Condado Beach Hotel** has been newly renovated, and a new mountain resort, El Barranquitas, has just opened. Best known country club is the Berwind, Rio Piedras.

**Native net fisherman** demonstrates possibilities for the sportsman. Puerto Rican waters are fished for white and blue marlin, sailfish, Allison tuna, many others.

**Fiesta Santiago,** celebrated for over 300 years by the villagers of Loíza Aldea, produces weird faces in coconut masks. Pageantry and parades last two weeks.

**Hotel Montemar** at Aguadilla offers cooling breezes, spectacular views from terrace high above the Atlantic. Here newlyweds need pay only for one instead of for two.

Photos: Hamilton Wright

**Napoleon's Empress Josephine** was born in Trois-Ilets, and a marble statue of her rises in the center of the Savannah or public park in city of Fort-de-France.

# MARTINIQUE IS "POMPEII OF THE WEST INDIES"

On May 8, 1902 Mont Pelée blew up with a roar and wiped out the whole 40,000 population of St. Pierre, with just one survivor, a prisoner in an underground dungeon. Martinique is one of the two main French islands in the Lesser Antilles, the other being Guadeloupe. 50 miles long by 19 wide, Martinique is very beautiful and a good place for relaxing because there's little night life. Large plantations grow substantial crops of sugar and bananas. The fishing is very good.

# Martinique

**Native net-thrower** fishermen in Ville-Fontaine show tourists how net is made.

**Colorful costumes** indicate native gaiety, also shown in dancing at *Select Tango*.

**Important influence** of Roman Catholic Church has helped control communists.

**Lido Hotel,** four miles from Fort-de-France, is place for bathing and loafing.

*Vieux Moulin, Chez Etienne, L'Auberge de Manoir* offer good French cuisine.

274

Photos: Pan American World Airways

# GUADELOUPE KEEPS ALIVE ITS CREOLE HERITAGE

About 80 miles north of Martinique, the other French possession of Guadeloupe is one of those "get-away-from-it-all" places where accommodations are far from luxurious, but the climate is ideal, scenery superb, and natives interesting.

Pointe-à-Pitre is the principal city and port. The official capital is Basse-Terre, about forty miles away. A jeepable track leads to the base of the extinct volcano, La Soufrière, a good stiff climb. People keep alive gay Creole customs.

# DISCOVER ANTIGUA FOR FRIENDLINESS

The coral island of Antigua is a British crown colony, capital of the Leeward Islands. It is a quiet, friendly place where every visitor is treated as an honored guest. St. John's, the principal town, is a neat, charming little seaport.

**Guests at the Mill Reef Club** enjoy a sunlit terrace overlooking the white sand beaches and clear blue-green water. Antigua has swimming, tennis and golf.

**Old winches** like this were used to haul Lord Nelson's ships onto beach for repair.

**Fishing boats** may be chartered; waters near reefs are perfect for spear-fishing.

Photos: Pan American World Airways

# EX-DANISH VIRGIN ISLANDS
# ARE TRANQUIL, CHARMING

**HILLSIDE STREETS OF CHARLOTTE AMALIE HAVE FLOWERING VINES.**

Purchased from Denmark in 1917, for $25,000,000, the three main American Virgin Islands of St. Thomas, St. Croix and St. John are still unspoiled by too many tourists. Since they have free-port status, it is possible to buy many wonderful things at a fraction of their U.S. prices. Most visitors come for the wonderful climate, with an average mean temperature of 79° F., the bucolic atmosphere, the delight of being "abroad" and yet still on home territory.

St. Thomas is 40 miles east of Puerto Rico, and St. Croix about 40 miles south of St. Thomas. Both of these islands may be reached by plane, but St. John is accessible only by regularly scheduled launch from Charlotte Amalie, port of St. Thomas.

St. Thomas is most highly developed island, with the new Virgin Isle and many fine hotels. St. Croix is the largest, most agricultural, with small but good hotels. St. John has most rugged primitiveness, limited but very delightful guest houses.

# Virgin Islands

**Distinctive tower** features Bluebeard's Castle Hotel, setting for many legends.

**Virgin Isle Hilton** is most luxurious. Swimming pool overlooks hills, harbor.

**From the terrace of Bluebeard's Castle** Hotel, you look out over the whole town

278

of Charlotte Amalie. On far side is the
French village, called Cha-Cha Town,
whose people are descendants of the early
French settlers. Shrine of St. Anne is here.

# Virgin Islands

Cruise ship "Mauretania" stays in harbor, ferries passengers to dock by motorboat.

Steep streets of Charlotte Amalie often require steps from one level to another.

Three youngsters grin for the tourist-photographer in hope of U.S. pennies.

Trunk Bay is on island of St. John, site of beautiful Virgin Islands National Park.

Christiansted on northeast (above) and Frederiksted on the west are the two principal towns on St. Croix.

This old Danish sugar mill is St. Croix Island landmark.

Photos: A. Milton Runyon; bottom row, Pan American World Airways

# TRINIDAD IS THE CAPITAL OF CALYPSO

**ON DRIVE "OVER THE SADDLE" TO MARACAS BAY YOU PAUSE HERE.**

Most colorful and polyglot of all the West Indies islands, Trinidad is home of Calypso, the satirical and haunting folk songs. As you walk through the streets of the capital, Port of Spain, you're likely to encounter East Indians, Hindus, British, Spanish, French, Chinese, Africans, Americans. There are Moslem mosques, Hindu temples, bazaars. Port of Spain is as exotic as Hong Kong or Singapore.

# Trinidad

**Beautiful Maracas Bay,** on North Coast, is reached by drive from Port of Spain that winds through bamboo groves, banyan trees, coffee and cocoa plantations.

**Donkey cart** loaded with coconuts is the Trinidad version of sidewalk "milk bar."

**Frederick Street** is Port of Spain's shopping center for British goods, silver.

Pitch Lake (Asphalt) is supposed to be 285 feet deep. You can walk on surface.

A Sikh, one of many East Indians living in Trinidad, stands before a mosque.

The local "steel bands" consist of steel drums of varying tones beaten to Calypso rhythm. The effect is surprisingly good. January is month of Calypso competition.

Queen's Park Hotel, center of social life, is located on 200-acre Savannah.

Trinidad's fertile soil yields sugar cane, cacao, coffee, citrus fruits, coconuts.

# TOBAGO IS UNSPOILED

Believed to be the spot where Robinson Crusoe was shipwrecked, Tobago is little-known place whose visitors would like to preserve its charm for themselves alone.

**Aquatic Club** beach has cabanas thatched with palm leaves and wonderful beach. It's at Pigeon Point, Man of War Bay. With sea goggles you may look at marine life.

**Exotic birds of paradise** are found only in Tobago and in New Guinea. They're shy, hard to find, but it's an unforgettable experience to see them on this tiny isle.

**Tobago is a land of leisure** and quiet beauty that you have often longed for. There are four main hotels and one guest house, an indication of the privacy here.

284

**WILLEMSTAD, BISECTED BY ST. ANNA BAY, HAS PONTOON BRIDGE.**

# OIL BRINGS RICHES TO DUTCH INDIES

The Netherlands West Indies consist of two widely separated units: the islands of Curaçao, Aruba and Bonaire, off the coast of Venezuela, and 500 miles away in the Lesser Antilles, the islands of Saba, St. Eustatius and southern half of St. Martin (the other half being French). Curaçao is noted for its sales of world-famed goods, liqueurs at bargain prices.

**Bird's-eye view** of Willemstad shows two halves, joined by "Queen Emma" bridge.

# CURAÇAO MIGHT BE HOLLAND AT SEA

Peter Stuyvesant became governor of Curaçao in 1643 and moved to New Amsterdam, now New York, in 1647. For 17 years he was Director General of the New Netherlands and Netherlands West Indies. Formerly a colony, this territory became in 1922 an integral part of the kingdom of the Netherlands. At first glance it looks like a slice of Holland, tidy and well scrubbed, moved out into the Atlantic 40 miles north of Venezuela. But you soon notice the West Indies influence. The buildings come in pastel, and sometimes more violent tints to soften the glare.

**Passengers on cruise steamer** get view of pontoon bridge as it swings to side.

Photos: Netherlands West Indies Tourist Committee

**Piscadera Bay Club,** foremost resort, has natural swimming pool with sea water.

**Everything** but liquor and tobacco is imported at 3.3% duty; it's almost free port.

**Floating market** forms daily on older side of town, with schooners from many ports.

**Foodstuffs** are peddled right from the decks. Many merchants are Venezuelan.

**West Point Bay** and beach, at the western tip of Curaçao, is a popular drive from Willemstad for lunch, bathing and fishing. Aloes cactus flourishes here.

# BARBADOS IS A TROPICAL BRITAIN

Said to have been originally discovered by the Portuguese and named "Los Barbados" because of the bearded fig trees Barbados was claimed by the British in 1605, settled by them beginning in 1627 and has been under the British flag ever since — something quite unusual in the history of a Caribbean island. Most easterly of the Lesser Antilles, Barbados juts far out into the Atlantic's open waters

**Sam Lord's Castle,** at St. Philip, is now operated as a residential club, one of several on Barbados, and there are good, small hotels. Life is simple, leisurely.

288

**Excellent roads** criss-cross Barbados Island, with its very English landscape.

**Swan Street,** Bridgetown, is filled with carts, cyclists, autos, and pedestrians.

**The Savannah,** big oblong of grass, is used for polo matches, race meetings.

At races the police band plays; the little horses bear colors raced for generations.

# GRENADA IS "THE SPICE ISLAND"

Most southerly of the Windward Islands Grenada is famous for its nutmeg, cloves and for some of the most beautiful white sand beaches in the world. It has Grand Étang, spectacular volcanic lake 1740 ft above sea level. Grenada's port city of St. George's is very popular cruise stop.

**Morne Rouge Beach Club,** St. George's, has excellent beach, dining and dancing.

Another fine spot to swim, or dream, is Grand Anse, with two miles of white sand.

**Guests** of the Santa Maria Hotel enjoy tea on veranda overlooking picturesque

St. George's. Its red-roofed houses are pale pink and green, its atmosphere quiet.

290

**Carenage Bay** is a calm harbor for fishing boats and cargo schooners. One section of St. George's is on the bay, another on the sea, connected by tunnel.

Photo: Pan American
World Airways

# ST. LUCIA WAS PORT FOR CLIPPER SHIPS

Directly in the path of the trade wind, on route of the sailing clippers of old, St. Lucia is largest of Windward Islands. Castries has sheltered harbor, one of finest in the West Indies and long an important coaling station. Landmarks are mineral springs near Soufrière and cones of the Twin Pitons Peaks. Castries has an airport, right on a fine strip of beach.

**Hotel Antoine** is high on a hill overlooking the city of Castries, its harbor and background of chocolate drop hills. Pigeon Island Beach Club is charming

Photo: Pan American World Airways

# CANADA

**CANADIAN PACIFIC'S "THE CANADIAN" CROSSES MISSISSIPPI RIVER.**

Because many parts of the United States are hot in the summer, nearby Canada has become a favorite vacation ground, offering cool lakes, rivers, beautiful mountains. And in winter, snow for sports is abundant in the Laurentians and Canadian Rockies.

One of Canada's many advantages is its excellent transportation. Canadian Pacific and Canadian National cover it with great railroad networks. There are Great Lakes steamers and St. Lawrence River steamers. Trans-Canada Air Lines will take you across Canada, or abroad. And because the highways are excellent, and less likely to be crowded, many tourists prefer to travel by car, especially on such a scenic drive as the one around the Gaspé Peninsula between Maine and the St. Lawrence. Another excellent idea is to make your trip abroad by way of the St. Lawrence River. The new Seaway makes it possible to embark on some transatlantic ships at Great Lakes ports. Many great liners leave from Montreal, traveling nearly a thousand miles in the quiet river waters before reaching the open ocean. On the west coast, Canada is the gateway to Alaska, via the 1000-mile "inside passage" route from Victoria and Vancouver up Georgia Strait to Prince Rupert, Juneau and Skagway.

In visiting Canada you will be amazed at the industrial developments in many places, but you'll enjoy some of the world's great resorts and explore great national parks covering 29,000 square miles.

Our photo tour of Canada starts in the Province of Quebec, home of the French Canadian nation, and Quebec City, the heart of that nation's loyalties. We then go on to Montreal, after Paris the second largest French city in the world. We then go east to the Atlantic Provinces — Nova Scotia, Prince Edward Island, New Brunswick, and Newfoundland.

We then ascent the St. Lawrence, with French names disappearing, and enter Ontario, the most populous province. It boasts two capitals — Toronto, the provincial capital, and Ottawa, capital of all Canada. It also has famous recreational areas — Niagara Falls, the Muskoka Lakes and other forested lakes north of Toronto, and the Lake of the Woods area in western Ontario, known for great fishing.

We cross Manitoba and Saskatchewan to the great resorts of Banff and Lake Louise in Alberta, and end our tour in spectacular British Columbia.

Photo: Canadian
Pacific Railway

# Canada

**Scale of Miles**
0   100   200        500

### (Inset map)
MONTREAL

ST. CATHERINE

ST. DENIS

ROCKLAND AV.

CÔTE DES NEIGES

MT. ROYAL PARK

UNIVERSITY OF MONTREAL

ST. LAWRENCE RIVER

NOTRE DAME

### (Main map labels)

Arctic Ocean

Atlantic Ocean

Pacific Ocean

Hudson Bay

NEWFOUNDLAND

St. John's

Gander

PRINCE EDWARD IS.

NOVA SCOTIA

Charlottetown

Grand Pré

Halifax

Bay of Fundy

NEW BRUNSWICK

Saint John

St. Andrews-by-the-Sea

Percé

GASPÉ TRAIL

SAGUENAY R.

Tadoussac

LAURENTIAN MTS.

Quebec

Montreal

Ottawa

St. LAWRENCE R.

Niagara Falls

Toronto

MUSKOKA LAKES

QUEBEC

ONTARIO

THE GREAT LAKES

Kenora

Winnipeg

Churchill

MANITOBA

SASKATCHEWAN

Regina

NORTHWEST TERRITORIES

YUKON

ALBERTA

Jasper Park

Lake Louise

Banff

Calgary

GLACIER NATIONAL PARK

ROCKY MOUNTAINS

BRITISH COLUMBIA

Victoria

Vancouver

VANCOUVER IS.

Seattle

Ketchikan

Juneau

YUKON R.

ALASKA

UNITED STATES

**CHATEAU FRONTENAC HOTEL IS LIKE A MEDIEVAL FRENCH CASTLE.**

# QUEBEC HAS CHARM OF THE OLD WORLD

Discovered by Jacques Cartier in 1534 and settled by the French under Champlain early in the 17th century, Quebec hasn't lost its Old World flavor. Hand looms, outdoor bake ovens, spinning wheels are still in daily use. Although French is spoken throughout the province, most people also speak English.

Calèches haul tourists up and down the hills as the driver tells of historic spots.

Rue Sous-le-Cap, in Lower Town, is said to be narrowest street in North America.

Quebec is deeply religious city, with Sisters of the Good Shepherd, and many shrines.

St. Louis Gate is one of several remaining from old fortifications of early days.

Hooked rugs, made during long winters, are good buys; so are carved wood figures.

Curling is kind of bowling played with heavy stones slid along ice toward a mark.

Photos: Canadian Pacific Railway; top left, Canadian National Railways

**Chateau Frontenac's toboggan slide** takes you at mile-a-minute speed from near top of Citadel hill down to Dufferin Terrace with spectacular view of St. Lawrence.

Photo: Canadian
Pacific Railway

**Ste. Anne de Beaupré,** a few miles east of Quebec City, is most famous shrine of the New World. The great Basilica burned in 1922, but has been built anew.

**Scala Sancta,** sacred stairway at Ste. Anne, is worn by the knees of worshipers.

**Montmorency Falls,** between Quebec and Ste. Anne, are even higher than Niagara.

**Round Lake Inn**, Weir, is one of many resorts of Quebec and the Laurentians.

Laurentides Park and Mt. Tremblant Park have 1500 lakes and cascading streams.

**Maple sugar camps** in the Laurentians gather their annual harvest each spring.

**Many** a rural Quebec family still goes to Mass on Sunday in a horse-drawn buggy.

**Husky races** are one of Canada's many winter sports: Scandinavian-type skiing

in the east, the dashing Alpine kind in western Rockies; skating, hockey, curling.

# Canada QUEBEC PROVINCE

**Bonaventure Island,** off end of Gaspé peninsula, is a sanctuary for gannets.

**River steamer** of Canada Steamship Lines passes Manoir Richelieu, at Murray Bay.

**Old Habitant houses** like this one on Isle of Orleans have been lived in 200 years.

**Percé Rock** is the high point of tour around Gaspé peninsula. It's the pierced rock that Cartier first saw beside the shore, a great stone buffeted by seas.

Photos: Canada Steamship Lines; Canadian National Railways; Canadian Pacific Railway; Office Provincial de Publicité, Quebec

**Mount Royal,** towering above the great city of Montreal, second largest French-speaking city in the world, has a lookout that gives magnificent view of the city.

**Open sightseeing trolley cars** are unique way to take in Montreal's historic points.

**Bonsecours Market** is the place where the habitant farmers sell their own produce.

**Brother André's** first chapel in Montreal.

**St. Joseph's Oratory** draws stream of pilgrims every day.

**St. Catherine Street** is one of the main shopping centers.

**The fame of McGill University** has gone around the world, especially for its medi- cine. Some think ice hockey was invented at McGill. Now skiing has taken over.

**Montreal** is the world's largest grain-shipping port, transshipment point for Great Lakes. Its extensive docks are busy when St. Lawrence is not ice-blocked.

**Grand Pré** was home of Longfellow's *Evangeline*.

**Evangeline's Memorial** is in a park full of flowers, memories.

**Chester Inlet** is quiet spot on the south shore.

**Port Royal Habitation** was first permanent white settlement north of the Gulf.

**From Dingwall,** Cape Breton Island, boats fish most fertile waters for swordfish, tuna.

**Old shipmodeler** at Plympton works on craft that brings back exciting memories.

**Ox cart** plods through village of Shag Harbour, known for its lobster, fisheries.

Photos: Canadian Pacific Railway; top right, Canadian National Railways; center right, Canadian Government Travel Bureau

**St. Andrews-by-the-Sea** is world-famous resort.

**Antique-hunting,** fishing, golf, are attractions at St. Andrews.

**Country** around Greenock Church looks Scottish.

**Famous "Reversing Falls"** at St. John are due to tremendous tides in Bay of Fundy.

As tide rises, the falls run uphill, inland from the sea, then they reverse.

**Fundy National Park** rises above tide-worn cliffs. It has sea and fresh-water swimming and fishing, including the heated salt-water swimming pool pictured.

Photos: Canadian Pacific Railway; bottom, Canadian Government Travel Bureau

# Canada PRINCE EDWARD ISLAND

**Nine to thirty miles** off Canada's coast, Prince Edward Island is reached by ferry.

**Articles of Confederation,** making Canada a Dominion, were drawn at Charlottetown.

**The crack clipper ship,** *Marco Polo,* was wrecked off Cavendish. The beach, now part of the Prince Edward Island National Park, is best-known resort on the Island.

Photos: Canadian National Railways; bottom, Canadian Government Travel Bureau

# Canada NEWFOUNDLAND

**Gander Airport** is main North American terminal for air services to all parts of Europe, built 1939. Though there is heavy snow, Gander is relatively free from fog.

**Lumbering** is important Newfoundland industry; there are plants for woodworking.

**At Cabot Tower,** St. John's, Marconi received first wireless across the Atlantic.

**Fishing** (cod, salmon, herring, lobster) on the Grand Banks and Labrador coast is the chief occupation. Newfoundland joined Confederation on March 31, 1949.

306

Photos: Canadian National Railways; top, Canadian Government Travel Bureau

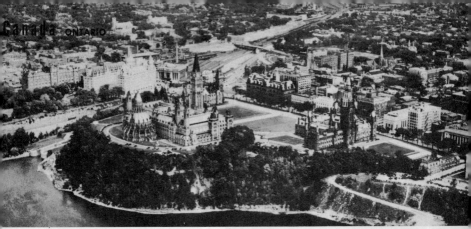

**Ottawa,** whose Parliament buildings on bank of Ottawa River are shown in this airview, was chosen capital by Queen Victoria, became seat of Dominion in 1867.

**Fort Henry,** overlooking Kingston harbor, built in 1812, is now history museum.

**Ship** passes through the Long Soo Canal. In background you see Long Soo Rapids.

**Peace Tower** is the dominating feature of Parliament buildings, rebuilt after fire.

Photos: Canadian Pacific Railway; center and bottom left, Canadian Government Travel Bureau

**This is one** of lakes in the Haliburton district, near Algonquin Provincial Park.

**Best vantage point** for the widest-angle view of Niagara Falls in the attractive

**Toronto,** on Lake Ontario, is Canada's second city, business center of flourishing

Ontario industry. Since 1912, Canadian National Exposition has been held here.

Photos: Herbert Ford; top right, Canadian Pacific Railway; bottom, Canadian Government Travel Bureau

top-floor big-windowed dining room of
the General Brock Hotel. You can watch

the *Maid-of-the-Mist* take honeymooners
for an exciting close-up near the falls.

**Queen Elizabeth Way** is excellent highway
running from Niagara Falls to Toronto.

**Lake Rosseau** is part of Muskoka Lakes
forest and resort area north of Toronto.

Photos: Canadian Government Travel
Bureau; bottom right, Wilfrid Ford

**This angler's paradise** is near border west Ontario; others are more remote

**Fishermen** at this lodge go after large and smallmouth bass, northern pike, and trout.

**Fish grow big** in Ontario's 750,000 lakes and ponds, and its many lively streams

**Fishermen's village** is near Kenora, Lake of the Woods, 120 miles east of Winnipeg.

**Sampling** the fresh-caught trout sizzling over campfire is one of real delights

Photos: A. L. Koolish

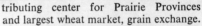

**Winnipeg,** capital of Manitoba, is midway between Atlantic and Pacific. It is distributing center for Prairie Provinces and largest wheat market, grain exchange.

**World's largest** privately owned railway yards are Canadian Pacific's at Winnipeg.

**A self-propelled combine** harvests barley in the vicinity of St. François Xavier.

**Riding Mountain National Park,** 100 miles north of Winnipeg, has hotels, cabins.

**At Churchill,** on Hudson Bay, grain is loaded for trip through Hudson Strait.

Photos: Canadian National Railways; center, Canadian Pacific Railway; bottom left, Canadian Government Travel Bureau

311

**Regina,** capital of Saskatchewan, is the first training center for famous Royal Canadian Mounted Police recruits. Above is Hotel Saskatchewan. City has many parks.

**Prince Albert National Park** and eight provincial parks in Saskatchewan provide many miles of forests, lakes, rivers. This is air view of Waskesiu and Lake Waskesiu.

**The magnificent Banff Springs Hotel** has a most spectacular setting overlooking the Bow River Valley. It's right in the Rockies, at an altitude of 4,538 feet,

Photos: Canadian Pacific Railway; bottom left, Canadian Government Travel Bureau

and is surrounded by several peaks over 9,000 feet high. Banff is in southern part of Banff National Park, 65 miles west of Calgary, and is famous as both summer and winter resort, with hot sulphur springs, museum, zoological garden, wild-animal paddock. For 64 years the Indian Days celebrations have been held here.

**The Canadian Rockies** are North American center of Alpine skiing, with snow 20 feet deep and powder fast. The peaks of the Rockies provide a majestic backdrop.

**Behind the Banff ski lift** you see peak of Mount Rundle, with Bow River Valley.

**Along the** Banff-Lake Louise highway you stop to feed Rocky Mountain sheep.

Photos: Canadian Pacific Railway; bottom right, Canadian Government Travel Bureau

**Banff Indian Days,** with their contests, reach climax with awards at the Hotel.

**Chieftains** parade in all their finery: Crees, Saracees, Blackfeet, and Stonys.

**Banff School of Fine Arts,** an extension of the University of Alberta, has held summer courses at Banff for twenty years. Students have beautiful scenes to paint.

Photos: Canadian Pacific Railway

Canada ALBERTA

**Lake Louise,** near Banff—sapphire blue in color and surrounded by perpetually snow-capped peaks—has been called most beautiful single scene in North America.

**Six Glaciers Tea House** looks out on Lake Louise and 11,365-foot Mount Victoria.

**Trail Riders'** packtrain crosses shallow Pipestone River on way to base camp.

Photos: Canadian Pacific Railway

**Canoeing** is probably best way to enjoy full beauty of Lake Louise and the giddy summits around it, in their ever-changing panorama. You may see bighorn sheep.

Photo: Canadian Pacific Railway.

**Steamer "Princess Elizabeth"** pulls into pier at Nanaimo, Vancouver Island. Such steamers ply daily between Victoria, Vancouver and Inside Passage to Alaska.

**Founded in 1843** by Hudson's Bay Company as a fur trading post, Victoria is now capital of British Columbia. Empress Hotel is attractive; roses bloom all year.

**Lumber,** pulp are important. Logs are dumped at Chemainus, Vancouver Island.

**Thunderbird Park** is one of several in Victoria; others are Beacon Hill, Gorge.

Photos: Canadian Government Travel Bureau; center and left, Canadian Pacific Railway; bottom right, Canadian National Railways

# MEXICO AND CENTRAL AMERICA

Just as Canada is a handy "foreign" land for vacations to the north, so are Mexico and Central America for southern vacations — and especially so for the residents of the border states of California, Arizona, New Mexico, Texas and other states near enough for travel by car. The well-paved Inter-American Highway leads from Laredo, Texas, through Monterrey to Mexico City, a comfortable 3-day trip of 764 miles. If you're coming from the East, you could cross the border at Brownsville and join the main highway at Ciudad Victoria. From California and Arizona, a popular auto trip south is through the Mexican state of Sonora which has recently been hard-topping its roads and preparing for North American visitors. From Nogales, just south of Tucson, Arizona, you head for Hermosillo and Guaymas. On the Gulf of California is the fishing mecca of Puerto Peñasco.

Air travel takes you speedily from many U.S. cities to Mexico City and other Central American points. Ships and passenger-carrying freighters call at such ports as Tampico and Vera Cruz in Mexico, Belize in British Honduras, Puerto Barrios on the Caribbean side of Guatemala and San José on the Pacific side, La Libertad in El Salvador, Puerto Cortés and La Ceiba in Honduras, Port Limon and Puntarenas in Costa Rica, Cristobal and Balboa in the Canal Zone. By railroad, you can go from New York to Mexico City in three days and three nights, from St. Louis in two days and two nights. And if you wish, you can go all the way on down to Guatemala City by rail.

Mexico offers temples and pyramids, palaces that recall the splendor of Napoleonic times, cathedrals, churches, museums. You'll see native costumes and dances, enjoy music and art, buy a variety

**Basket vendor waits beside a Taxco road.**

of handicrafts, hear fascinating legends.

As you travel from one to another of the six republics of Central America, you find that each has its own personality, and charming differences. The people of Guatemala are predominately pure-blooded Indian, those of Nicaragua are nearly 70% mestizo, and the population of Costa Rica is almost exclusively European. The scenery differs, too, with hot, moist, tropical seacoasts — temperate plateaus in the interior regions — and high mountains, many of them volcanic cones of spectacular beauty.

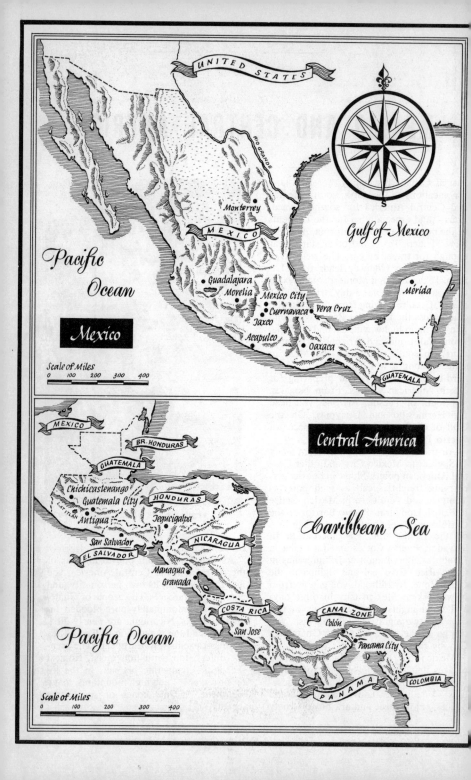

**THIS GATE OPENS ON VERSAILLES-LIKE CHAPULTEPEC CASTLE, PARK.**

Travelers from the U.S. are spending more than 180 million dollars a year in Mexico, land of the ancient Aztecs, where the charm of Old Spain lives on in a magnificent modern setting. The land is enchantingly beautiful, with misty blue mountains, tropical seas, placid villages, quaint colonial towns, great modern cities.

Photo: A. L. Koolish

**The Zócalo,** old Mexico City square, is setting for the great cathedral, Church of the Asunción de María Santísima. The foundation is on stones of Aztec temple

**Dressed for the Fiesta:** There are many festivals, some local, some nation-wide.

**Benito Juárez,** memorial above, was the leader who instituted the Reform Laws.

**Palace of Fine Arts** is center of art and music, with National Theater, murals.

**The National Palace,** with offices of the President, flanks east side of the Zócalo.

**Hotel Reforma** has 25 skyline suites looking out over the nearby mountains.

**Paseo de la Reforma** leads from center of Mexico City to Chapultepec Castle.

**Modern business section** is at crossing of Avenida Juárez, Paseo de la Reforma.

**From fashionable symphony** of Chávez to strolling players, Mexico is musical.

# Mexico

**Temple of Quetzalcoatl,** the wind god of the ancient Toltec civilization which preceded the Aztecs, is 29 miles from Mexico City, at San Juan Teotihuacán

**The great Pyramid of the Sun** is also at San Juan Teotihuacán. Once used as altar and observatory, it is 217 feet high has bigger base than Pyramid of Cheops

**Plaza de Toros:** Mexico City's bull ring is largest bullfighting arena in world.

**Pre-fight ceremonies** and parade have a fascinating array of color and costume.

**Bullfight begins** with grand entry of all the bull's antagonists: Three toreros, three banderilleros, three picadors, and the matador, who is responsible for the kill.

**Action of bullfight** is effectively told in Hemingway's *Death in the Afternoon*.

**The audience** at a bullfight is perhaps most interesting part of the spectacle.

Photos: Richard Joseph

**Floating Gardens of Xochimilco** are most popular on Sundays when people of all social classes come to ride the flower-decked boats, poled by Aztec Indians.

**Xochimilco punts** are called *canoas*, are furnished with chairs and table for food.

**Chapultepec Park** is one of world's most lovely natural parks, with shaded walks.

Photos: Kurt Severin (Black Star); bottom left, Pan American World Airways; bottom right, Victor de Palma (Black Star)

**Festivals,** like this Harvest festival at Ocoyoacac, are very colorful, interesting.

**Conversation piece:** From balcony of your hotel you observe scenes like this.

**Inter-American Highway traffic at Zimapán:** This road is great building achievement, sometimes at sea level, sometimes rising to heights more than 8,000 feet.

**Massive cathedral** in Cuernavaca was begun by Cortez in 1529, is very Spanish in character. Much of the city retains atmosphere of days of the conquistadores.

**Tepoztlán,** Aztec for *Where there is Copper*, puts on an outstanding festival.

**Teloztlán,** unspoiled village 12 miles from Cuernavaca, adheres to old ways of life.

# Mexico CUERNAVACA, TAXCO

**Community laundry** is a feature of old picturesque silver-mining town of Taxco.

**Perched on side of a mountain,** Taxco rivals the hill towns of Italy for beauty.

**"Heavy Traffic"** in fascinating Taxco: There's "a picture around every corner."

Indian market, on Sundays, offers baskets, silver, tinware, many other handicrafts.

Photos: A. L. Koolish; top right,
Georgia Engelhard (Camera Clix)

329

# Mexico

**Morelia's main square:** Towers of great cathedral are more than 200 feet high.

**Aqueduct at Morelia** was built, 1785–89 to give employment during a famine

**Spectacular mountains** and lush tropical foliage are reflected in swimming pool

near Veracruz, city whose name stems from Cortez landing on Good Friday.

**Amecameca** ("Many Water Holes" in Aztec) is point of ascent to Popocatepetl and Ixtaccihuatl (in background of photo), the two magnificent volcanoes.

**El Castillo** is huge 100-foot pyramid at Maya ruins of Chichén Itzá, near Mérida.

**Temple of the Warriors** surrounds 4½ acre area that was probably a Mayan market.

**Church of San Francisco** at San Miguel de Allende is in Spanish colonial style.

**Monterrey,** 3rd largest city, is 140 mi. from Laredo, on Inter-Am. Highway.

**Deep-sea fishing** is famous at Acapulco; witness this magnificent sailfish catch.

**Favorite "morning" beach** is Caleta. In the afternoon, Los Hornos is preferred.

Photos: A. L. Koolish

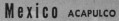

**El Mirador Hotel,** on Quebrada Cliffs, below) has a magnificent water view.

**Daredevil divers** leap from 100-foot cliff into waters between Quebrada rocks.

Photo: Above, Eric M. Sanford (Black Star)

333

# Mexico

**Loaves of bread** aren't cellophane-wrapped in rural areas, but taste is good!

**The festival** for blessing the sugar cane: almost every day sees a fiesta somewhere.

**Mexican musicians** start young, and play impromptu concerts anywhere, any time.

**This is the sort** of café entertainment you get anywhere in the south of Mexico.

**Street merchant** in Oaxaca offers Aztec patterns in hand-loomed cotton and wool.

**Mexicans excel** in making costumes out of things at hand; note inverted lampshades!

334

Photos: Samuel E. Lessere

# GUATEMALA IS LAND OF HILLS AND LAKES

If you're seeking a land of great scenic beauty, with jungle highlands, ancient cathedrals, Indian villages, you'll find them all in Guatemala. But you won't get night life or conventional entertainment.

**Calvary Church,** built 1618, is located at Chichicastenango, the Indian village that is a "must" for Guatemalan visitors. Faithful worshipers come by thousands.

Photo: National Tourist Bureau, Guatemala

335

# COFFEE DOMINATES ECONOMIC LIFE OF TINY EL SALVADOR

El Salvador is almost a one-crop nation, coffee—mostly of the "mild" variety—furnishing 80% of all exports. Country has 170 mile coastline on Pacific, but none on Atlantic, is not easily reached.

Smallest of the Central American republics, El Salvador is the most densely populated, with 144 persons per square mile. The climate is subtropical, with moderately heavy rainfall of 68 inches.

**San Salvador,** capital of El Salvador, centers on Parque Barrios, with the National Palace (above) being the most imposing building in city of 160,000.

**Tegucigalpa** was founded 1578 as mining settlement, became capital of Honduras in 1880. City centers on Plaza Morazán, site of cathedral and municipal palace.

# HONDURAS EXPORTS ITS BANANA GOLD

Bananas, the golden agricultural crop of Honduras, are grown in the north on plantations once run by big U.S. fruit companies, now controlled by local interests. It's little-known by tourists.

**Inspector looks over bananas.** At left, Mayan seat in the park at Tegucigalpa.

Photos: Copyright, Charles Perry Weimer

337

# NICARAGUA OFFERS SECOND CANAL SITE

Lake Nicaragua, Lake Managua and the Tipitapa River that connects them have long been considered for a canal from the Atlantic to the Pacific. Nicaragua is largely mountainous, thinly peopled.

**La Merced church** is one of many colonial churches in León, once the capital.

**Las Isletas,** in Granada, is lovely area reached by the Inter-American highway.

**Managua** was made capital of Nicaragua in 1855 to end the rivalry between the cities of León and Granada. This is the National Palace, facing Parque Central.

**Parque Darío,** in Managua, is named for poet Rubén Darío. City was almost destroyed by an earthquake in 1931, and the government was moved temporarily.

**Club Managua** is one of city's numerous impressive buildings. Beauty of the city is enhanced by its location on the southeast shore of 38-mile-long Lake Managua.

**Ministry of Public Health,** Managua, deals with a population that is principally of mixed Spanish and Indian extraction. The main agricultural crop is coffee.

# PANAMA CANAL IS "A DREAM OF CENTURIES COME TRUE"

An idea that occurred to the earliest Spanish explorers, the Panama Canal took many years to build and surpasses all other man-made waterways both in cost and in difficulty. It is 50.72 miles long from channel entrance in the Caribbean to deep water in the Pacific. Because the canal runs generally southeast from

**Constant dredging** is required to keep channels at proper depth. Landslides have sometimes blocked passage of the Gaillard cut, 8 miles long, 45 feet deep.

ts Atlantic ports of Colón and Cristobal, the Pacific entrance is paradoxically 27 miles east of the Atlantic one. Trip through the canal takes 7 to 8 hours.

**Ship's passengers** have excellent view of the locks in action. Traffic moves in both directions, since all locks are double. Over 5,000 ships a year use canal.

Photos: A. L. Koolish

# PANAMA IS A MINIATURE SPAIN

Fiestas, bullfights, colorful costumes and the gay nightlife of Panama City may make you think you're in Spain. People of Panama call their nation "The Crossroads of the World" because of its trade routes.

**Ruins of Cathedral** in old Panama remind you of country's historic past, when it was route by which treasures of the Inca empire were carried to Spain.

**Hotel Internacional**, Panama City, has up-to-date facilities, old world charm.

**El Panama** has Cabana Sun Club by pool, roof garden, air-conditioned rooms.

**Panama City** is near Pacific end of canal, is capital of Panama, industrial center.

**Famous San Blas Indians** make their home on the picturesque Mulatas Islands, near Cape San Blas, a point in north Panama which juts out into Caribbean.

San José, capital of Costa Rica, is a bustling city on main business street. **Airport at La Sabana, west of San José.**

Residential section has great charm, with many Spanish balconies and patios. **Even small towns have palatial churches.**

# COSTA RICA: HEART OF THE AMERICAS

Located in the geographical center of the Americas, Costa Rica is a country of high culture, education, and political stability. Coffee is its principal crop. Air and steamer services are plentiful.

Photos: Ewing Galloway; bottom left, Ace Williams (Black Star)

# SOUTH AMERICA

Jet air travel makes it easy for you to make an extensive trip to South America even if you have just two weeks for your vacation. The classic trip is down one coast and up the other. You fly from New York and Miami to Panama City, Lima, La Paz and Santiago, then cross the Andes to Buenos Aires. Heading northward you may stop at Montevideo, São Paulo, spectacular Rio de Janeiro, and possibly the new capital, Brasília.

If you have time to travel by ship, that is the way for a vacation of real relaxation. Many cruises stop at La Guaira for a visit to Caracas, capital of Venezuela. Three steamship lines offer regular cruises down the East coast, calling at Rio, Santos, Montevideo and Buenos Aires. And there are cruises from both New York and California ports to South America's West coast, for visits to Colombia, Ecuador, Peru and Chile.

Venezuela is the gateway for our picture tour of South America. Half again as large as the state of Texas, it is a country of great contrasts, with high mountains that slope precipitously to the sea, with snow-capped peaks just a few miles from steaming jungles, with fine homes of the oil-wealthy and modest adobe palm-leaf-thatched huts.

Hopping over to Brazil we find some of the world's greatest natural beauty, and one of the most dynamic civilizations of today. There's the breath-taking beauty of Rio de Janeiro, with its green mountains rising abruptly from the sea and bay; there is the bustle of the industrial São Paulo, and the magnificence of the new capital built in the wilderness — Brasília.

After a brief visit to the beaches of Uruguay and attractive Montevideo, we come to Argentina and the tree-lined city of Buenos Aires, often called the "Paris of South America." In many ways, though,

the country resembles the United States — with the level Pampa that is like our prairies, places on the Paraná River that are like Florida's Gulf Coast, and inland Argentina that has much in common with our West.

There's a side-trip to Paraguay, and then we visit Chile, that great shoestring of a land whose length of more than 2,600 miles gives it the greatest north-south span of any country on earth. Going beyond the big cities of Santiago and Valparaiso, we enjoy the breath-taking scenery of the Lake District, America's Switzerland, dotted with lakes ringed by virgin forests and reflecting the snow-capped cones of volcanic mountains.

Directly north of Chile is another country dominated by the Andes, Bolivia, with its famous Lake Titicaca, 12,000 feet above sea level, the world's highest navigable body of water . . . and with La Paz, at nearly 12,000 feet above the sea, the world's highest large city.

Peru consists of three parallel sections that present great contrasts of climate and landscape — the narrow strip of desert along the Pacific, the great mass of the Andes, and a tropical jungle lowland to the East. The city of Lima, too, is a contrast — between charming old mansions, modern offices and apartments. Ecuador, just north of Peru, has the same three parallel strips, hot lowland by the sea, high plateau of the Andes, steaming, rain-soaked Amazon jungle.

Colombia is distinguished from other Andean lands by the fact that it borders on both the Pacific and Atlantic Oceans — with three gateway ports, Buenaventura on the Pacific, Cartagena and Barranquilla on the Atlantic. Bogotá, capital and largest city, is proud of the cultural tradition that won it the title of "Athens of America."

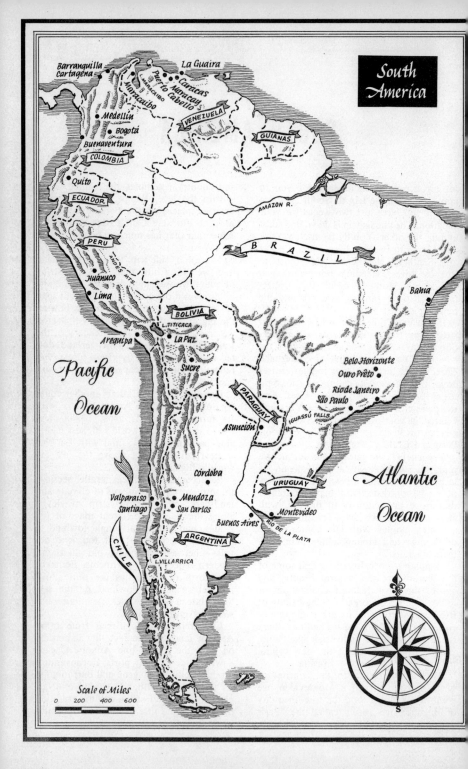

# BOLIVAR AND THE ANDES DOMINATE VENEZUELA

**NEW AUTOPISTA HIGHWAY, LA GUAIRA TO CARACAS, COST $70,000,000.**

Simon Bolivar was born in Caracas, 1783. Now, more than a hundred years after his death, the people remember with awe and reverence "the great Liberator" who freed Venezuela and five other countries and ended Spanish power in South America. The fabulous human career of Bolivar is matched by a stupendous natural phenomenon, the great *cordillera* of the Andes flowing from Venezuela 4,600 miles south.

Photo: Hamilton Wright

347

# Venezuela

**Capitol building's** most famous room is the Salon Eliptico, with heroic paintings.

**The Pantheon** is the "Westminster Abbey" of Caracas, with tombs of national heroes.

**Center of Caracas** is Plaza Bolivar, with statue of Liberator, important buildings.

**"Casa Natal,"** birthplace of Bolivar, has become a national shrine, with mementos.

**Cathedral** is one of impressive buildings of old Spanish city, with narrow streets.

**Country club** has swimming pool, golf course, view of surrounding mountains.

**Altamira** is one of several new residential sections of Caracas, with broad boulevards.

The city is in a hollow, with the mountains towering around it on every side.

**28-story twin sky-scrapers** overlooking Centro Bolivar will house government offices when finished. Beneath the Centro lies a bus station, parking space for autos.

Photos: Hamilton Wright

Rio de Janeiro's trade-mark is 1,296-foot Sugar Loaf Mountain, guarding the entrance to Guanabara Bay. The summit is reached by aerial railroad, has fine view.

# BRAZIL'S CITIES DEFY WILDERNESS

Brazil, covering almost half the land area of South America, is larger than the continental United States and is exceeded in size only by the U.S.S.R., China and Canada. Most of the country is vast, untamed wilderness, but its pioneers have carved out some of the world's most interesting cities, fabulous Rio de Janeiro, São Paulo, and the new capital, Brasília.

**Copacabana Beach** is the promenade spot of Rio, like the Champs-Elysées in Paris.

**Praça Paris** is one of Rio's bayside parks, its formal gardens unsurpassed in world.

**Mosaic sidewalks,** palm-lined boulevards make walking pleasant for Rio's citizens.

**Palatial residences** like this testify to wealth of fashionable Avenida Beira Mar.

# Brazil

**President's Palace in Brasília,** the new capital, is symbolic of nation's "new look."

**Business buildings** in São Paulo, "world's fastest growing city," suggest Hollywood

**São Paulo's great avenues** have underpasses and viaducts to speed traffic. The

Triangulo at heart of city is much like Chicago's Loop. Population is 2,600,000.

# URUGUAY, WITH ITS FAMOUS BEACHES, IS PLAYGROUND OF SOUTH AMERICA

Smallest, but one of most progressive of South American nations, Uruguay is often compared to Denmark and to Switzerland, and its renowned beach area is known as "the Riviera of South America." Uruguay is about size of New England. It was claimed by both Portuguese and Spanish. After the wars of independence, it emerged as a buffer state between Brazil and Argentina and was recognized by foreign powers in 1828. Uruguayans make no attempt to match power with their larger neighbors, but concentrate on earning a living—largely from agriculture—and on making their country a well-run republic with a deep belief in democracy.

**Plaza Independencia,** on Montevideo's main artery, features statue of national hero, José Gervasio Artigas. Calle Sarandi leads downtown, Avenida 18 de Julio up.

Photo: Copyright, Charles Perry Weimer

# Uruguay

**Another view** of Plaza Independencia shows the modern Victoria Plaza Hotel.

**Skyscraper Palacio Salvo** contains Hotel Palacio Salvo, with 10th fl. dining room.

**La Carreta monument** in the Parque de los Aliados (Park of the Allies) represents the spirit of undiscourageable pioneering. Done in bronze, it is wonderfully real.

**Avenida 18 de Julio** takes name from date of Uruguay's proclamation of freedom.

**Avenida Agraciada,** lined with beautiful buildings, leads to Legislative Palace.

Photos: Oficina Nacional de Turismo del Uruguay; top right and center, A. L. Koolish

**Distinctive modern apartment** has flamboyant exterior decoration.

**Playa Carrasco** is just outside city limits of Montevideo. The beach has an immense casino.

**Music,** dancing and gaiety feature the annual Montevideo carnival.

**Playa Pocitos** is another in the string of famous beach resorts that surround Montevideo.

**Punta del Este** is one of the top sea resorts of all South America.

**Legislative Palace,** containing 30 kinds of marble, is matched in splendor only by Cuba's *Capitolio.*

# ARGENTINA BOASTS MIGHTY METROPOLIS

Buenos Aires, the "City of Fair Breezes," is as cosmopolitan a city as any in the world. It is largest in South America, with population of nearly three million, and covers 80 square miles. It offers theaters, opera, concerts. There's a modern subway system, hundreds of trams and thousands of busses. Café-sitting has developed almost to the point it has in Paris. In spite of strange new winds, Buenos Aires can be a place to have a lot of fun.

**Palermo Park** has fine rose gardens, statue of Carlos María de Alvear, hero of revolution.

**Argentine National Congress** building faces Congress Plaza, with monu-

**Luxurious Plaza Hotel** faces Plaza San Martín, is well known to North American visitors.

**Plaza de Mayo** is in the heart of old Buenos Aires. Directly across

...ents and fountains that recall the ...rand manner of European capitals.

**Kavanaugh Building** is second tallest in South America. Alvear Palace Hotel is next door.

...ou see the dusty-pink Casa Rosada ...Pink House), residence of President.

**Subway stations** (entrance above) have artistic tile work depicting scenes in Argentine life.

**Teatro Colón**, municipal opera house, seats 3500 and is one of best equipped in world.

# Argentina

Mendoza (San Martín monument above) is wine and fruit center, "Garden of Andes."

Córdoba, 400 miles northwest of Buenos Aires, is noted for beautiful Cathedral.

Gauchos are more colorful than U.S. cowboys. Pampas cover 200,000 square miles.

Hotel Llao-Llao (pronounced by Argentines Jao-Jao, with the "j" soft as in French) is most famous of the mountain inns in the Lake District, near Chile.

**Monte Tronador** is an Andean peak of 11,200 feet, with number of waterfalls and glaciers. Nearby is Swiss-settled San Carlos de Bariloche, like Alpine village.

**Spectacular** Nahuel Huapí National Park, in Argentine Lake district, is one of most scenic regions in all Latin America. It's a thousand miles west of Buenos Aires.

# PARAGUAY IS OFF BEATEN TRACK

Paraguay and Bolivia are South America's two wholly inland countries. Paraguay's Asunción (founded Assumption Day 1536) has a strong lure for travelers who are fed up with big cities. It is thoroughly primitive, and thoroughly charming

**Asunción** may be reached easily by air, or by 4-day voyage by river steamer from

Buenos Aires, up Paraná and Paraguay. Lace made at Itaguá village is famous

**Asunción Palace** is newest hotel. Gran Hotel del Paraguay was once residence.

**You'll often see** countrywomen riding to market, sitting side-saddle on donkeys

# CHILE'S MOUNTAINS STRETCH 2,600 MILES

**INDIAN PONCHOS SHOW YOU THIS IS NOT SWITZERLAND BUT CHILE.**

Averaging barely 110 miles in width, Chile is a narrow strip extending from Peru down to the tip of South America, a distance greater than that from New York to Los Angeles. Within a short distance of the coast the formidable Andes rise to some of the hemisphere's highest peaks. The Chilean lake district, with 12 lakes all differing in the color of their water, offers magnificent scenery, great sport.

Photo: Pan American World Airways

# Chile

**The Alameda,** in Chile's capital of Santiago, is also known as Avenida Bernardo O'Higgins, named for one of the patriots who led the movement for independence.

**Hotel Puyehue,** famed hot springs resort, is among most sumptuous in South America.

**In a Chilean rodeo,** *huasos* are judged by speed and accuracy in stopping steer.

**Golf Club at Los Leones:** Sports in Chile take precedence over almost everything.

**Club Hípico** in Santiago, offering horse racing, is one of show places of continent.

Photos: Grace Line; center left, Pan American World Airways; bottom left, Pan American-Grace Airways; bottom right, Panagra

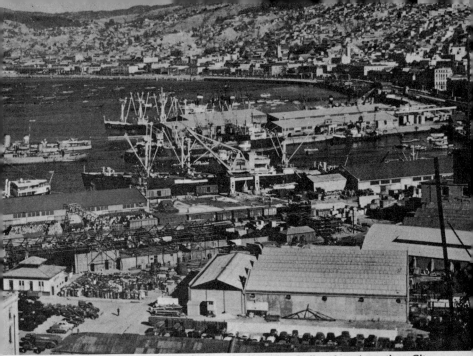

**Valparaiso,** most important port on west coast of South America, is terminus of the Transandine Railroad to Argentina. City is bounded by hills, reached by funiculars.

**Pucón** on Lake Villarrica is outstanding resort, dominated by snowy volcano.

**Valparaiso** attracts tourists to its nearby beaches, like Playa Torpederas (above).

Photos: A. L. Koolish; bottom left, Grace Line; bottom right, Panagra

**One of main streets** of La Paz is Avenida
16 de Julio. At left is office of Patino
Mines, fabulous enterprise that put Bolivia 3rd among world producers of tin.

**Cathedral at La Paz,** on Plaza Murillo, is
one of largest churches in South America.

**Equestrian statue** of General Antonio
José de Sucre is prominently located.

Photos: Panagra

# BOLIVIA'S LA PAZ IS HIGHEST BIG CITY IN WORLD

At an altitude of 11,909 feet, La Paz is the highest large city in the world, with 320,000 residents living more than two miles above sea level. Some say it's the world's highest capital, but accurate research indicates that Lhasa, Tibet, is slightly higher, although it is a comparatively small place with only 20,000 population. Then too, La Paz is not the legal capital of Bolivia (Sucre is), but La Paz developed more rapidly because of better transportation and has been since 1900 the actual seat of the government. Nearest seaport is Mollendo, in Peru.

**Lake Titicaca** is largest lake in South America and highest large lake in world.

**El Prado** is the main boulevard of La Paz. Visitors often find high altitude hard to get used to at first; it is advisable to take cabs for sightseeing rather than walk.

Photos: Grace Line

# PERU IS QUEEN OF WEST COAST

This mountain valley is near Huánuco, reached by rail, crossing 15,000 ft. passes.

Lima, capital of Peru, is one of the world's most fascinating cities. A mixture of Indian and Spanish tradition, it is gay and sophisticated. It's a spectacular country physically: the narrow strip along the coast, the stupendous Andes, the Amazon lowlands. The road from Lima up the Andes rises 15,948 feet in 85 miles!

Torre Tagle Palace in Lima is a beautiful survival of seventeenth-century design.

Cornerstone of the Cathedral, on Plaza de Armas, was laid by Francisco Pizarro.

Peruvian folk dancers exhibit their gay costumes. February has 3-day carnival.

October is month of annual Fair. Andes Memorial stands before Fair Grounds.

**In Lima's streets,** advertising signs contrast with dignified Spanish buildings.

Lima's shops are good place to buy silver, leather, antiques and Incan curiosities.

**Church of San Marcello,** an excellent example of Spanish style, was built in 1584.

**Arequipa,** in the south, is a picturesque city. This is the Church of San Augustin.

**Aroya Indians** (Peru's population has 3 million Indians) sell silver and baskets.

**Machu Picchu ruins,** amazing Inca city, weren't discovered by white men till 1911.

# COLOMBIA HAS COLOR, CULTURE

Colombia, perhaps the most purely Spanish of all South American nations, is a country of infinite variety and color. In Bogotá, its isolated mountain capital, there are more bookshops than cafés, and the city is frequently referred to as the "Athens of America." Its theaters are very fine and there is an excellent conservatory of music and a national orchestra. Orchids grow in wild profusion in Colombia and are one of the principal sights in Cali and Medellín. Colombia is only South American country which fronts on both Atlantic and Pacific.

**Parque Nacional** is largest, most beautiful park in Bogotá, with extensive gardens, promenades.

**Bell Tower** of the San Felipe Fortress, Cartagena, gave warning of enemy ships.

**Circo de Santamaria**, in Bogotá, is one of world's greatest bull-fighting rings.

**Cartagena** is one of oldest cities in the Western Hemisphere, founded 1533. It be- came "treasure city" of the Spanish Main, where conquistadores kept their spoils.

Photos: Grace Line; bottom, Foto Mangini

Swimming pool of the Del Prado Hotel, Barranquilla, is a favorite tourist spot.

Medellín is Colombia's leading industrial city, center of the rich gold-mining area.

A visitor picks orchids growing wild in jungle near Buenaventura, a leading port.

Cali is old colonial city with eight fine parks, churches, magnificent haciendas.

Puente Roman in Cartagena is the bridge which joins the city with island of La

Manga, one of main residential sections. Principal beach resort nearby is Marbella.

# ECUADOR CLAIMS OLDEST CITY OF THE NEW WORLD

Quito, capital of Ecuador, makes what may prove a valid claim to being oldest city in Western Hemisphere. Once occupied by the Quitu Indians, it was captured in the 15th century by the Incas.

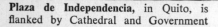

Plaza de Independencia, in Quito, is flanked by Cathedral and Government Palace. Quito, under Spanish till 1822, joined Gran Colombia, then broke away.

Guayaquil is largest city of Ecuador and its principal seaport, about 60 miles from ocean on the Guayas River.

Simple monument marks the Equatorial Line in Ecuador.

Photos: Pan American-Grace Airways; bottom, Grace Line

# SOUTH PACIFIC

World War II opened up new interest in the South Pacific for thousands of Americans. You may never have been nearer than reading *Tales of the South Pacific* by James Michener, or seeing the great musical show based on it, but you have an idea of its romance, and the vigor of the great frontier lands, Australia and New Zealand.

One of the fascinating things about travel in the Pacific area is that nearly every day you run across some sort of local celebration. In Fiji, for instance, the New Year is welcomed with the "Vakatawase," including fireworks, floral decorations and boisterous merrymaking. Queen Elizabeth's birthday celebration is highlighted by an impressive military review at Albert Park in Suva. Throughout August there are exhibitions of Indian fire-walking; and at mid-September comes the Hibiscus Festival. October sees the Day of Cession, re-enactment of the day the Fijian chiefs ceded Fiji to the British crown in 1874.

Australia also welcomes the New Year with all sorts of sports events, and there are surf carnivals each weekend during January. Australia Day, at the end of the month, celebrates the landing of the First Fleet at Sydney in 1788. The Royal Hobart Regatta, biggest aquatic carnival in the Southern Hemisphere, comes in mid-February. Highlight of the year is the Moomba Festival in Melbourne, with pageants, concerts, fairs, outdoor art shows, races, fireworks, and a gigantic parade. ("Moomba" is Aborigine for "Let's get together and have fun.") Anzac Day, in April, is a solemn holiday commemorating the 1915 landing at Gallipoli by Australian and New Zealand troops. Many horse racing events take place during June, July and August. The Royal Adelaide Show and the Royal Melbourne Show in September combine all the elements that make up a fair: exhibits, amusements and competitions. It's typical of the reversed seasons "down under" that the flower shows take place in September and October. The Melbourne Cup, biggest horse race in Australia, is run in November. John Martin's Christmas Pageant, in Adelaide, is forerunner of many Christmas celebrations in churches and city gardens.

New Zealand begins the year, in mid-January, with the Auckland Birthday Carnival, featuring sideshows, trade exhibitions, a grand parade, a three-ring circus, racing, fireworks, and the largest one-day yachting regatta in the world. February brings Waitangi Day, the annual commemoration of the signing of the treaty between the Maoris and the British in 1840. In March there is the Easter Show in Auckland, and the Ngaruawahia Regatta, an aquatic carnival with Maori participation. April features the Scottish Highland Games at Hastings. In May and June there are Arts Festivals, and an Industries Fair at Palmerston North. August and September bring Ski Championships and Golf Championships. Carnival Week takes place at Christchurch in early November. As Christmas approaches, there are many seasonal events — Mardi Gras at Napier, Summer Holiday Festival at Nelson, and Christmas Carnivals at Tauranga and Rotorua.

In Tahiti, last stop on our photo tour of the South Pacific, the biggest event is "La fete du 14 Juillet," an annual week-long event built around Bastille Day and celebrated with unbridled enthusiasm all over Tahiti. Dancers and singers from all districts, as well as from outlying islands, compete for honors in their colorful costumes.

# FIJI'S 250 ISLANDS ARE TROPIC HEAVEN

Most important British colony in Pacific, the Fiji Islands are 2500 miles southwest of Hawaii. Some say there are 250 isles, others up to 320. 80 are inhabited. The largest is Viti Levu, with capital of Suva.

**Natives of Suva** were once cruel cannibals; converting them was a religious triumph. Population is now about 40% Fijian, 50% Indian and 10% other races.

**Grand Pacific Hotel** in Suva is one of the best known Pacific hostelries. It entertained during the war hundreds of U.S., British, and other Allied officers.

**SYDNEY IS DOMINATED BY GREAT BRIDGE OVER ARM OF THE HARBOR**

# AUSTRALIA IS BIG AS UNITED STATES

The smallest of the continents, Australia is still very nearly as large in area as the United States—but it has only about nine million inhabitants. Known as "the sunshine continent," it is a land where you can live outdoors much of the time, with such sports as golf, skiing, fishing, bathing on wonderful beaches.

**Eighteen footers** take part in yachting regatta in beautiful harbor of Sydney.

**Sydney is the largest city,** with over a million and a half population. Other principal cities are Brisbane, Melbourne, Adelaide, Perth, and Hobart on island of Tasmania, lying to the south, 150 miles from Melbourne. Australia, up-and-coming British dominion, has a vitality and an optimism that appeal to Americans.

**Canberra** is federal capital of Australia, with Parliament House, lovely gardens.

Photos: Australian National Publicity Association; Australian News and Information Bureau

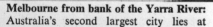

**Melbourne from bank of the Yarra River:**
Australia's second largest city lies at the head of Port Phillip Bay, an almost land-locked inlet just over 30 miles long.

**There's good fishing** for trout in mountain streams and in spillways of big dams.

**Riding is popular** in Melbourne, and city has the Melbourne Cup race each fall.

Photos: Australian National Publicity Association

**In Melbourne's** trim Fitzroy Gardens is cottage in which Captain Cook lived.

**Skiiers** find new chalets at Mt. Hotham (above), Mt. Buffalo, Mt. Kosciusko.

**Hobart,** capital of island of Tasmania, lies at the foot of Mt. Wellington. It has swinging bridge across Derwent River, with a floating portion 3,168 feet long.

Photos: Australian National-
al Publicity Association

# Australia

**The Great Barrier Reef** extends over 1,200 miles along the Queensland coast.

**Australian bushland** is world-famous for its dense growth of trees, ferns, flowers.

**Cattle crossing at river in Queensland:** Dairy cattle are raised in the richer coastal areas, and much beef is raised for local use and for export to England.

**Flowering trees** of Brisbane frame its City Hall. Brisbane is capital of the pastoral state of Queensland with its coastal plantations of fruit, sugar cane.

**The wattle,** with pale-golden blossoms, is Australia's national tree and flower.

**Koala Bears** are easily tamed, perfectly harmless, feed exclusively on eucalyptus.

Photos: Australian National Publicity Association; bottom right, Pan American World Airways

# NEW ZEALAND HAS MATCHLESS BEAUTY

New Zealand is a wonderland of scenery: The Southern Alps have over 200 peaks of 7,500 feet and more, with Mount Cook rising to 12,349. There are lakes and waterfalls, fertile farms and bushland.

**Wellington,** capital of the Dominion, is built on steep hills about a magnificent harbor, 3 miles wide and 12 long. The hills are climbed by trams, cable cars reminiscent of those in San Francisco.

**Rotorua** is center of Maori life, with wonderful carvings; also has thermal spa.

**Wanganui River** runs through primeval forest in beautiful thermal wonderland.

**Auckland,** built on the shores of deeply indented Waitemata harbor, is chief port and largest city of New Zealand. This is view of the north shore from Mount Eden.

**Wellington** has tunnels that take roads, trolley lines through encircling hills.

**University Tower, Auckland:** Nation is proud of education, social legislation.

Photos: New Zealand Government; Three Lions; Ewing Galloway

**Christchurch,** the largest city on South Island, is the most typically English town outside of England. The River Avon sweeps through it in graceful curves.

**Sutherland Falls,** 1,904 feet high, is one of world's tallest, most beautiful.

**Pohutu Geyser** is one of many in the Hot Springs district health resort, Rotorua.

Photos: Three Lions; bottom left, Ewing Galloway; bottom right, New Zealand Government

**GAUGUIN DID MANY PAINTINGS IN SOUTH SEA PARADISE OF TAHITI.**

# TAHITI IS THE END
# OF OUR WORLD TOUR

*Kon-Tiki* brought home to thousands of readers the lure of primitive life in the South Seas, and especially the tiny islands of Polynesia. Queen of them all in the dreams of men is Tahiti, supreme symbol of living for the simple joy of living . . . a good place to end our trip.

# "AROUND THE U.S.A."

# "FROM SEA TO SHINING SEA"
# —THE MOODS OF AMERICA
## by Paul J. C. Friedlander

For the purposes of the tourist, "America the Beautiful," as described in the Katharine Lee Bates poem and song from which the heading of this Foreword is taken, consists of thirteen separate regions. Each is as big as, if not bigger than, many world powers. Each is an entity in itself. Each has a personality, and characteristics of geography and agriculture, of people and industry, of scenery and climate—both physical and intellectual—that make it distinct from all other regions. Just as the traveler can tell when he crosses from England to Wales or from German Switzerland into Italian Switzerland, so he can tell in this country without recourse to an atlas when he is in New England, the Midsouth or the Deep South.

To aid the vacationist about to plan a tour of his own country, the armchair traveler anxious to learn more about his native land, and the returned traveler who wants to kindle anew the memories of the places he has visited, the editors of this book have selected well over a thou-

*Mr. Friedlander is Travel Editor, The New York Times*

sand pictures showing America in its many moods, at work and at play. They have identified each picture with pertinent and often intriguing facts. And they have reprinted with permission character studies of the eleven regions written by correspondents of *The New York Times* who live and work in the various sections they describe.

Because the editors have already covered in their attractive book, *Around the World in 1,000 Pictures,* such outlying sections of the United States as the Virgin Islands and Puerto Rico, this book deals only with the fifty states of our Union and with the District of Columbia. Emphasis is placed on the natural wonders of our country and the places of greatest interest to the pleasure traveler and the vacationist. Yet these alone cannot convey the moods of America. The strength and spirit of our country today are compounded of 160,000,000 people and of their forebears, and of the things they believed in and worked and fought for, the same principles we honor today at our historic shrines.

So among these 1,000 photographs you will find more than the grandeur of nature as it spreads in a 3,000-mile panorama from sea to shining sea. You will see many of the great historic shrines that bring to life those great occasions in New England, Pennsylvania, Virginia and in many other regions when Americans wrote the history of the New World in bold, unfrightened hands. You'll see their descendants at work today—on the farms, in the automobile factories and the industries that make this nation, and the fishermen who still go down to the sea under sail. And, to complete the picture, you'll see Americans at play in their National Parks where the wilderness of this continent is preserved as it was when the first explorers and hunters came through; on the broad sandy beaches that encircle this land like a golden necklace; and at the fabulous man-made resorts like Reno and Palm Springs and Miami Beach, and the biggest tourist attraction of them all—New York City.

Many of the pictures were taken by world-famous photographers, but most of them were made by men and women who live in the various regions and have had the opportunity to capture on film the places they love best. The photos have been selected, not for the qualities that would win prizes in a competition, but for their ability to show America's colorful scenes and people and events in the same way you might like to preserve them in your own photo album. This is a tremendous undertaking, to picture this great nation in one volume. To do it as successfully as they have, the editors had to touch lightly, or not at all, a few sections of the country. They beg, herewith, the indulgence of the loyal partisans thereof.

It is their hope, and I commend this volume to you in the belief that they have achieved their goal, that this book will help Americans to become more familiar with their own ball park, our friends abroad to see us in our true lights, and inspire both to travel from sea to shining sea to see for themselves the great sights pictured in these pages.

# NEW ENGLAND

## by JOHN H. FENTON

The westward migration across America opened new lands and new vistas for a growing population. Among the pioneers who opened the new country were Yankees. But sooner or later the Yankees' descendants come back to New England, if only for a visit. And along with them come other Americans, for this relic-filled corner of the United States exerts a compelling influence. So much of it, from the Atlantic's breakers and Old North Church to the piny hills and bouldered fields and the Yankees themselves, has been changeless for 300 years.

The sounds of New England are many: the wind in the sand dunes of Cape Cod, the water lapping the sun-bleached fishing wharves of Maine, the rush of a mountain-fed stream in New Hampshire and the twitter of birds in the Berkshire hills of Massachusetts. Voices from the past whisper in the Colonial burying grounds of Boston, in the House of Seven Gables in Salem, beneath the bridge at Concord and in the Old Stone Mill at Newport.

The architecture is a conglomerate blend of graceful Colonial, sterner Federal, utilitarian Cape Cod and the best and worst of the contemporary. In places like Boston, Newburyport and Newport it is possible to turn a corner and go back 300 years.

By and large, the native Yankee has been pictured as a bleak character, with an inborn suspicion of all strangers, inhospitable and clannish. Actually, by nature and heritage, he has a respect for individual opinion. And he is inclined to keep the latchstring of his hospitality withdrawn on the theory that he himself would not knock without good reason.

There are many aspects to this region,

"The Atlantic's breakers . . . changeless."

but a specific tradition marks New England as the national cornerstone. It is found in Boston, in Lexington, in Concord, in Bennington and Newport and Salem. Visitors from all over the world have come to see the shrines and view the relics of the American Revolution that changed the trend of history.

They walk the Boston streets where British muskets rattled in the massacre. They climb the stairs of the Old North Church where the signal lights for Paul Revere were hung. They drive through the Middlesex countryside where the hoofs of Revere's horse echoed in the night. They visit Plymouth and walk where the Pilgrims marched to church. And they wander through a hundred churchyards where fading slate stones tell the story of departed pioneers and patriots.

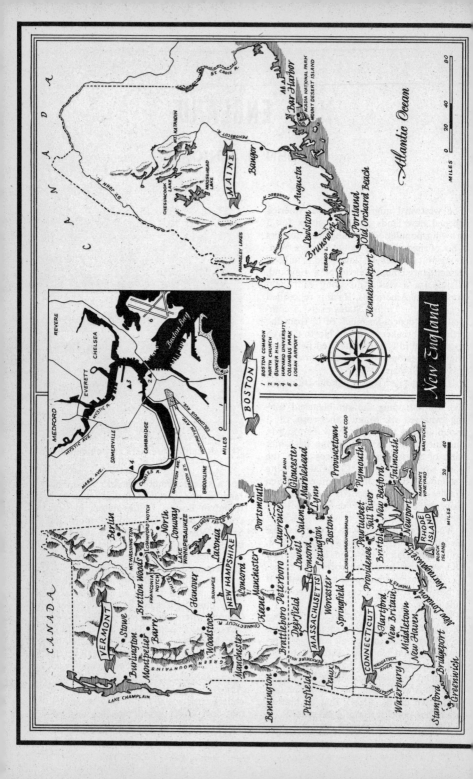

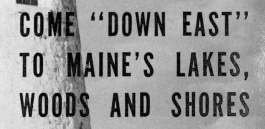

COME "DOWN EAST"
TO MAINE'S LAKES,
WOODS AND SHORES

**Pemaquid Light** is at the tip of one of the many points that jut into the ocean north of Portland. Established 1827, it warned clipper ships of rocky peninsula.

Photo: Grant M. Haist

# Maine

**New Harbor** is fishing village and resort three miles from Pemaquid Point. It was home of Samoset, the Indian who startled the Pilgrims at Plymouth with his welcome.

**Maine's rolling slopes** and the consistency of its snows make for ideal ski country.

**Henry Wadsworth Longfellow** taught at Bowdoin College. This is the Chapel.

Photos: Grant M. Haist; Konstantin Kostich; Stephen Merrill

**Acadia National Park** is on Mount Desert Island which also includes Bar Harbor.

Nearly cut in half by a fjord, with many hills and lakes, the island is beautiful.

**Rockland and Camden** on Penobscot Bay, are home ports for windjammer cruises.

**"Alice S. Wentworth"** is one of sailing ships offering salt-water vacation trips.

**This scene** in Camden harbor is typical of many of Maine's bay and river harbors.

**Early morning stillness** made possible the perfect reflections in this Maine cove.

Photos: National Park Service; Alice S. Wentworth Cruises; Maine Development Commission; Grant M. Haist

# Maine

**Pleasant Point** is up near Passamaquoddy Bay, on the Canadian border. Lobster pots show it's one of the many places where Maine lobsters are caught for market.

**Lakes near Bridgton,** 35 miles northwest of Portland, are good for trout and bass.

**The Rangeley Lakes** have such lovely names: Mooselookmeguntic, Umbagog.

Photos: Maine Development Commission; Konstantin Kostich; Alfred E. Reichenberger

# GREAT WHITE HILLS, LOVELY LAKES BECKON TO NEW HAMPSHIRE

**The Old Man of the Mountain** stands guard at Franconia Notch, scenic defile in the White Mountains. There is an aerial tramway and the famous Flume is nearby.

Photo: White Mountains Region Association

395

# New Hampshire

**Concord** has been the capital since 1808; imposing State House was built in 1819.

**Mt. Washington Cog Railway,** completed in 1869 was first of its kind in the world.

**Boyhood home of Franklin Pierce,** 14th President of U.S., is in Hillsborough.

**Skimobile Tramway** at Mt. Cranmore, near North Conway, carries passengers

**Dartmouth College,** founded 1769, is one of country's most distinguished liberal

Berlin's 80-meter ski jump has highest
steel ski tower (171½ ft.) in the U.S.

nearly a mile, with vertical lift of 1300 ft.
It's used by skiers, summer sight-seers.

The White Island lighthouse, Isles of
Shoals, lies off the coast near Portsmouth.

arts colleges for men. Dartmouth Winter
Carnival is big social event at Hanover.

The Balsams, at Dixville Notch, is Swiss-
like hotel on sparkling Lake Gloriette.

Photos: Eric M. Sanford; Cranmore Skimobile, Inc.;
Dartmouth College News Service; Berlin Chamber
of Commerce; Douglas Armsden; The Balsams

# New Hampshire

**Newmarket** is attractive little industrial community on shores of the Lamprey.

**Village of Walpole** has distinguished Unitarian Church, many lovely old homes.

**New Hampshire granite** has been used to fashion many U.S. buildings, monuments.

**John Goffe's Mill,** made famous by recent best seller, attracts many art students.

**Visitors** enter Hall of Ships at Lost River Reservation, near North Woodstock.

**Chair lift** at Mt. Sunapee State Park offers summer visitors a superb view.

Photos: Douglas Armsden; Monadnock Region Association; John Swen Granite Company, Inc.; White Mountains Region Association; Eric M. S ford, from New Hampshire State Planning and Development Commiss

# VERMONT MEANS ELM-SHADED TOWNS, QUIET COUNTRY, HIKING OR SKIING

**Lake Champlain** at sunset is typical of the peaceful scenes to be found in the Green Mountain State. This tremendous lake borders western Vermont for 100 miles.

Photo: Vermont Development Commission

# Vermont

**Playhouse at Weston** is a fine 100-year-old structure that was formerly a church.

**Ethan Allen,** colonel of "Green Mountain Boys," stands at State House, Montpelier

**Half a hundred centers** have been built up to accommodate winter sports fans in Vermont. These skiers are at the foot of the lift at the Snow Valley resort.

**Derrick** hoists granite block at Rock of Ages quarry, Barre, world's granite center.

**Famous "Round Church"** at Richmond is actually 16-sided. It was built in 1812.

Photos: Vermont Development Commission

**Basin Harbor Club,** Vergennes, is one of delightful resort areas along shore of Lake Champlain. This air view shows the Adirondacks across the lake in New York.

**Hikers arrive** to spend night at one of bunk houses on the 261-mile Long Trail.

**State constitution** was adopted here at Old Constitution House, Windsor, in 1777.

Photos: Basin Harbor Club; Vermont Development Commission

# Vermont

Bay Psalm Book was printed on this press, now at Historical Museum, Montpelier.

Hazen Road Monument at East Hardwick commemorates military road built in 1779.

Historical Museum at Bennington has relics, documents, utensils of early days.

Mt. Mansfield, 4,393 ft. high, is summit of the Green Mountains. This area, near Stowe, is world renowned as winter sport center and also as summer vacationland.

Photos: Vermont Development Commission

# IN MASSACHUSETTS YOU RE-LIVE THE BIRTH OF AMERICA

**Bunker Hill monument** on Breed's Hill, Charlestown, commemorates the stand of raw American militia against the cream of British troops, at start of Revolution.

# Massachusetts BOSTON

**Old South Meeting House** shares with Faneuil Hall momentous oratory of 1770's.

**Faneuil Hall,** scene of important protest meetings, is called "Cradle of Liberty."

**Paul Revere statue** stands near the Old North Church, where the lanterns hung.

**Blooming magnolias** indicate that Spring has come to Commonwealth Avenue.

**Iron grillwork** distinguishes old houses on Beacon Street, opposite Boston Common.

**Old waterfront,** once host to ships from all over world, now has mostly fishing boats.

Photos: Massachusetts Department of Commerce; center right, TWA Trans World Airlines; bottom right, Konstantin Kostich

**From Memorial Drive in Cambridge,** you look across the Charles River Basin to the downtown skyline. Tallest buildings are Courthouse, Custom House, Post Office.

**Agassiz House** is recreation building at Radcliffe College for women, Cambridge.

**Sightseeing boat on Charles** passes one of Harvard's dormitories, Dunster Hall.

**Public Garden,** with its celebrated swan boats, has been treasured feature of city for generations, as has also the Common where free speech is honored every day.

# Massachusetts

**Old Deerfield** is known for its historic houses. This is room of "Indian House."

**Nearby Conway** has beautifully simple old house with a "ballroom" on second floor.

**Berkshire Music Festival** is annual series of public concerts at Tanglewood estate in Stockbridge. Famous conductors draw music lovers from all of North America.

**Farm house kitchen** at Old Sturbridge village shows early American methods.

**House of the Seven Gables,** in Salem, is said to be setting of Hawthorne's novel.

Photos: Alfred E. Reichenberger, center and bottom right; A. Milton Runyon, top right; Pioneer Valley Association, top left; Old Sturbridge Village

**Mt. Greylock,** some 3,500 feet, is tallest of the Berkshire Hills and highest mountain in the state. In winter dress, or autumn colors, it has majestic beauty.

**Williams** is known as "the college of gentlemen." This is Chapin Hall auditorium.

**"Sweetheart Gate"** is revered fixture of Mohawk Trail curio shop, Charlemont.

**Covered bridges** are a New England feature that may disappear before onslaught of wide new roads. This fine example spans the Deerfield River near Charlemont.

# Massachusetts

**Gloucester fishermen** unload cod at this port with 300-year seafaring tradition.

**Hadley's** First Congregational Church has spire designed by Christopher Wren.

**This view** of Connecticut River valley from Mt. Sugarloaf is typical of lovely farm country around South Deerfield and Sunderland, part of the "Pioneer Valley."

**Plymouth Rock,** one of America's most revered shrines, is protected by imposing granite portico of classical design. It is visited by some half million annually.

**Rock itself** bears 1620 date as reminder of year Pilgrims used this stepping-stone.

**Each May** traditional corn-planting is re-enacted at the Old Fort-Harlow House.

**Three famous statues:** "Hail to the Sunrise" greets visitors to Mohawk Trail. Kitson's "Minuteman" stands on green at Lexington, the one by French at Concord.

**Giant blue fin tuna,** weighing 300 to 600 pounds. are landed at a Cape Cod harbor.

**Cape Cod's** 300 miles of coast provide scores of safe bays, inlets for sailing

**Provincetown's** narrow streets and lanes delight visitors to its famous art colony.

**Sandwich Congregational Church:** Famous colored Sandwich glass was made in town

**Harvesting cranberries:** The September landscape is brilliant with the crimson bogs and the colorful costumes of the berry pickers, some of Indian descent.

**Melody Tent at Hyannis** presents operetta, musical comedy in theater-in-round style.

**Hooked rug exhibition** shows present-day examples of favorite early American art.

**Stoney Brook Mill** at Brewster is first water power grist mill in the country.

Photos: Cape Cod Chamber of Commerce; bottom right, Massachusetts Department of Commerce

**Nantucket Island** (25 mi. off Cape Cod) once was the great whaling port of world.

**Jethro Coffin house,** genuine "salt box" style, is oldest on island, built 1686.

**Old Mill** on Nantucket has spar so fixed that vanes will turn only for West wind.

**Martha's Vineyard** is triangular isle off elbow of Cape Cod. This is Edgartown.

**Gay Head Cliffs** on Martha's Vineyard are noted for brilliant colors, especially when reflected by the late afternoon sun. Wampanoag Indians make souvenirs of clay.

Photos: Massachusetts Department of Commerce; top right by Eric M. Sanford

# NEWPORT HEADS STYLISH RESORTS OF RHODE ISLAND, OUR SMALLEST STATE

**Newport's** famous 3-mile Cliff Walk along the Atlantic Ocean passes many fabulous summer residences built by millionaires. At left is Vanderbilt's "The Breakers."

Slater Park in Pawtucket has 193 acres of winding drives, flower gardens, a lake, and lagoons with artificial islands which contain the noted Shakespearean Garden.

State House overlooks busy Providence. It has world's second largest marble dome.

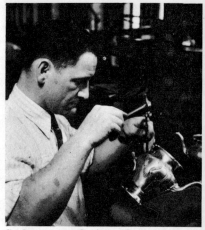

Craftsman at Gorham Company works on an exquisite sterling silver tea service.

At Brown's University Hall, French and U.S. troops were housed in Revolution.

Green Hall at University of Rhode Island houses library and administrative offices.

414

**John Brown House,** built 1786, is now the headquarters of R. I. Historical Society.

**Samuel Slater** built first textile mill in America on this Pawtucket site in 1790.

**Naval War College** at Newport teaches officers, logistics to advanced tactics.

**Huge yachts** line up at Newport for start of race to Bermuda, a sailing classic.

# Rhode Island

**All-steel Motor Vessel "Viking"** takes to water at Blount Marine Works, Warren.

**Block Island,** fishing center and resort, is 12 miles off the Rhode Island coast.

**"The Towers"** at Narragansett, designed by Stanford White, has been a landmark of this noted resort since the turn of the century. It was originally a casino.

**Old Colony House,** Newport, is considered one of nation's best Colonial buildings.

**Newport's Old Stone Mill** was probably windmill, but legend calls it Norse relic.

Photos: Rhode Island
Development Council

# CONNECTICUT IS KNOWN FOR SKILLED ARTISANS, EDUCATION, TRIM COUNTRY

**Old Lyme,** where "a sea captain once lived in every house," is an elm-shaded village that typifies Connecticut. Present Congregational Church copies 1816 one.

Photo: Connecticut Development Commission

417

**The Sterling Memorial Library at Yale:** According to tradition, the founders of the college donated books from their own libraries to start the school in 1702.

**U.S. Naval Submarine Base,** New London, operates "submarine escape training tank."

**Choate School,** exclusive prep school for boys, has 500-acre campus at Wallingford.

Photos: Connecticut Development Commission; Official United States Navy Photograph; The Choate School

**The Corps of Cadets** of the United States Coast Guard Academy, New London, lines up for review on the parade ground. Academy is "Annapolis" of Coast Guard.

**Cadet Training Ship "Eagle"** is part of floating equipment of $2,500,000 school.

**Stanton House** in Clinton is one of the many historic early homes in Connecticut.

**Home office** of the Aetna Life Affiliated Companies in Hartford is the largest colonial-style office building in the world. It's one-eighth of a mile long.

# Connecticut

Intricate work of skilled craftsmen is shown at U. S. Time plant in Middlebury.

Stonington lighthouse, now a museum, stood up under bombardment by British

Nathaniel Allis House, at Madison, is kept as in old days. This is the kitchen.

The Barnum Museum, Bridgeport, honors founder of Greatest Show on Earth.

Clock Tower at Waterbury was modeled after the Torre del Mangia, Siena, Italy.

Gillette Castle, Hadlyme, is perched on cliff like medieval strongholds it copies.

**Mystic Seaport** is 19th century coastal village being recreated by the Marine Historical Association. At left is the *Charles W. Morgan*, Yankee whaleship.

**Pratt & Whitney Aircraft** plant at East Hartford shows state's industrial power. In 1851 the Sharps Company began making the famous Sharps rifles on this site.

Photos: Official Mystic Seaport Photo, Louis S. Martel; Pratt & Whitney Aircraft

Connecticut

**Meriden's** Broad Street-Memorial Boulevard parallels the long Green. World War I monument stands in front of two churches, both over a hundred years old.

**The War Office** at Lebanon was supply headquarters for Revolutionary troops.

**Nathan Hale,** of "I have but one life" fame, taught school here at East Haddam.

# MID-ATLANTIC STATES

## by PAUL J. C. FRIEDLANDER

The Middle Atlantic States — New York, New Jersey, Pennsylvania and Delaware — constitute a kind of old, established and, therefore, respectable *avant garde* of the United States of America. They set the pace for the rest of the country in finance, communications, industry, science, education, and in the civilizing influences of culture and of fashions.

With their roots deep in the history of pre-Colonial days, these four states need not bluster over their origins, their patriotism or devotion to America's ideals, for they were among the very first to fight for, achieve and practice them since the days when this continent was parceled out in royal grants. They are able to face life more calmly, with the stability of a mature population, than some of their sovereign cousins to the west. Their outlook is of necessity broader, international and global because of their vantage point on the Atlantic seaboard.

The highest compliment a visitor can give a San Franciscan is to tell him that his city has the feel, the pace of an eastern metropolis. A traveler through the United States, and particularly an Easterner come home again, immediately feels this drive, this concentration of purposeful energy that moves people, that gets things done. This is the keen spirit of the "major league" of accomplishment, the sophistication of a cruelly competitive market for talent and ideas.

Here, too, are the universities, the book publishing houses, the newspaper and magazine offices where much of the nation's thinking is shaped. Here are headquarters for the media of communications—radio, television, advertising, entertainment. Here are the highest buildings, the deepest subways, the largest cities and biggest seaside playgrounds,

and even deserted, barren areas remote in time and customs, if not miles, from seaboard civilization. Here are the largest banks, the biggest corporations, the richest of the rich, and just down the block in cold-water hovels the poorest of the poor. Here parade the intellectuals and the very smartest smart set and, by extension of this law of superlatives, the dumbest of the dumbbells.

The region owes much of its character to the Appalachian Mountain Range that runs from northeast to southwest, paralleling the Atlantic Coast. They were a barrier against the earliest arrivals, forced the colonizers to build cities and towns on the coastal plain. The few water gaps to the west channeled trade and commerce to and from the great deepwater ports of New York, Newark and Philadelphia, making these big cities grow bigger than ever.

Over 30 million people — one-fifth of the nation's total population—live in these four states, a population cosmopolitan because of the diversity of its origins, yet homogeneous in the sense of being "Easterners." Immigrants and sons of immigrants sit in the legislatures, on the courts and in the governors' mansions, and so do descendants of the men who signed the Declaration of Independence. There are regional and city accents within each state; election campaigns show conflicts between farmers and industrial centers.

Perhaps it is these great diversities in such a great concentration of people in a comparatively small area that gives this region its peculiar character — not as a cross section of America, not the common denominator, but rather a kind of show window of what this country has been, what it is and what it can hope to be.

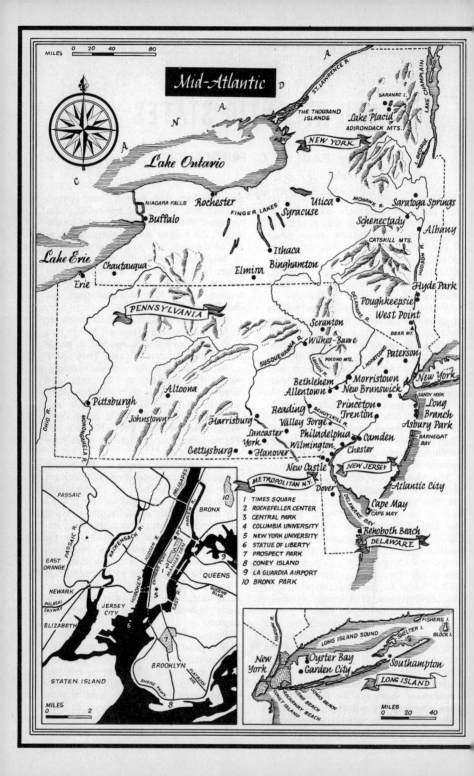

MILES 0 20 40 80

# Mid-Atlantic

ST. LAWRENCE R.

THE THOUSAND ISLANDS

SARANAC L.

Lake Placid

ADIRONDACK MTS.

LAKE CHAMPLAIN

L. GEORGE

NEW YORK

CANADA

Lake Ontario

NIAGARA FALLS    Rochester    FINGER LAKES    Utica    MOHAWK R.    Saratoga Springs

Buffalo    Syracuse    Schenectady    Albany    HUDSON R.    CATSKILL MTS.

Lake Erie    Chautauqua    Ithaca    Binghamton    Elmira

Erie

PENNSYLVANIA    DELAWARE R.    Poughkeepsie    West Point    BEAR MT.

Scranton    Wilkes-Barre    LEHIGH R.    POCONO MTS.    L. HOPATCONG    Paterson

SUSQUEHANNA R.    New York    SANDY HOOK

Altoona    Bethlehem    Morristown    Long Branch

Pittsburgh    Johnstown    Allentown    New Brunswick

OHIO R.    MONONGAHELA R.    Reading    SCHUYLKILL R.    Princeton    Trenton    Asbury Park    BARNEGAT BAY

Harrisburg    Valley Forge    Philadelphia    Camden

Lancaster    Chester

Gettysburg    York    Hanover    Wilmington

New Castle    NEW JERSEY

METROPOLITAN N.Y.    Dover    Atlantic City

DELAWARE BAY    Cape May    CAPE MAY

Rehoboth Beach    DELAWARE

1  TIMES SQUARE
2  ROCKEFELLER CENTER
3  CENTRAL PARK
4  COLUMBIA UNIVERSITY
5  NEW YORK UNIVERSITY
6  STATUE OF LIBERTY
7  PROSPECT PARK
8  CONEY ISLAND
9  LA GUARDIA AIRPORT
10 BRONX PARK

PASSAIC    PALISADES    BRONX

PASSAIC R.    HACKENSACK R.    HARLEM R.    10

EAST ORANGE    HUDSON R.    MANHATTAN    QUEENS

NEWARK    HOBOKEN    EXPRESS PKWY    EAST R.    QUEENS BLVD.

PULASKI SKYWAY    JERSEY CITY

ELIZABETH    BROOKLYN    FLATBUSH AVE.

STATEN ISLAND    SHORE PKWY.    8

MILES 0    2

FISHERS I.    BLOCK I.

LONG ISLAND SOUND    SHELTER I.

HUDSON R.    New York    Oyster Bay    Garden City    Southampton

LONG ISLAND

CONEY ISLAND    JONES BEACH    ROCKAWAY BEACH

MILES 0    20    40

# NEW YORK BOASTS THE WORLD'S LARGEST CITY AND GREATEST HARBOR

**Looking south** from 70th floor of RCA Building at dusk, you see lights aglow in Empire State Building (1472 ft. with television tower) and lower Manhattan.

# New York NEW YORK CITY

**Bartholdi's Statue of Liberty** welcomes ships as they arrive in New York harbor.

**United Nations Secretariat Building** has two sides entirely of glass, two of marble.

**Ferry "Miss Liberty"** carries half million visitors yearly from Battery to Statue.

**Sightseeing yachts** provide pleasant way of viewing all of Manhattan's skyline.

**Sub-Treasury Building,** Wall and Nassau streets, is of Greek Revival architecture.

Photos: New York State Department of Commerce; Trans World Airlines; Circle Line-Statue Ferry, Circle Line-Sightseeing Yachts, Inc.; Konstantin

**New York's City Hall** has welcomed visitors from all over world for 150 years.

**Heart of financial district,** at lower tip of island, is seen from across river.

**"The Bowery,"** famed in song and story, is a battered relic of its early days.

**The "canyons"** of the financial center are pictured at Pine Street and Broadway.

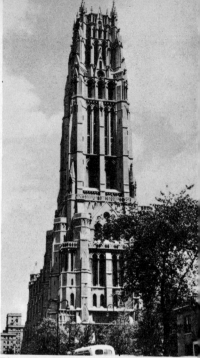

**St. Patrick's Cathedral** occupies whole block across from Rockefeller Center.

**Riverside Church** has impressive tower containing carillon of seventy-two bells.

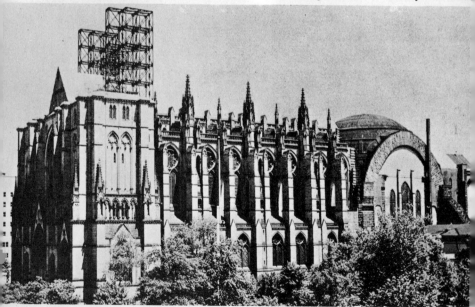

**Cathedral of St. John the Divine,** when completed, will be the largest Gothic cathedral in the world. It has seven chapels clustered around soaring apse.

Photos: Konstantin Kostich

**Rockefeller Center,** 16-building group in mid-Manhattan, is world's largest private-ly owned business and entertainment area. New Time & Life Building is at top right.

**The city's nighttime lights** sparkle for vis-itors to the Observation Roof of the 70-story RCA Building, Rockefeller Center. You see the U.N. building, many others.

Photos: Thomas Airviews, Edward Rat-cliffe, from Rockefeller Center, Inc.

"Sunday in the Park" is favorite recreation of New Yorkers who boat or skate on its lakes, loll on grassy fields, visit the menagerie, use the many playgrounds.

Columbia University, founded in 1754 as Kings College, has over 22,000 students.

Hall of Fame at New York University honors American men and women of note.

**At Times Square,** Broadway becomes the "Great White Way," aglow with hundreds of spectacular electric signs. Theaters make it the amusement center of nation.

**Sherman Billingsley's Stork Club** is one of most famous night clubs in country.

**Christmas** brings enormous decorated tree to Rockefeller Plaza, songs by Choristers.

**Jack & Charlie's "21"** always has autograph hunters waiting for celebrities.

**Stage shows** at Radio City Music Hall are famous for precision *Corps de Ballet.*

**Brooklyn Bridge,** built in 1883 by the Roeblings, was first to span East River.

**George Washington Bridge,** with Lincoln and Holland tunnels, cross Hudson River.

**Metropolitan Opera House** is premier home of grand opera in the United States.

**Washington Arch,** at lower end of Fifth Avenue, is gateway to Greenwich Village.

**Chinatown** is center for restaurants and curio shops, about 4,000 Chinese residents.

**Grant's Tomb,** Riverside Drive landmark, honors Civil War general, 18th President.

432

**Coney Island** often attracts a million to its ocean beach, boardwalk and amusements.

**Rockefeller Plaza** outdoor ice skating pond has twenty onlookers to each skater.

**Llamas from Peru** are among the curios in Bronx Zoo, one of world's largest.

**Japanese Garden,** Rose and Rock Gardens are found in Brooklyn Botanical Garden.

**Parades** up New York's great Fifth Avenue honor holidays, heroes, special events.

**Sidewalk art shows** encourage looking and buying in bohemian Greenwich Village.

**Montauk Point** is the eastern tip of Long Island. Its lighthouse, with black-and- white-striped tower, was built in 1796. Fishing grounds off the point are famous.

**Ducks on the hoof:** Duck farms flourish along the many creeks of the South Shore.

**Whalers Church** at Sag Harbor lost its spyglass-shaped tower in 1938 hurricane.

**Shelter Island** nestles between the two eastern points of Long Island, Orient Point on the north and Montauk to the south, connected with both by ferries.

**Once** an almost inaccessible sandbar, Jones Beach is now state's best play spot.

**Watertower,** floodlighted at night and visible for 25 miles, dominates Jones Beach.

**Sagamore Hill,** recently opened to public, was home of Pres. Theodore Roosevelt.

**Souvenirs** of Rough Rider days, of big-game hunting, fill Teddy Roosevelt home.

**Walt Whitman Birthplace** in West Hills: Good Gray Poet was born here in 1819.

**Country Life Press,** Garden City, is one of world's great book publishing centers.

**Franklin D. Roosevelt Library,** at Hyde Park, houses six million of his papers.

**Taylor Hall** is at entrance to Vassar College for women, at Poughkeepsie.

**At West Point,** the buildings of the U. S. Military Academy seem carved out of the hillside rocks. Admitted as cadets, graduates are named second lieutenants.

**Harness racing at Goshen** is climaxed by the internationally famous Hambletonian.

**Mid-Hudson Bridge** is at Poughkeepsie, half way between New York and Albany.

Photos: New York State Department of Commerce

**Bear Mountain Bridge,** about 40 miles north of New York, leads to Palisades Interstate Park, with variety of sports for New York-New Jersey residents.

**Catskill Game Farm,** in Greene County, exhibits animals from all over the world.

**Actors rehearse** for summer theater at Woodstock, widely known artist colony.

**Tower in Catskills** gives wide view. This is noted as "Wish You Were Here" land.

# New York ADIRONDACK REGION

**Kayak sailing** on Seventh Lake: There are hundreds of lakes in the Adirondacks.

**Ausable Chasm** is a wonderland of rock forms: Pulpit Rock, Devil's Oven, etc.

**Schroon Lake** is lovely 9-mile-long body of water that attracts many vacationists.

Legend says it was named after Madame de Maintenon, widow of Paul Scarron.

**State operated bathing beach** is one of many facilities of 33-mile Lake George.

**Whiteface Mountain** has elevator to lookout tower that gives a magnificent view.

**Saratoga Race Track,** Saratoga Springs, is scene of internationally famous horse races during August, including the Travers and the Hopeful, test for two-year-olds.

**Central Adirondacks** offer winter sports thrills for youngsters and for grownups.

**Snow tractor** transports skiers in comfort at the Whiteface Mt. ski development.

**Lake Placid ski jump:** This village on Mirror Lake is famous as sport center.

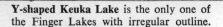

**Y-shaped Keuka Lake** is the only one of the Finger Lakes with irregular outline.

About 19 miles long, it is noted for the many vineyards on the surrounding slopes.

**The Krebs,** Skaneateles, is one of most famous eating houses in upstate area.

**Baseball Museum** at Cooperstown reveres Abner Doubleday's invention of the sport

**McKinley Circle,** Buffalo: This is the second largest city (580,000) in state.

**Elmira** was summer home of Mark Twain for many years. This is writer's studio

**Sailboats** are towed to anchorage after a race on Cayuga Lake, largest of the six Finger Lakes. Chief city on the lake is Ithaca, the home of Cornell University.

**Watkins Glen:** The Gorge Trail is 2 miles long, has some 700 steps, many bridges.

**Taughannock Falls,** 50 feet higher than Niagara, is highest east of the Rockies.

Photos: Bill Ficklin; Alfred E. Reichenberger;
New York State Department of Commerce

The **"Thousand Islands"** actually number about 1700. About 20 of them are visible in this picture of the American channel of the St. Lawrence near Alexandria Bay.

**Boldt Castle** was built on Heart Island by George C. Boldt, who rose from dishwasher to presidency of the company that owned New York's Waldorf-Astoria hotel.

Photos: Alexandria Bay Chamber of Commerce; New York State Department of Commerce

**Lighthouse on Cape Vincent:** Many French settled here at time of Napoleon's exile.

**Water tours** visit the six state parks and view Thousand Island luxury estates.

**International highway,** with several bridges, crosses the St. Lawrence via Wells and Hill islands. It was opened in 1938. From mainland to mainland, it's 6 miles.

Photos: New York State Department of Commerce

**Niagara Falls** is the largest cataract in North America with total width of 4,750 feet. This is American Falls which altered shape with recent erosion of rock.

Photo: Grant M. Haist

# FIFTY MILLION A YEAR ENJOY
# NEW JERSEY'S FAMOUS BEACHES

**Atlantic City's** fabulous boardwalk, immense hotels, Municipal Auditorium, Steel Pier all combine to make it one of world's most patronized year-round resorts.

# New Jersey

**Skyline of Trenton,** New Jersey's capital, is dominated by dome of Statehouse.

**This tall electric beacon** marks Thomas A. Edison's workshop at Menlo Park.

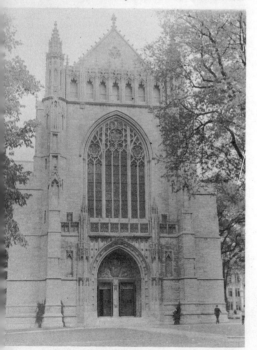

**Princeton University Chapel** ranks with Chicago and Cambridge as world's largest.

**This is Voorhees Chapel** of N. J. College for Women, a part of Rutgers University.

Photos: New Jersey Department of Conservation and Economic Development.

**Asbury Park** is best-known of the resorts along the northern part of New Jersey's coast. This is view of boardwalk looking north from Casino to Convention Hall.

**Chalfonte-Haddon Hall** is meeting-place of many of Atlantic City's conventions.

**Cape May** is at southernmost point of the state, between Delaware Bay and Atlantic.

**Barnegat Lighthouse** was replaced by lightship off-shore.

**Manasquan and Brielle,** on the Manasquan River where it flows into the Atlantic, are fishing headquarters.

Photos: Asbury Park Municipal Publicity Dept.; Chalfonte-Haddon Hall; New Jersey Department of Conservation and Economic Development.

# New Jersey

**George Washington** slept here, at Wallace House, Somerville, near winter camp.

**Walt Whitman** lived in this modest Camden residence from 1884 until his death.

**Alexander Hamilton monument,** in a small park on the brink of the Palisades at Weehawken, marks spot of Burr-Hamilton duel. Across Hudson is New York skyline.

**Basking Ridge oak,** in Somerset County, has amazing branch spread of 140 feet.

**Paulins Kill** is one of many lakes and streams that provide good sport-fishing.

448

Photos: center, G. A. Reims· New Jersey Department of Conservation and Economic Development

# PENNSYLVANIA HAS HISTORIC SHRINES FROM EARLY DAYS OF INDEPENDENCE

**Philadelphia's Independence Hall,** which houses Liberty Bell, witnessed the signing of the Declaration of Independence in 1776. Constitution was framed here, too.

Photo: TWA Trans World Airlines

# Pennsylvania PHILADELPHIA

**Franklin Institute** has many exhibits, including Benjamin Franklin Printing Shop.

**Liberty Bell** developed crack in 1835 when tolling death of Chief Justice Marshall.

**University of Pennsylvania** was first in the country officially designated as such.

**First Continental Congress** assembled here in Carpenters' Hall on September 5, 1774.

**Old Original Bookbinder's** is a favorite restaurant, filled with mementoes of past.

**Old Swedes Church,** built in 1700, is the oldest church building in Philadelphia.

**Betsy Ross House** is reputed place where first American Flag was designed, sewn.

**Wissahickon Valley,** Walnut Lane Bridge show a pastoral section of Philadelphia.

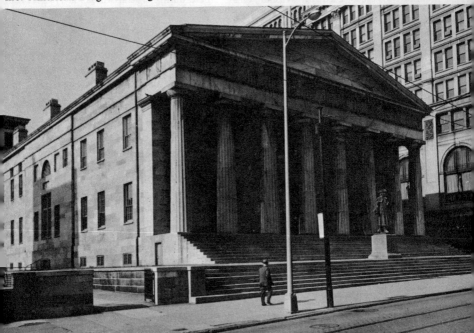

**Old Custom House** was originally home of the second Bank of the United States.

In front stands a statue of Robert Morris, a chief financier of American Revolution.

**These soldiers' huts** at Valley Forge are similar to those used by Washington's 11,000 ragged Continentals who camped here during crucial winter of 1777–1778.

**Washington's Headquarters** was scene of conferences with Lafayette, Knox, others.

**Washington Memorial Carillon** has 49 bells, one for each state, one for Union.

**Gettysburg** was scene of three-day battle that marked turning point of Civil War.

**Monument** honors General Meade who led Union forces against General Lee's.

**Soldiers' National Cemetery** has graves of 3,604 soldiers who died in battle be-tween forces numbering 70,000 to 80,000 on each side. Cemetery covers 17 acres.

**Pennsylvania Memorial** honors 34,530 men of state who took part in the battle.

**National Monument** is near spot where Abraham Lincoln gave Gettysburg speech.

# Pennsylvania

**Bucknell University,** Lewisburg, is one of state's leading educational centers.

**University of Pittsburgh's** 42-story skyscraper is called "Cathedral of Learning."

**Pittsburgh's "Golden Triangle"** is area between Allegheny and Monongahela rivers.

**One of the great steel centers** of world is Pittsburgh's gigantic "Steel Valley."

**Quaint buggies,** homespun garb typify the Amish, one of state's many religious sects.

**Hopewell Village,** near Reading, has been re-created as it was in Revolutionary days.

Photos: Pennsylvania State Department of Commerce; top left, A. Milton Runyon; center left, Robert V. Pivirotto

**Delaware Water Gap Bridge** spans river between New Jersey and Pennsylvania.

**Capitol at Harrisburg** was dedicated by President Theodore Roosevelt in 1906.

**Cambria Inclined Plane** connects Johnstown with Westmont, 504 feet higher.

**Shaft** commemorates Washington's crossing of Delaware in attack on Trenton.

# Pennsylvania

**U. S. Brig "Niagara"** took decisive part in Battle of Lake Erie, during War of 1812.

**Buck Hill Falls** is hidden in deep gorge. Photo shows the Upper and Middle Falls.

**The Inn** at Buck Hill Falls in the Pocono Mountains was established in 1901 by a group of Philadelphia Quakers. It is one of America's prominent resort hotels.

**Horseshoe Curve** of the Pennsylvania Railroad, constructed in 1852, is an outstanding engineering feat. The curve, with 220-degree central angle, is 2,375 ft. long.

Photos: Pennsylvania State Department of Commerce; top right and center, Buck Hill Falls Co.

# DELAWARE IS PROUD OF ITS HISTORIC LANDMARKS

**The County Court House** at New Castle has served Delaware's government since the days of William Penn, making it oldest U. S. Court House in continuous use.

Photo: Delaware State Development Department

# Delaware

**First powder mill** of E. I. duPont de Nemours used power of Brandywine Creek.

**University of Delaware** pioneered in Foreign Study, with exchange students.

**Christ Church,** Dover, possesses a Bible presented in 1767 by Benjamin Wynkoop.

**Old State House,** built in 1787, stands on the Green in Delaware's capital, Dover.

**Rehoboth Beach,** largest summer resort in Delaware, occupies one of the few spots along the South Atlantic coast where the mainland extends right to surf's edge.

**Wilmington** is Delaware's one big city, of 110,000 people. This is old City Hall.

**Zwaanendael Museum,** Lewes, commemorates settlement by the Dutch in 1631.

**Tourinns Motor Court,** near Wilmington, is typical of modern highway facilities.

**Old Swedes Church,** built at Wilmington in 1698, has mementoes of many pioneers.

**Old Drawyers Presbyterian Church** dates from 1773. It is located near Appoquini-mink Creek, in Odessa. Many founders of the state are interred in its cemetery.

# THE MIDSOUTH

## by STACY V. JONES

The Midsouth is New England with the corners rounded. It is more Colonial than Confederate, and this in spite of the fact that roadside markers recall Manassas and Appomattox. Perhaps it would be fairer to call New England a rough-edged Midsouth, for the adventurous businessmen of Jamestown did beat the Puritans to the New World by a few years. At any rate, there are similarities between the two regions: oldness and reverence for age; a pervading sense of duty and the fitness of things; close identification with the finding and founding of America and with the Revolutionary War.

The tourist is likely to see more boxwood than battlefields, for much of the area's history is preserved in the old homes and gardens of the men who made it. Energetic clubwomen have restored numerous eighteenth-century mansions; they collect visitors' half-dollars and see that everything indoors is dusted and everything outdoors is green. Stratford Hall, on Virginia's northern neck, was the birthplace of Robert E. Lee, and also of two earlier Lees, who signed the Declaration of Independence. There is George Washington's birthplace on what was once Pope's Creek and his later home at Mount Vernon on the Potomac; George Mason's Gunston Hall just below the latter, and Jefferson's Monticello at Charlottesville. A whole Colonial capital has been restored at Williamsburg. And colonial plantation houses dot Maryland's Eastern Shore and the banks of the James in Virginia.

Mount Vernon was George Washington's later home and place of burial. It is on Potomac, 14 miles south of Washington.

The Midsouth has great topographic variety, which makes it congenial country for casual touring. In orderly progression tidewater plains cut by widening estuaries give way to rising piedmont farmland, which in turn is broken by the wooded Appalachians—a handsome but tamed range in these parts, well suited to vacationing. And of course there is Washington, a national capital but definitely a Southern city.

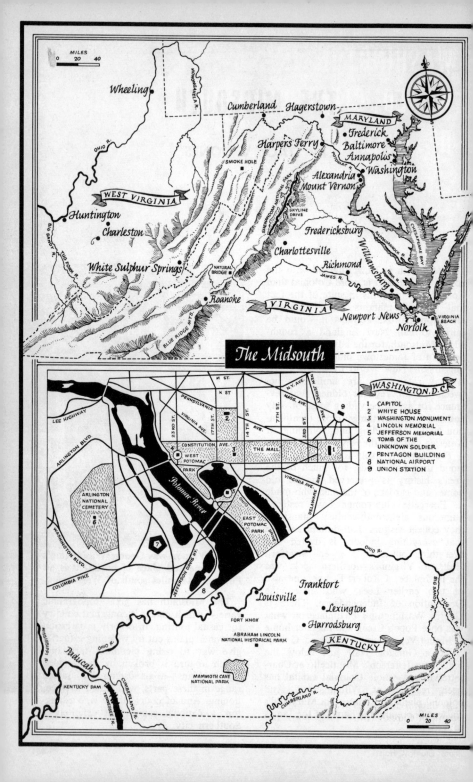

# WASHINGTON IS WORLD CITADEL OF FREEDOM

**U. S. Capitol** dominates Washington from summit of Capitol Hill. George Washington laid the cornerstone in 1793; statue of Freedom was placed atop dome in 1863.

Photo: Grant M. Haist

# Washington, D.C.

**Washington Monument,** opened in 1888, is the world's tallest structure of masonry.

**Air view of the Capitol** shows its 120 acres of grounds. In the north wing, to

the left, is the Senate, and in the south wing, the House of Representatives meets.

The building is 751 feet long, 350 wide, and its dome rises to height of 285 feet.

**Visitors** to the top of 555-ft. Washington Monument have a spectacular view of the city, and especially of the White House and its 18 acres of grounds. Every U.S

President has lived here since President John Adams moved to the unfinished building in 1800. It was completely rebuilt, within the original walls, in 1950–1952.

# Washington, D.C.

**Arlington Memorial Bridge,** built at cost of $10 million crosses Potomac from the Lincoln Memorial to Arlington National Cemetery. Photo shows end-of-day traffic.

**Lincoln Memorial,** built in general form of a Greek temple, is one of the world's most impressive memorials. 36 columns represent states at time of Presidency.

Photos: Grant M. Haist; Greater National Capital Committee

**Interior of Lincoln Memorial** contains gigantic 19-ft. seated figure of Lincoln by Daniel Chester French, in which the artist has captured his brooding sadness.

Photo: Grant M. Haist

**Jefferson Memorial,** completed in 1943, was dedicated on the 200th anniversary of the birth of Thomas Jefferson. Its Pantheon design was one he often used

Photo: Konstantin Kostic

**Towering statue of Jefferson,** the great statesman who wrote the Declaration of Independence, is principal feature of the Memorial. Quotations are carved on walls.

Photo: Grant M. Haist

471

**National Gallery of Art** is one of most famous in world. It was gift of Andrew W. Mellon. This view shows Constitution Avenue entrance and the 7th Street side.

**Rotunda in National Gallery** has fountain surmounted by Giovanni Bologna's bronze Mercury. In famed collection are paintings by Stuart, Renoir, Vermeer, Homer.

**Pentagon Building** is across Potomac in Virginia, but so much a part of life in Washington that we include it here. It's the largest office building in the world.

**Smithsonian Institution** houses amazing scientific exhibits, most popular being *The Spirit of St. Louis,* the plane in which Lindbergh made solo flight to Paris.

**The Supreme Court,** completed in 1935, is one of newest and most beautiful of the major buildings in Washington. Decisions by Court reflect history of the nation.

**Abraham Lincoln** was fatally shot, here at Ford's Theater, by John Wilkes Booth.

**Old Peterson House,** where Lincoln died, in April 1865, is across from theater.

**Occidental Restaurant** is noted eating place next door to famous Willard Hotel.

**Photographs** of military men and other celebrities line walls of the Occidental.

Photos: Library of Congress;
bottom, Occidental Restaurant

# JUST BELOW THE MASON-DIXON LINE, MARYLAND BLENDS NORTH AND SOUTH

**The Third State House** to be built on the same site in Annapolis, this one dates back to 1772. It is the oldest state capitol in America still in daily use, and the only one in which the Congress of the United States has convened.

Photo: Maryland Department of Information

# Maryland

"Tecumseh" is revered by midshipmen at United States Naval Academy, Annapolis.

Academy Chapel has crypt containing tomb of daring hero, John Paul Jones.

St. John's College, Annapolis, was the first free school in original 13 colonies.

Annapolitans model fashions of ancestors at historic Hammond-Harwood house.

Photos: Maryland Department of Information

**Ocean City** is Maryland's only resort by the sea. Located on sandy strip between Sinepuxent Bay and the Atlantic, it has ocean and bay swimming, fishing, yachting.

**Fort McHenry** repulsed British in 1814; was birthplace of "Star Spangled Banner."

**And battle-scarred Fort Frederick** dates back to 1756, in days of the Indian wars.

**Antietam Battlefield,** near Hagerstown, was scene of one of the hardest-fought Civil War battles, on September 17, 1862. Markers show ebb and flow of fierce battle.

Photos: M. E. Warren, Maryland Department of Information

# Maryland

**Hagerstown,** a manufacturing city, boasts Museum of Fine Arts, in a lovely setting.

**The "Narrows,"** near Cumberland, was famous gateway to the west 200 years ago.

**Fairchild Aircraft plant,** near Hagerstown, is responsible for the city's nickname, "The Home of the Flying Boxcars." Other plants make furniture, pipe organs, shoes.

**Wye Oak** is the state tree. Maryland has twelve extensive park and forest areas.

**Princess Anne,** one of the earliest settlements, has old homes like Teackle House.

Photos: top left, Raup, Maryland Department of Information, top right, Cumberland Chamber of Commerce; center, Maryland Department of Information; bottom, M. E. Warren, Maryland Department of Information.

# VIRGINIA, "MOTHER OF PRESIDENTS," HAS WEALTH OF SCENERY, HISTORY

Photo: Court House, Charlottesville,
by Henri Cartier-Bresson (Magnum)

# Virginia WILLIAMSBURG

**Williamsburg** is delightful replica of our Colonial past. Magazine was built 1715.

**In this 18th century Capitol,** Patrick Henry made speech against the Stamp Act.

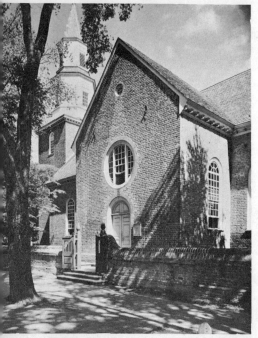

**Bruton Parish Church** has been restored to its appearance when built in 1710–15.

**Raleigh Tavern** has been refurnished according to inventories of early keepers

**Public Gaol:** Minor offenders were punished in the stocks and pillory in front

**Governor's Palace,** considered one of the handsomest estates in colonial America, was the official residence of the king's representative in the Virginia Colony.

**Williamsburg Inn,** just outside restored area, has fine facilities for visitors.

**Early costumes** recreate lavishness of colonial life under the British crown.

# Virginia

**Skyline Drive** is 107 miles long, from Front Royal on the north to Rockfish Gap near Waynesboro on the south. There it links up with the Blue Ridge Parkway.

**Shenandoah National Park** is 300-square-mile tract of mountains and ridges that extends on either side of the Skyline Drive. It has 200 miles of hiking trails.

**The Homestead,** at Hot Springs, is one of the world's famous hotels. First inn on the site dates from 1765. The modern building radiates from 12-story tower.

**James Monroe,** as a young attorney, used this modest Law Office, Fredericksburg.

**University of Virginia** was founded 1819 by Thomas Jefferson. This is the Rotunda.

**James Monroe built Oak Hill,** near Aldie, during his first term as President. He spent much time here, making journeys to and from the Capital on horseback.

# Virginia

**Monticello,** the home of Thomas Jefferson, was designed and built by the states-man himself. He died here on July 4, 1826, fiftieth anniversary of Independence Day.

**Luray Caverns,** beneath western slopes of Blue Ridge, have great underground halls.

**Shenandoah** is another of Virginia's nine caverns. This is the Grotto of the Gods.

Photos: Virginia Department of Conservation and Development

**Here at Mount Vernon,** plantation home overlooking the Potomac River, George Washington lived the life he loved best —that of a prosperous country squire.

**Stonewall Jackson** taught at "V.M.I."— Virginia Military Institute, Lexington.

**Natural Bridge,** 215 feet high, is one of the seven natural wonders of the world.

# Virginia

**State Capitol** at Richmond is one of many buildings designed by Thomas Jefferson.

It contains Houdon statue of Washington, only one of the President made from life.

**Kenmore** was home of Washington's sister, Betty, and her husband, Colonel Lewis.

**Westover,** home of the famous Byrd family of Virginia, is along the James River.

**Girls from Mary Washington College** serve tea in the stately dining room at Kenmore.

Photos: Virginia Department of Conservation and Development

**Valentine Museum,** Richmond, houses work of sculptor Edward V. Valentine.

**White House of Confederacy,** at Richmond, was the home of Jefferson Davis.

**Stratford** was birthplace of the Lees of Virginia, including the famous Robert E.

**"Mother's Room"** at Stratford: The great plantation, now restored, borders Potomac.

**This is gracious dining room** of house in which George Washington was born, 1732.

**Exterior of Birthplace:** Rebuilt like the original, it is now a National Monument.

**Arlington House,** in Arlington National Cemetery, was built by step-grandson of George Washington. Robert E. Lee was married here, lived in house until 1861.

**Woodrow Wilson** was born in this square house at Staunton, on December 28, 1856.

**Presbyterian Meeting House, Alexandria:** Unknown Soldier of Revolution lies here.

**Gunston Hall** was home of George Mason, outstanding author of the Bill of Rights.

**St. Luke's Church,** near Smithfield, is one of nation's oldest, built in 1632.

**Shirley,** one of the largest of Tidewater Virginia mansions, was built between 1720 and 1740 by Thomas West and his three brothers. Lawn slopes to James River.

**James Monroe** built Ash Lawn near Monticello, so he could be near his friend and mentor, Thomas Jefferson. Estate is known for its beautiful boxwood hedges.

# Virginia

**Old church tower, Jamestown:** This was site of first permanent English settlement.

**St. John's Church,** Richmond, echoed to Patrick Henry's cry for "liberty or death."

**Virginia Beach,** on the Atlantic near Norfolk, is an outstanding shore resort.

Virginia's best-known Chesapeake Bay resorts are Ocean View, Buckroe Beach.

**George Washington Masonic National Memorial Temple** towers over Alexandria.

**Boyhood home of Patrick Henry,** this old house became Michie Tavern in 1746.

Photos: Virginia Department of Conservation and Development; bottom right, Michie Tavern

# WHITE SULPHUR IS NOTED RESORT OF "MOUNTAIN STATE," WEST VIRGINIA

**The original** White Sulphur Springs Hotel was renowned for more than half a century as the Old White. Belle, in front of Greenbrier, re-creates ante-bellum days.

Woodburn Hall is symbol of West Virginia University, situated at Morgantown.

West Virginia's State Capitol is located at Charleston, in Appalachian foothills.

Greenbrier College for Women, originally Lewisburg Seminary, was founded in 1812.

Harewood, in Eastern Panhandle, was built by Washington for his brother, Samuel.

"Old Stone Face" gazes across creek at Beckwith Cut-Off, near Chimney Corner.

Photos: West Virginia Industrial and Publicity Commission

**Hawks Nest State Park** provides breathtaking view of the New River Gorge, east of Charleston. The towering rock is named for the fish hawks that once nested there.

**At Blackwater Falls,** the dark hued river drops over broken ledge to huge boulders.

**Smoke Hole Cavern** was used by Indians and early white settlers to cure meats.

**Monument above and "John Brown's Fort"** at right commemorate the stand which the

famed abolitionist made against force of marines prior to start of the Civil War.

Photos: West Virginia Industrial and Publicity Commission

**Indian Burial Mound,** in Staunton Park at South Charleston, is 175 feet around at base and 30 feet high. Many Indian ornaments, stone weapons have been found.

**The Castle,** Berkeley Springs, was built by Judge Soult as a "castle in the air."

**Carbide and Carbon Chemicals Corporation** is one of state's many industrial plants.

Photos: West Virginia Industrial and Publicity Commission

# KENTUCKY IS A LAND OF BLUEGRASS, RACE HORSES, AND GRACIOUS LIVING

**Horse farm region** of Kentucky centers around Lexington. Visitors may see the thoroughbreds that have made history and watch gambols of promising young colts.

# Kentucky

**Bluegrass** name comes from steel-blue tint of May blossoms. It's ideal for grazing.

**Capitol,** built in 1909, is at Frankfort in center of state, along Kentucky River.

**Mammoth Cave** covers an area ten miles in circumference and has 325 explored passageways which extend 150 miles. This is Crystal Lake, an outstanding feature.

**Churchill Downs** in Louisville is scene of America's most celebrated horse race, the Kentucky Derby. More than 100,000 fans gather here first Saturday in May.

**Air view of Calumet Farm** shows beautiful barns, outdoor track, miles of rolling blue-grass where many thoroughbred winners have been raised. It covers 1,000 acres.

Photos: Kentucky Division of Publicity

# Kentucky

**Kentucky Dam** is major TVA dam, finished 1944, 206 ft. high, 8,422 ft. long.

**Kentucky Lake,** formed by dam, is sport center with three state parks on shores.

**Laurel Cove,** Pine Mountain State Park, is scene of the annual Mountain Laurel

Festival. High point of 3-day event is crowning of the queen by the Governor.

**Liberty Hall,** in Frankfort, was home of John Brown, state's first U.S. Senator.

**Diamond Point** is one of Harrodsburg's old homes in southern plantation style.

Photos: top left, Robert H. Faith
Kentucky Division of Publicity

**This memorial** honors the birthplace of Abraham Lincoln, near Hodgenville, in central Kentucky. The birth cabin is preserved inside the memorial building.

**Log house** where Lincoln's parents were married stands at Pioneer Memorial Park.

**Split-rail fence** appropriately marks boundaries at Lincoln Memorial Park.

**Marriage Temple** shelters cabin where Thomas Lincoln married Nancy Hanks.

**At Federal Hill,** near Bardstown, Stephen Foster wrote "My Old Kentucky Home."

499

# Kentucky

**Restored buildings** at old Fort Harrod are furnished in manner of pioneer days.

**Fine burley tobacco** is grown in bluegrass section and taken to market at Lexington.

**Monument to Jefferson Davis,** President of the Confederacy, stands at Fairview.

**Boone Tavern at Berea** is operated by Berea College as a student industry.

**Graves of Daniel and Rebecca Boone** are on a high bluff in Frankfort cemetery.

# THE SOUTH

## by JOHN POPHAM

The South is a kaleidoscopic parade of natural scenery and human attitudes, both of them etched sharply. The land and the people are undergoing great economic and social changes. The past and the present tilt lances in a setting as colorful as any pageantry in history.

The South is a land rich with historical continuity, a land of long days, bright in the sun and slow to cool in the evening shadows. On a summer's day the heat dances visibly along macadamized highways and dusty country roads. The ubiquitous screen doors shut with loud report on hollow stillness. Soft Southern voices add to the muted effect.

Everywhere there is a sense of something old and stable. Go west in North Carolina through the Great Smokies to Cherokee at twilight and watch Cherokee Indians from the near-by reservation act out the tragic story of their ancestors' trek across the "trail of tears" in the days of Andrew Jackson.

Then go down into the valley where the Tennessee River forms the famous Moccasin Bend at Chattanooga and visit the great dams of the Tennessee Valley Authority, where turbines and generators pour out the electrical power that has helped remake the face of this section.

At Memphis one reaches the banks of the Mississippi River and for miles around the country is flat, the soil black with Old Man River's largesse. This bustling city is a modern commercial hub for much of Tennessee, Mississippi and Arkansas but over its business section there yet remains the aura of plantation society. Along the river front cotton is yet the economic king. The shouts of river roustabouts have long since drifted downwind, side-wheelers no longer churn muddy waters and W. C. Handy's jazz is held in escrow on LP records. But trucks loaded with Negro handlaborers still roll out of the city for chopping and weeding in the cotton fields. Men with necks burned red from the sun, wearing broad-brimmed hats and white shirts with open collars, shop in the stores and talk incessantly of cotton prices and Government parity programs.

Southward from Memphis the hand of history remains heavy, but it is the clash of old and new architecture that catches the eye. There are the great pillared mansions in Vicksburg and Natchez, vast stretches of delta cotton land, dotted with sharecroppers' cabins.

New Orleans is a special South within the South. The gems of architecture of the French quarter are perhaps unmatched in this country. Eighty miles upriver is Baton Rouge, where Huey Long built a skyscraper capitol.

The Gulf Coast makes a wide arc from Biloxi to the southern tip of Florida's west coast, a coastal vacation land running down to the citrus groves and cattle farms and thriving tourist towns of Florida.

For all the changes, when the midday sun has softened, when afternoon shadows dapple tree-shaded streets, when children return to play after their naps, there is always a Savannah or Charleston with red-brick sidewalks and colonial architecture and patio gardens to take the visitor back into the past of the South.

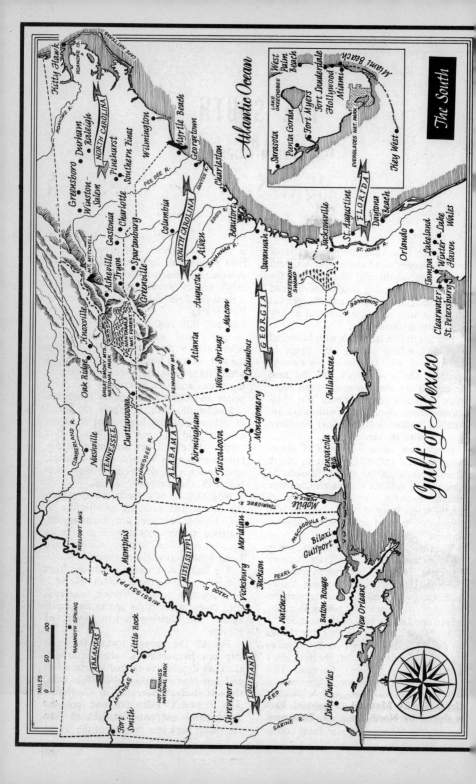

The South

# FROM HATTERAS TO GREAT SMOKIES, NORTH CAROLINA OFFERS INFINITE VARIETY

**Great Smoky Mountains National Park** is shared by North Carolina, Tennessee.

The "Great Smokies" take their name from bluish perpetual haze found here.

Photo: National Park Service

# North Carolina

**Mile-High Overlook** is on new section of the Blue Ridge Parkway, extending from Soco Gap to Black Camp Gap at boundary of Great Smokies Nat'l Park.

**Chimney Rock,** Eastern America's greatest monolith, rises 315 feet from its base.

**Old Market House,** built 1838, stands "where all roads meet" in Fayetteville.

504

**Near Asheville,** the mountain-top Craggy Gardens may be seen from Blue Ridge Parkway. In late May and June, acres of rhododendrons bloom in a blaze of color.

**Old Well,** in classic little temple, is landmark of University of North Carolina.

**Floodlighted,** North Carolina's Capitol stands out from surrounding oak grove.

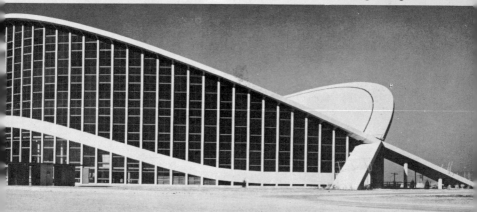

**North Carolina State Fair Arena,** five miles west of Raleigh, is one of the most remarkable buildings ever constructed. It has seating capacity of more than 9,000.

Photos: North Carolina News Bureau, bottom by Gus Martin

**Mount Mitchell,** in western part of state, is 6,684 feet—the highest in Eastern America. State park on the summit may be reached by five-mile paved highway.

**Home Moravian Church** is one of historic buildings in industrial Winston-Salem.

**A million azaleas** greet early spring in Wilmington at many garden plantations.

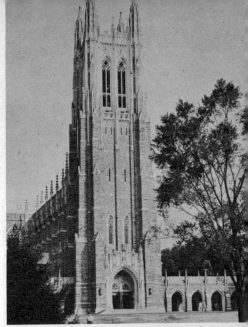

**Wright Brothers National Memorial**, near Kitty Hawk, marks birth of powered flight.

**Chapel at Duke University**, Durham, is beautiful example of Gothic architecture.

**Pisgah National Forest** is million-acre tract in western part of state, parts of which may be reached by motor roads. This is trail beside river at North Mills.

Photos: North Carolina News Bureau; bottom, U. S. Forest Service

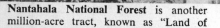

**Nantahala National Forest** is another million-acre tract, known as "Land of the Noonday Sun," in southwestern part of state. This is the Nantahala gorge.

**Tobacco production** in state is valued at over $460 million. This is auction room.

**Principal cigarette factories** are located at Durham, Reidsville and Winston-Salem.

**Biltmore House**, near Asheville, was George Vanderbilt estate, built in 1890.

**Governor's Mansion**, Raleigh, is Queen Anne style. Furnishings are magnificent.

Photos: U. S. Forest Service; North Carolina News Bureau, center left by Sebastian Sommer, bottom right by Gus Martin

# LOVELY OLD GARDENS ARE MEMORABLE FEATURE OF SOUTH CAROLINA

**The great gardens of South Carolina** lure thousands of visitors each spring. Among the principal ones are Magnolia, Cypress, Middleton (above), and Brookgreen.

# South Carolina

**Fort Sumter,** in Charleston Harbor, was scene of first shot fired in Civil War.

**Charleston's Dock Street Theater** was formerly the famous Old Planters Hotel.

**Lofty octagonal steeple** of St. Philip's Episcopal Church is Charleston landmark.

**Stuart House,** with arched entrance and fluted columns, is beautiful old home.

**Miles Brewton House** is most elegant example of Charleston Georgian residence.

Photos: Charleston Chamber of Commerce, top left by Ronald A. Reilly, others by Alma Crenshaw; top right, Delta-C&S Air Lines

**Many great estates** like Bonny Hall were built on rice plantations. The tidewater cultivation of rice, with elaborate dikes and canals, once produced half U.S. crop.

**Inky waters of Cypress Gardens** reflect the great trees and brilliant azaleas. Visitors may view the gardens, open from Thanksgiving to May 1, from little boats.

# South Carolina

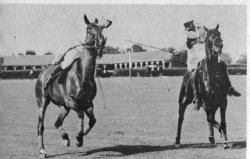

**Aiken,** in the west central sandhills, is known as the "Polo Capital" of the South.

**State House at Columbia** was bombed by General Sherman while it was being built.

**Library at University of South Carolina** was first separate library by U.S. college.

**Marine base at Parris Island,** Beaufort, has trained thousands of U. S. Marines.

**Crofut House** is one of many old homes that give Beaufort an Old World charm.

**Four former rice plantations** were joined to form 4,000-acre Brookgreen Gardens.

Photos: South Carolina State Development Board, Columbia

# GRACIOUS GEORGIA HAS VARIED TOPOGRAPHY, VARIED INTERESTS

**Savannah River,** 314 miles long, forms the boundary between Georgia, South Carolina. Nicknamed "Cracker State," Georgia is the largest state east of the Mississippi.

# Georgia

**Atlanta,** state capital and largest city, is called the "Gateway to the South."

Capitol is at right, city hall left, and Peachtree Street shopping center at top.

**Cyclorama** depicts Battle of Atlanta, at start of Sherman's "March to the Sea."

**Municipal Auditorium in Hurt Park:** Atlanta has many colleges and universities.

Photos: Delta-C&S Air Lines, Georgia Department of Commerce, lower left by Carolyn Carter

**The Cloister** is famous resort on Sea Island, one of the "Golden Isles" off Georgia's coast, with Atlantic on one side, Intracoastal Waterway on the other.

**Okefenokee Swamp** covers 700 square miles, is nation's most famous, primitive.

**National cemetery at Marietta** is burial place of 3,000 soldiers of Confederacy.

**Savannah,** Georgia's oldest city, is port of entry, industrial and shipping center.

**Independent Presbyterian Church** is one of proud buildings in tree-shaded Savannah.

**Old stone wall** leading to water: Savannah was once busiest port in the whole South.

**Monterey Square** is one of more than 50 parks that dapple the city with green.

Photos: Carolyn Carter, Southern Photo Service; Ralph Jones—Georgia Department of Commerce; bottom right, Chamber of Commerce of Savannah

**Air view of Savannah,** looking east, with Savannah River at the left: City is 17 miles from river's mouth on the Atlantic. Mild climate attracts many winter visitors.

**The Old Pink House** dates from 1771, way back in Savannah's days of crinolines.

**Herb House,** built as tool shed in 1734, is considered oldest building in state.

**Cotton merchants** once made big fortunes in these historic houses on Bay Street.

# Georgia

**Fort Pulaski,** on Cockspur Island, is named for hero of the Revolutionary War.

**Iron lacework** decorates porch of Juliette Low house, one of ante-bellum homes.

**Warm Springs Foundation,** for polio aid, was established by Franklin D. Roosevelt.

**Ocmulgee National Monument,** near Macon, has museum run by Park Service.

**Henry W. Grady,** journalist and orator, lived in this stately mansion at Athens.

**Grove Point** is one of great plantations reminiscent of Gone with the Wind's Tara.

Photos: Southern Photo Service, Inc. Hubert Dunlap, Harden, Edgar Orr— Georgia Department of Commerce

# FLORIDA ENJOYS 1,200-MILE COAST, YEAR-ROUND MILD CLIMATE

**Sun, sand, surf and wind-swept** palms have attracted millions of visitors to Florida's coasts, both Atlantic and Gulf. This is Delray Beach, near Lake Worth.

Photo: Charles L. Sherman

Miami's Crandon Park beach boasts miles of wide, white ocean sand. The "Gold Coast," from Miami north to Hobe Sound, is nearest thing to an America Riviera.

Dade County Courthouse, downtown Miami, is tallest building south of Baltimore.

Horses round the first turn at Gulfstream, one of three tracks in Greater Miami area.

Miami's new "Torch of Friendship" is symbol of good will toward all nations.

Photos: City of Miami News Bureau; bottom right, Florida State News Bureau

**Miami Beach's** fabled mile of gigantic hotels: Each has its own swimming pool and span of beach. Biscayne Bay causeways connect Miami Beach with Miami.

**Miami skyline from across Biscayne Bay:** The city's growth has been little short of miraculous. Little more than a village 50 years ago, population is now 250,000.

Photos: Florida State News Bureau; bottom, City of Miami News Bureau

**Jacksonville** has 4 bridges over St. Johns River. Newest is Gilmore Street Bridge, foreground, opened to traffic in 1954. The city was named for Andrew Jackson.

**Hemming Park** is tropic oasis in midst of bustling Jacksonville business district.

**Jacksonville's huge Union Terminal** is junction point for East Coast, West Coast.

**Castillo de San Marcos,** also called Fort Marion, is oldest fort standing in the U.S. Begun in 1672, but not finished until 1756, it is now National Monument.

**St. Augustine's** "Oldest House," now a museum, was reputedly built in 1500's.

**This well** is said to be Fountain of Youth that Ponce de Leon drank from in 1513.

**Ponte Vedra Club** is delightful resort five miles south of Jacksonville Beach.

# Florida EAST COAST

**Daytona Beach** is famed for hard-packed sand on which automobiles can be driven.

The 25-mile strip, 500 feet in width, has often been used for auto speed trials.

**Coral Sands cottages,** at Ormond Beach, are typical of modern resort facilities.

**Motorcycle races,** too, have been held on the hard white sand of Daytona Beach.

**Marineland,** just south of St. Augustine, is the world's largest oceanarium, with

leaping porpoises and other denizens of sea in tremendous 700,000 gallon tank.

Photos: Florida State News Bureau; center left, A. Milton Runyon

**Palm Beach** is exclusive resort, on tip of 18-mile island between Lake Worth and the Atlantic. It ranks with Newport as vacation center for the socially elite.

**McKee Jungle Gardens,** just south of Vero beach, have 80 acres of luxuriant tropical plants, with thousands of orchids and other exotic flowers, trees, shrubs.

**Boca Raton Hotel and Club,** once private club for millionaires, is now luxurious resort hotel. It's between Delray Beach and Fort Lauderdale, has own golf course.

**Hollywood Beach Trailer Park:** Florida offers world's best facilities for trailers.

**Hollywood is winter home** of Riverside Academy, a preparatory military school.

**Palm-lined boardwalk at Hollywood Beach:** This resort, south of Fort Lauderdale, was founded by a Californian, but bears no resemblance to movie capital.

Photos: Richard B. Hoit; Florida State News Bureau; Walter Gray, Hollywood By-the-Sea

**Mid-winter** finds Fort Lauderdale Beach lined with hundreds of gay beach cabanas.

City has many natural waterways, 90 miles of canals, Port Everglades harbor.

**Crowd lines Intracoastal Waterway** for Fort Lauderdale water-skiing, boat races.

**Sightseeing tours by boat** leave for New River, Pan-American Park, Everglades.

**Pleasure boat traffic on New River:** Fort Lauderdale is called "Venice of America."

**Fabulous Bahai-Mar yacht basin** offers berths for 400 yachts and power cruisers.

University of Florida, at Gainesville, has upwards of 10,000 students enrolled.

Rollins College, Winter Park, has 600-acre campus on shore of Lake Virginia.

Singing Tower, near Lake Wales, memorial to Edward Bok, has 71-bell carillon.

More than a hundred ferns and related tropical plants are found in the state.

Air plants, small spiny growths, derive their sustenance entirely from the air.

**Orlando, from across Lake Eola:** Recent rapid growth has made it largest inland city in the state. Often called the "City Beautiful," it is year 'round playground.

**Orlando's Lake Ivanhoe** is large enough for sailboat racing. Orlando Yacht Club is on Lake Conway at Pine Castle. There are 44 lakes within Orlando city limits.

**Orlando** is citrus-fruit shipping center, with nurseries, packing houses, canneries.

**Kissimmee,** known locally as Cow Town, is one of the state's chief cattle areas.

Photos: Greater Orlando Chamber of Commerce; bottom, Florida State News Bureau

**Tarpon Springs** is one of largest sponge markets in world, with fleet of 70 or more boats. Fishing with Greek deep-sea divers, begun 1905, is now major industry.

**Tallahassee,** with its State Capitol, is attractively set among hills and lakes.

**Silver-scaled tarpon** make tremendous leaps as they battle fisherman in Gulf.

Photos: Florida State News Bureau; bottom left, Wm. Lavendar

**Clearwater Beach** is on island in Gulf, connected by Memorial Causeway with the mainland. Clearwater itself is center for growing, shipping citrus fruits, gladioli.

**DeSoto Oak,** one of state's biggest, is at entrance to University of Tampa campus.

**Latin-American Fiesta** is annual event at Tampa, biggest port and industrial city.

# Florida WEST COAST

**2,400-ft. Municipal Pier** is trademark of the "Sunshine City," St. Petersburg.

**Many** of St. Petersburg's 3,800 sidewalk benches are placed along Central Avenue.

**Sailboats** pass Vinoy Park hotel on way to a day of sport in sheltered Tampa Bay.

**Al Lang Field:** Two major league teams Cards and Yankees, train at St. Pete

**New $22 million Sunshine Skyway** extends 15 miles, St. Petersburg to Palmetto.

**Spring Fiesta** at St. Petersburg is 3-day frolic, with parades and Coronation Ball.

**Jungle Gardens,** just north of Sarasota, has thousands of native and imported trees, plants and shrubs in junglelike setting. It's outstanding tropical botanical garden.

**Flamingoes,** other rare birds, wade in the beautiful dark waters of Jungle Gardens.

**Ringling Museum of Art at Sarasota** has 700 old masters collected by showman.

**Thomas A. Edison** home at Fort Myers: The inventor came here 1886 for experiments with his incandescent lamp. Each February, Pageant of Light honors him.

**"Money tree" in Edison garden:** Over 60 kinds of tropical palms are found here.

**Yacht basin:** Fort Myers is situated on the mile-wide Caloosahatchee River.

**Sanibel Island,** in Gulf off Fort Myers, is noted for number, variety of sea shells.

Photos: Florida State News Bureau; bottom left, Atlantic Coast Line Railroad

**Everglades National Park** is our newest, dedicated in June, 1947. It is 1¼ million acres of tropical scene, a wilderness of strange, exotic plant, bird, animal life.

**After Seminole Wars,** many Indians were removed to Oklahoma, but a number stayed in Everglades and Big Cypress. Above is Musa Isle Village, in Miami.

Photos: Florida State News Bureau; Konstantin Kostich; City of Miami News Bureau

**Key West** is southernmost city in U.S. Fishing boats go after shrimp, turtles.

**Lighthouse** is known as only one in the country within corporate limits of a city.

**Fort Jefferson,** now a National Monument, is on Garden Key of the Dry Tortugas, 60 miles from Key West. It was from here that the *Maine* sailed for Havana.

**Florida National Bank building** shows the "different" appearance of Key West.

**This home,** with its Captain's Walk, is typical of the Bahamas-style residences.

**Turtles,** weighing up to 600 pounds, are brought by fishermen to the soup plants.

536

# ALABAMA MEANS AZALEAS, COTTON, CATTLE, LUMBER

**Bellingrath Gardens** has fabulous collection of rare azaleas and camellias. It is a must on the itinerary of winter and spring visitors to Mobile's Azalea Trail.

Photo: Wm. Lavendar

Alabama

**Statue of Vulcan,** made for St. Louis Exposition, dominates hill near Birmingham.

**Mardi Gras Carnival at Mobile,** instituted in 1704, rivals the one at New Orleans.

**Famous oak drive at Spring Hill College on the Mobile Azalea Trail:** The annual flower festival is held in February or early March when azaleas are in full bloom.

**Birmingham,** largest city in Alabama, is a leading iron and steel center and is often called "Pittsburgh of the South." Downtown is laid out in planned squares.

**First White House of the Confederacy** was Montgomery home of Jefferson Davis.

**Timepiece** above entrance to Capitol was the town clock of Montgomery until 1852.

**Members of Azalea Trail "court"** are shown during a visit to the Bellingrath Gardens. The trail begins in Mobile's Bienville Square, is well marked by signs.

Photos: Birmingham Chamber of Commerce; Official State of Alabama; Montgomery Chamber of Commerce; Mobile Azalea Trail

# Alabama

**Alabama State Coliseum,** Montgomery, is outstanding in its modern architecture.

**Tuskeegee Monument** honors the great Negro educator, Booker T. Washington.

**Helen Keller,** who won out over deafness, blindness, was born here in Tuscumbia.

**Rosemount** is 20-room plantation mansion near Eutaw which took five years to build.

**Gorgas House,** with typical portico, is at University of Alabama, Tuscaloosa.

**Cotton raising** is still a major occupation, but hand-picking is on way out.

Photos: Official State of Alabama

# DEEP-SOUTH TRADITION IS STRONG
# IN MAGNOLIA STATE OF MISSISSIPPI

**Gloucester,** open to visitors during the Natchez Pilgrimage, is oldest mansion in the district. It was home of Winthrop Sargent, the first Territorial governor.

**Mississippi River at Vicksburg:** A major river port, Vicksburg overlooks junction of Yazoo Canal and the Mississippi. It was known as "Gibraltar of Confederacy."

**Dunleith** is stately mansion, with tall Doric columns, on outskirts of Natchez.

**This cypress swamp** is on Natchez Trace, new Parkway following historic old road.

**Iuka Mineral Springs** were discovered by Indians, later became noted health resort.

**MacArthur Hotel, Biloxi:** This was first French settlement in Mississippi Valley.

Photos: Mississippi Agricultural & Industrial Board

**Melrose** is especially popular with visitors during the Pilgrimage because it is one of the best-preserved old homes, with furnishings much as in the 1840's.

**Jefferson Military Academy,** Washington, was scene of Aaron Burr trial for treason.

**Lyceum Building,** erected 1848, is center of University of Mississippi at Oxford.

# Mississippi

**Biloxi Lighthouse** dominates new 28-mile sand beach along Mississippi Sound, near the Gulf of Mexico. The city is noted as packing center for oysters and shrimp.

**Swimming pool** is one of Biloxi's many attractions for entertainment of tourists.

**Percy Quinn State Park,** at McComb, is one of eight state parks in Mississippi.

**The Walter Place,** Holly Springs, is fine example of a luxurious home of the 1850's.

**Old Capitol Building, Jackson:** Henry Clay, Jefferson Davis spoke from balcony.

544

Photos: Mississippi Agricultural & Industrial Board

# LOUISIANA MEANS PLANTATIONS, BAYOUS, AND FABULOUS NEW ORLEANS

**From balcony of Pontalba Apartments,** visitors to New Orleans' historic *Vieux* *Carré* see famous St. Louis Cathedral, on Chartres Street and Jackson Square.

"Dinner at Antoine's" added fame to an already internationally known restaurant.

Above is exterior, and at left the front desk of Antoine Alciatore's restaurant.

Pirates Alley runs between St. Louis Cathedral and Cabildo, where Spanish ruled.

French Market coffee stand is place for coffee and doughnuts in the wee hours.

Old Absinthe House has secret room where Jackson met Laffite to plan city's defense

Photos: Antoine's Restaurant; Louisiana Department of Commerce and Industry; bottom right, Delta-C&S Air Line

**Browsing in the numerous antique shops** is favorite occupation in the old French Quarter. Many buildings are adorned with lovely wrought-iron projecting balconies.

**There are many shops,** too, featuring the mouth-watering Creole pecan pralines.

**Seen through intriguing doorways** are magnificent patios, verdant courtyards.

Photos: Henri Cartier-Bresson (Magnum); Delta-C&S Air Lines

**Tulane University's 93-acre campus** is scene of the Sugar Bowl football game.

**The International Trade Mart** exhibits products from South America, Europe

**Huey P. Long Bridge** is $13 million span carrying automobiles and trains across the Mississippi, which is 2,200 feet wide here, and as much as 180 feet deep.

**Canal Street** extends 3½ miles, from the Mississippi to Metairie. It is one of the widest thoroughfares in the world 171 feet, and one of most brilliantly lit

Photos: Louisiana Department of Commerce and Industry; center, Bureau of New Orleans News

**At Mardi Gras time,** and on New Year's Eve, Canal Street is real maelstrom. Mardi Gras, the festival that ushers in Lent, brings 100,000 visitors to the city.

**The Mississippi** winds around New Orleans in a great crescent, lined with docks for ships that have come down the river and ships that have come through the Gulf.

Photos: Louisville & Nashville Railroad; Shell Oil Company

# Louisiana

**Memorial Tower** clock and chimes keep time for students at Louisiana State.

**Louisiana's** towering Capitol at Baton Rouge soars 33 stories, cost $5 million.

**Statue of Evangeline** is in St. Martinville, the heart of the Acadian country.

**Snowy egrets** sun themselves in famed Bird City sanctuary at Avery Island.

**Still waters of Bayou Teche** are guarded by cypress trees overhung with Spanish moss. Bridge in background crosses over into Longfellow-Evangeline State Park.

**At Oakley,** John James Audubon did much research for his great *Birds of America*.

**San Francisco** is "Steamboat Gothic" home, Garyville, built before Civil War.

**One of loveliest** of plantation homes is Greenwood, 1830–35, St. Francisville.

**The Shadows,** at New Iberia, stands in lush gardens bordering Bayou Teche.

**But for the automboile on deck,** this photo of the Mississippi at Baton Rouge might have been taken in Mark Twain's time. Ferries cross from Port Allen to city.

**Pirogue races** are held at Barataria Bay each year. Smugglers and pirates once made this their headquarters. It is now the heart of Louisiana's shrimp country.

Photos: Henri Cartier-Bresson (Magnum); Louisiana Department of Commerce and Industry

# ARKANSAS IS HOME OF HOT SPRINGS, WORLD FAMOUS SPA

**Along the lower reaches** of the White River before it joins the Mississippi:

Commercial fishing on Arkansas rivers brings an income of $1½ million annually.

**Giant bluffs** dwarf fishermen on a float trip down the White River. The Arkansas River, flowing nearly 1,500 miles from Rockies, is state's principal waterway.

**Mystic Cave,** above, Wonderland Cavern, Diamond Cave are underground marvels.

**Eden Falls, Lost Valley:** In mountain country, streams are clear, swift, cold

Photos: Arkansas Publicity and Parks Commission, top by Harold Phelps

**Hot Springs National Park,** America's oldest, was dedicated in 1832. It covers 1,000 acres in Ouachita Mountains. View shows Army and Navy General Hospital.

**Arkansas' old State House,** in Little Rock, is now official history museum.

**Beautiful new State Capitol,** designed by Cass Gilbert, was finished in 1916.

**Oaklawn Jockey Club,** Hot Springs, has glass-enclosed, steam-heated grandstand.

The climax of each meet is the Arkansas Derby, famous event for three-year-olds.

Photos: Arkansas Publicity and Parks Commission, top and center left by John Blundell; center right, Little Rock Chamber of Commerce

**Little Rock Country Club** is high above Arkansas River, once busy steamboat route. North Little Rock, on the other side of the river, is reached by five bridges.

**Railway ferry "Pelican"** carries freight cars across the Mississippi at Helena.

**Outboard motor racing** is popular at Lake Hamilton, Hot Springs, and at Batesville.

**Arkansas Post State Park** adjoins town which was first capital of the Territory.

**Artistry** or "land of cross-bow" is shown at Blanchard Springs, Mountain View.

Photos: Arkansas Publicity and Parks Commission, bottom right by Harold Phelps; top, Little Rock Chamber of Commerce

# TENNESSEE IS KNOWN FOR SMOKIES, T.V.A., ANDREW JACKSON, ATOM BOMB

**Gatlinburg** is on the edge of Great Smoky Mountains National Park, which covers 643 square miles in Tennessee and North Carolina. Photo shows the smoky mist.

**"Gordon C. Greene"** on the Tennessee River near Chattanooga: After the Civil War, more than fifty steamboats were in operation carrying passengers, freight.

**Hiking party tackles Mt. LeConte,** 6,595-foot peak in the Great Smoky Mountains.

**Lookout Mountain Incline Railway** goes from Chattanooga to summit of mountain.

Photos: Paul A. Moore,
Tenn. Conservation Dept.

**Memphis,** largest city in Tennessee, is a metropolis for that state and for the nearby states of Mississippi, Arkansas. It is named after ancient city on Nile.

**Marble quarrying** ranks with textiles and furniture as top Knoxville industries.

**Spinning,** hand-weaving, coverlet-making are prized arts of Tennessee mountain folk.

**From top of Lookout Mountain,** Chattanooga, you can see more than 100 miles on clear days. This vantage point is near upper end of Incline Railway (photo left).

**Oak Ridge** is site of laboratory at which uranium for the world's first two atom bombs was separated. Community housing 30,000 was built here almost "overnight."

**Fort Negley,** built 1862, overlooks Nashville from the summit of St. Cloud Hill.

**Tennessee State Capitol** stands on Cedar Knob, highest point in city of Nashville.

**Reelfoot Lake,** formed by earthquake in 1811, is noted for its huge cypress trees and abundant plant life. 18 miles long, 2½ miles wide, it's only 2 to 9 feet deep.

Photos: Paul A. Moore, Tenn. Conservation Dept.; center left, W. Lincoln Highton

# THE MIDWEST

## by RICHARD J. H. JOHNSTON

"Twin Zephyr" with vista-domes rolls along scenic route beside Mississippi River.

Contrary to popular misconception, the Midwest, from the lakes of Minnesota and Wisconsin and the Great Lakes down through Illinois and Indiana and Ohio, is not barren flat land, always more of the same. There is, perhaps, more homogeneity in the people who live in these states than in their landscapes, though the contrasts between the big cities and the rural areas is as sharp as that between one section of this country and another.

For variety, there are in Indiana and Michigan those strange natural wonders, the sand dunes along the eastern shore of Lake Michigan.

One would normally expect the tang of salt air and the roar of ocean surf beyond the dunes, but instead the lake lies quietly in midsummer, shimmering in the sun. Like an isolated world by itself stands the dune country; similarly the Midwest stands almost as distinctly a sheltered world of its own within the United States.

The approach from the East leads through industrial Ohio, then rural Indiana, and then the traveler plunges into the seemingly endless expanse of smoking mills that border Lake Michigan near the Illinois line. Here the great works of the country's major steel companies belch soot and flames, fouling the air and the approach that catapults the motorist suddenly from a maze of factories onto Chicago's South Lake Shore Drive.

In Wisconsin, northern Michigan and Minnesota, the country turns woodsy and green, sprinkled with lakes and fishing streams and with wilderness as unspoiled as it was when the French missionaries and explorers and fur traders first opened up this territory. South in Illinois, across the prairie, one reaches the Abraham Lincoln country and the shrines at Springfield.

The Mississippi by now has run its majestic course down through the bluffs and is flowing smoothly across the flat country beyond which the prairie runs off through Iowa into the neighboring Plains States. The nation's railroads and airlines spoke out from the Midwest, her products and her cities feed the nation's industry and commerce.

This is a cross-section of latter-day America. Once the wild Northwest Territory, it has long been tamed. It lacks the majesty of some other regions; it is America at home and at work. After all, the internal combustion engine and the automobile, the truck and powered farm implements and the mail order house—developments that made possible the present state of America at home and abroad —came out of the Midwest.

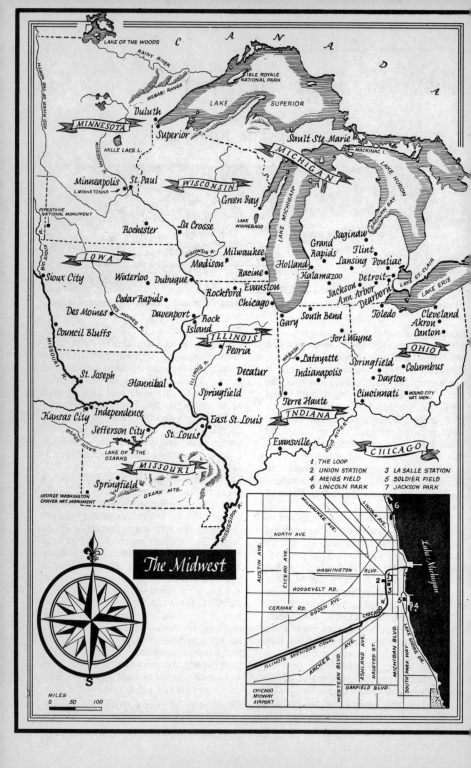

The Midwest

1 THE LOOP
2 UNION STATION
3 LA SALLE STATION
4 MEIGS FIELD
5 SOLDIER FIELD
6 LINCOLN PARK
7 JACKSON PARK

MILES
0   50   100

# A 31-MILLION ACRE FARMLAND, ILLINOIS ALSO HAS GREAT MIDWEST METROPOLIS

**Chicago,** with more than 3½ million population, is the youngest of the world's great cities. Its nickname is the "Windy City." This is North Michigan Avenue.

Photo: G. A. Reims

**Grant Park's 303 acres** provide the mile-long Loop with an open view of the lake.

This is Buckingham Fountain, with the new Prudential skyscraper at the right.

**Randolph Street** is fun center of Loop at night, with theaters and night clubs.

**Wrigley Building** is across Michigan Avenue from Tribune Tower, Sheraton Hotel.

**Flaming sword service** is a distinctive feature of Pump Room, Ambassador East.

Photos: Kaufmann & Fabry Company; bottom left, Delta-C&S Air Lines; bottom right, Shiro, Hotels Ambassador

**Oak Street Beach,** most widely used public bathing spot, fills a corner on North Lake Shore Drive. Pedestrian tunnel connects it with Michigan Avenue and Drake Hotel.

**Chicago's Union Stockyards** are world's biggest; recently celebrated arrival of one-billionth animal. Nearby Amphitheater had the 1952 presidential conventions.

**Merchandise Mart** is second in floor area only to Pentagon Building, Washington.

**Chicago Art Institute** has 6,000 students, world-famous paintings and many exhibits.

**Northwestern University** has Chicago campus, above, for professional schools and divisions of night study. Main school is at Evanston, on shore of Lake Michigan.

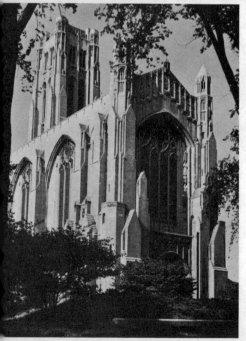

**Rockefeller Memorial Chapel** is one of stately University of Chicago buildings.

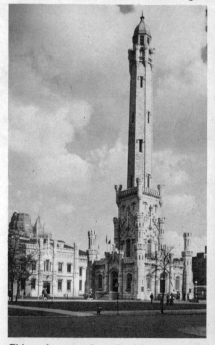

**Chicago's great fire of 1871** spared this historic water tower, now much revered.

Photos: Northwestern University; Wayne Miller, University of Chicago; Kaufmann & Fabry Company

**Rodgers-Hammerstein Night** brought big crowd to the Band Shell in Grant Park.

Nationally known guest conductors and soloists are featured at free concerts.

**Garfield Park Conservatory** has 5,000 species of flowers, valued at $1½ million.

**Air view** shows North Lake Shore Drive sweeping southward from Lincoln Park.

Photos: Chicago
Park    District

**Lincoln Tomb,** in Oak Ridge Cemetery, Springfield, was financed by citizens all over the nation. 117-ft. monument has four bronze groups and statue of Lincoln.

**Lincoln Log Cabin State Park** has cabin lived in by Lincoln's father, stepmother.

**This is Lincoln-Berry store,** now in New Salem State Park, northwest of Springfield.

Photos: Illinois Division of Department Reports

**Cave-in-Rock,** now State Park, was once he lair of Ohio River pirates, outlaws.

**Time rolls back** millions of years for those who explore canyons of Giant City Park.

**Dyche Stadium,** Northwestern University, at Evanston, can accommodate 54,000 at football games. McGaw Hall, background, is used for indoor meets, convocations.

**Since 1850,** Illinois has been a top-rank agricultural state, and today its 195,000 farms are valued at $5 billion. 43 field crops are grown, with corn the largest.

**General U. S. Grant** received this Galena home as gift on his return from Civil War.

**This house in Springfield** is the only home that Abraham Lincoln ever owned.

**"Wedding of the Wine and Cheese"** is a feature of the annual grape festival at Nauvoo, historic old Mormon city built by the Mormon prophet, Joseph Smith.

Photos: Illinois Division of Department Reports; bottom, Illinois Division of Parks

# INDIANA, THE HOOSIER STATE, ADDS BUSTLING INDUSTRY TO RURAL CHARM

Sacred Heart Church and Administration Building with Golden Dome are features of Notre Dame University at South Bend, home of Rockne's "Four Horsemen."

Photo: University of Notre Dame

**Executive Building** houses administrative offices of Purdue University, noted for engineering courses. Behind it is Hall of Music Auditorium, seating 6,200 people.

**Student Building** is outstanding landmark of Indiana University, at Bloomington.

**The French Lick Springs Hotel** has been known since 1840 as a luxurious resort

**Indianapolis Motor Speedway**, built 1909, is site of the annual 500-mile automobile speed classic. Some 150,000 attend the race, held each year on Memorial Day.

**Trotting races** are feature of Indiana State Fair, held each September at the Indianapolis Fairgrounds. It's been an annual feature for over a hundred years.

# Indiana

**Soldiers' and Sailors' Monument** marks heart of Indianapolis, state's chief city.

**At far end** of impressive World War Memorial Plaza is the Central Library

**Indiana State House** is located on 9-acre square in downtown Indianapolis. Erected in 1878–88, of Indiana limestone, it i Neo-Roman design. Basement is Museum

574

**Lincoln Memorial,** Lincoln State Park: It was in this neighborhood that Lincoln's family settled in 1816, when he was 7, and Indiana had just been made a state.

**From all over world,** Christmas parcels come to be mailed from Santa Claus, Ind.

**Oldest covered bridge** in state, once at Raccoon, now spans Clinton Falls creek.

**City park in New Harmony** has "golden rain trees" brought from China by Wm. Maclure. These small round-topped trees produce large yellow flowers in June.

# Indiana

**Lanier mansion,** at Madison, was thought "last word" when built, 100 years ago.

**Indiana Dunes State Park** covers 3½ sq. miles on southern tip of Lake Michigan.

**Wyandotte Cave** is one of largest in the country, with its 23 miles of passages.

**Brown County State Park** and adjoining Game Preserve constitute largest publicly owned land in Indiana. Ten miles of fine roads show off this lovely hill country.

# OHIO FARMS AND INDUSTRIES ARE SERVED BY LAKE ERIE, OHIO RIVER

**Cleveland,** Ohio's largest city, is big center for steel mills and refineries.

**Ohio farm and range lands** cover 22 million acres, with corn the major field crop.

Photos: Ohio Development and Publicity Commission

**Cleveland from Lake Erie:** At left is the Municipal Stadium. The city's landmark, tower of Union Terminal, dominates the background. City population is 914,808.

**Ohio's Capitol,** at Columbus, is one of purest examples of Greek Doric in U.S.

**Toledo** is 3rd largest railroad center of nation, with new Central Union Terminal.

**Zanesville** is divided into three parts by the Licking and Muskingum rivers. It is noted as site of only "Y" Bridge in country, spanning both of the rivers.

Photos: Ohio Development and Publicity Commission

**Akron** is known as rubber capital of the world. B. F. Goodrich Rubber Company,

above, produces automobile tires and over 30,000 kinds of other rubber articles.

**Akron is the chief supplier** of tires to nearby automobile-making city of Detroit.

**Molten steel** is "teemed" into molds at Republic Steel's plant at Cleveland.

Photos: Ohio Development and Publicity Commission

Ohio

**New group of "fledglings"** is graduated from Ohio University, oldest college in what was formerly Northwest Territory. Ohio now has 52 colleges and universities.

**Memorial at Ft. Recovery** marks site of General Wayne's defeat of Indians, 1794.

**Air view of Ohio State University,** Columbus, shows 400-acre campus, stadium.

Photos: Ohio Development and Publicity Commission

**Memorial at Hamilton** reproduces stockade used in campaigns against the Indians.

**Wright Brothers Monument,** Dayton, honors inventors of first successful plane.

**Allen Memorial Art Building** at Oberlin was modeled after Brunelleschi's Hospital of the Innocents. It houses the finest college art museum in the United States.

**Campus Martius Museum,** at Marietta, has wonderful collection of pioneer relics, including restoration of Rufus Putnam house, built by one of the first settlers.

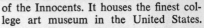

# Ohio

**Ohio Caverns,** West Liberty, are noted for coloring and diversity of formations.

**Old Man's Cave,** at Logan, is overhanging ledge that once formed home for hermit.

**Constructed of stone and yellow clay** by prehistoric Indians, the Great Serpent Mount extends for 1,330 feet. It is the most remarkable effigy mound in the U. S.

# MICHIGAN IS WORLD'S AUTO CENTER AND VACATIONLAND OF GREAT LAKES

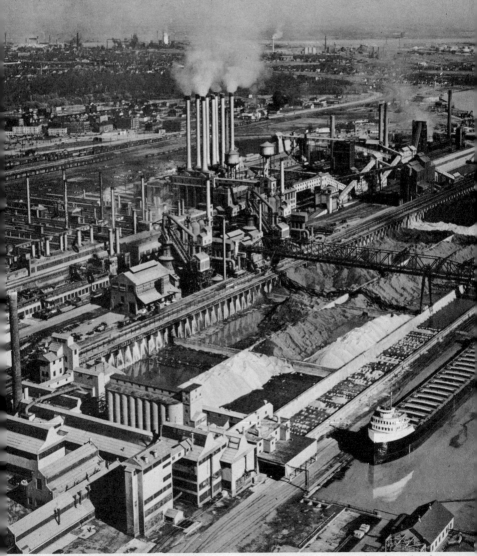

**River Rouge Plant** of the Ford Motor Company, near Dearborn, is one of largest mass-production automobile factories in world. Henry Ford was born at Dearborn.

**Detroit,** nation's fifth city, is noted as automobile-manufacturing center, with plants of General Motors, Chrysler, and others. It fronts on the Detroit River.

**General Motors Technical Center,** Warren, is headquarters for automotive research.

**Sleeping Bear,** 480 feet above Lake Michigan, is largest shifting sand dune in world.

**Five-mile-long Mackinac bridge** links the two peninsulas of Michigan's vacationland.

Reaching from Mackinaw City to St. Ignace, it is framed by north country pine, cedar.

**Isle Royale National Park,** rock fortress in Lake Superior, is a real wilderness.

**Lansing's skyline** is dominated by the State Capitol and 25-story Olds Tower.

**Greenfield Village,** at Dearborn, was established by Henry Ford in 1933 to

re-create a colonial village. At left is Martha-Mary Chapel, above, old mill.

**General Store** at Greenfield Village is complete with Cigar Store Indian.

**Village** also has river boat, and complete reproduction of Edison's first laboratory.

# Michigan

**The "Soo" Locks** at Sault Ste. Marie enable the lake boats to travel along the canal between Lake Huron and Lake Superior, avoiding St. Mary's rapids

**Carriages line main street** of auto-less resort on historic Mackinac Island.

**Porch** of Mackinac's luxurious Grand Hotel is said to be world's longest

**Straits of Mackinac** cut Michigan in two, between the Upper Peninsula and the Lower Peninsula. Ferries take autos and their passengers across this barrier.

**University of Michigan** is at Ann Arbor, on Huron River. This is Law Quadrangle.

**Tahquamenon Falls:** This river plays prominent part in Longfellow's Hiawatha.

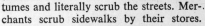

**On opening day of Tulip Festival** in city of Holland, citizens don their Dutch costumes and literally scrub the streets. Merchants scrub sidewalks by their stores.

**Port Huron,** on St. Clair River, connects with Canada by an international bridge.

**Lake o' the Clouds** is high in the Upper Peninsula's remote Porcupine Mountains.

# Michigan

**Ishpeming** is the ski center of Northern Michigan, with one of state's first clubs.

**State has 18 million acres** of farm and range land, varied field and truck crops.

**Interlochen** is scene of summer music camps for high school boys and girls.

Programs, often with famous leaders, are given frequently in camp's concert bowl.

**Pictured Rocks,** multicolored cliffs on Lake Superior shore, extend 27 miles.

**Memorial** on Au Sable River perpetuates spirit of Michigan's pioneer lumbermen.

Photos: top right, Grant M. Hais
others, Michigan Tourist Counc

# LAKES, WATERFALLS, GREEN WOODS BLESS WISCONSIN'S VACATIONLAND

**Wisconsin** has some 8,500 lakes, 10,000 miles of trout streams, and 500 miles of shoreline on Lakes Superior, Michigan. This is High Lake, near Michigan border.

# Wisconsin

**From dome of State Capitol,** Madison, you can see five lakes. Three girdle city, Lakes Mendota, Monona and Wingra Lakes Kegonsa and Waubesa are nearby

**Wisconsin River** is one of many stream in Badger State for canoeing, fishing

**Near Wisconsin Dells,** seven miles of sandstone rocks have been etched by river.

**First Capitol Building,** at Old Belmon was used by the legislature in 183

Photos: Wisconsin Co servation Departmer

**At Pattison State Park,** the Black River plunges 165 feet over Big Manitou Falls.

**U. S. Forest Products Laboratory,** Madison, conducts research on the use of wood.

**A summertime class** at the University of Wisconsin meets below Carillon Tower.

**St. Croix River** cuts through castellated bluffs in Interstate Park, recreation area that is shared between Wisconsin and Minnesota. Park covers 730 acres.

# Wisconsin

**Devils Lake** is hemmed in by horseshoe of cliffs, some 500 feet high. Formed by glacial action, it is a paradise for geological students hunting its oddities.

**Tank Cottage,** at Green Bay, is the oldest house standing in Wisconsin, built 1776.

**Villa Louis** was built at Prairie du Chien by the fur-trader, Hercules L. Dousman.

**Potawatomi State Park,** on the peninsula between Green Bay and Lake Michigan, is one of Wisconsin's 21 state parks. Many trails wind through Norway pines.

# THE "SHOW ME!" STATE OF MISSOURI IS CENTER OF TRANSPORTATION AND COMMERCE

**Missouri River** joins the Mississippi just above St. Louis. Including its 500-mile frontage on the Mississippi, state has over 1,000 miles of navigable water.

# Missouri KANSAS CITY, ST. LOUIS

**Union Station with downtown Kansas City skyline:** On route of the Santa Fe and Oregon trails, Kansas City is today an important railroad and airline center.

**Kansas City's Eleventh Street area** has the major stores, theaters and hotels.

**Liberty Memorial** is 217-foot shaft, in honor of those serving in World War I.

**Swope Park,** with 1,346 acres of hills, ravines is the 3rd largest U.S. city park.

594

**Jefferson Memorial,** St. Louis, is built on site of Louisiana Purchase Exposition.

**Shaw's Garden,** modeled after London's Kew Gardens, has 12,000 plant species.

**St. Louis,** state's largest city, is 2nd only to Chicago in importance as railway center. Union Station, with train sheds and power house, covers more than 20 acres.

Photos: Massie—Missouri Resources Div.

# Missouri

**Thomas Hart Benton's lively murals** are in house lounge of Capitol, Jefferson City.

**Missouri's capital,** known locally as "Jeff City" is named after Thomas Jefferson.

**Home of Ex-President Truman** is in town of Independence, in western Missouri.

**Santa-Cali-Gon Parade,** at Independence, commemorates days of wagon caravans.

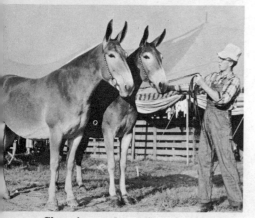

**Champion mules:** Missouri mules have long been known for quality, mulishness!

**Henry County** is noted for its dairy and poultry farms, for these Roberts' horses.

596

# IOWA, SYMBOL OF CORN BELT
# IS RICHEST FARM STATE

**Old Capitol Building,** Iowa City, now administrative center of State University of Iowa, was State Capitol from 1846 to 1857, when Des Moines became capital.

Photo: State University of Iowa

Iowa

**Old water mill, Panora:** Town's name is contraction of "panorama," the story being that pioneers, viewing site from a hill, exclaimed, "What a beautiful panorama!"

**Davenport** stretches along Mississippi River for five miles, where it widens to form Lake Davenport. Rock Island and Moline, Illinois, are across river.

598

Photo: Iowa Development Commission

**State Capitol** looks down on Des Moines from an eminence east of the Des Moines River. Design of the gilded dome recalls that of the Hotel des Invalides in Paris.

**About 30% of Iowa's land** is in pasture, with the eastern and western sections leading in meat production, the northwestern part being chief dairying region.

# Iowa

**Iowa is symbol of the Corn Belt,** with 95% of the land in farms. The state leads the nation in corn and oats, in hogs, poultry and eggs, and in fattening cattle.

**Cutler Bridge, Madison County:** Most of the state is a gently rolling plain, with many winding rivers. Hilly northeastern region is called "Little Switzerland."

Photos: Iowa Development Commission, top left by James A. Kent

# 10,000 LAKES, BEAUTIFUL FORESTS LURE VISITORS TO MINNESOTA

**Split Rock Lighthouse,** on sheer cliff high above Lake Superior, warns of dangerous reefs. Light and siren are important because metal in rocks throws compasses off.

Photo: W. A. Fisher, courtesy Lake
Superior North Shore Association

**At Silver Creek Cliff,** the highway from Duluth to Canada follows the scenic north shore of Lake Superior. Nearby is lake made famous in *Hiawatha,* Gitche Gumee.

**Winter waves of Lake Superior** pile up windrows of ice, 20 feet high, miles long.

**John Jacob Astor trading post** was center of fur trading more than 100 years ago.

**Mighty Mississippi,** "Father of Waters," has its source here, in Itasca State Park.

**Ice-bound Iron Ore Carriers:** Frequently ships trying to open the season early find further headway impossible. Then they must wait for a shift in the wind.

Photos: Barney Thomas; top, W. A. Fisher; lower-center right, Minnesota Division of Publicity

**Minneapolis** is state's largest city, the banking and wholesale center of the area. It adjoins St. Paul, Minnesota's capital, and the two are known as "Twin Cities."

**Fur trappers** use skis to run their lines in the wilderness of Northern Minnesota.

**Palisade Head** is 80-acre headland of volcanic rock jutting from Lake Superior.

Photos: Northwest Orient Airlines; Barney Thomas; W. A. Fisher

**Air view of St. Paul** shows Capitol at upper left, main business section with

First National Bank skyscraper, and three of many bridges across Mississippi.

**Girl scouts** paddle huge "war canoe" near their camp on Northern Minnesota lake.

**Giant statues** of Paul Bunyan and his Blue Ox stand on shore of Lake Bemidji.

**Falls of Minnehaha,** immortalized in poem by Longfellow, are in Minneapolis park.

**Kensington Runestone,** shown in replica, says Vikings came to Minnesota in 1362.

Photos: Kenneth M. Wright; center left, Barney Thomas; center right, Minnesota Division of Publicity; bottom left, Northwest Orient Airlines

# THE PLAINS STATES

## by SETH S. KING

The moment a traveler crosses the Mississippi River and heads west he begins to encounter the one dominant quality of the Plains States—space. Starting with the rolling, compact corn fields and pasture lands of Iowa, and extending beyond the Missouri River to the great wheat plains and ranges of Nebraska, Kansas, and the Dakotas, his horizon broadens until it is almost limitless.

From the rich black and green of the corn country he moves into the grayer, lighter green and gold of the wheat lands and then to the brown ranges that stretch clear to the foot of the dark blue mountains. From the great white barns and silos of Iowa and Minnesota, past the towering grain elevators and sprawling feed lots of eastern Nebraska and Kansas, the traveler crosses on to the Great Plains, where the small ranch houses and corrals are almost lost in the expanse of land.

In the Plains States, people earn their living from the land; they do not merely live on it. Because of this, the people change as the land changes.

In Iowa there is a tendency toward conservatism. Here the people have been established for several generations, and they are more secure in the knowledge that theirs is one of the most consistently productive farm areas in the world. Beyond the Missouri, nature is more uncertain. As the yearly rainfall diminishes, the gamble on livelihood or even on survival increases. The people more often are imbued with a casual disregard for formality and are generally sustained by a persistent optimism. Still farther to the west, the land becomes rougher. It makes a greater demand on the people there, and they, like their pioneer fathers, take pride in having withstood the fierce winter

**Six combines cut wide swath through the wheat of an enormous Plains States farm.**

blizzards, the dust and the summer heat. They are marked by their independence.

The great sweep of plains from the Missouri westward to the Rockies is a relatively new country. But it is rich with the history of this nation's drive toward the Pacific. And most of its sections are still wild enough for a traveler to visualize, with ease, the wagon trains that once labored over the plains or the keel boats and war canoes that struggled up the rivers in search of a route to the Western Sea.

The great expanses of North and South Dakota beyond the Missouri can also be fascinating, if one looks across the unbroken rangeland and remembers that the wild Sioux Indians once came plunging over these same rolling hills in pursuit of buffalo or the white man.

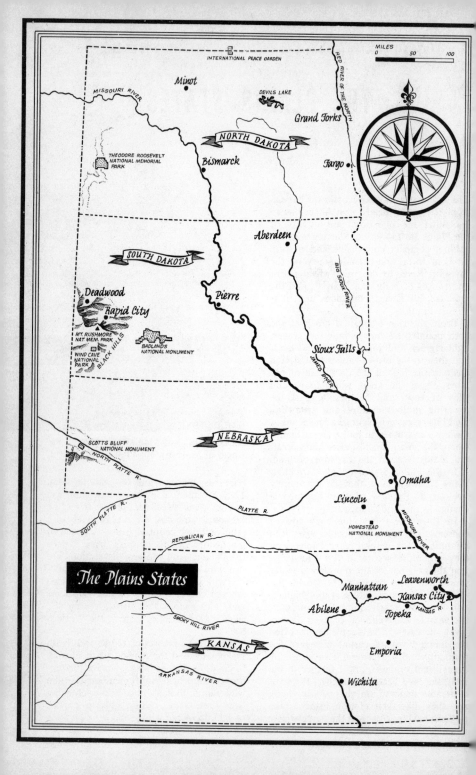

The Plains States

# NORTH DAKOTA HAS UNBOUNDED PLAINS, HILLS, COLORFUL BADLANDS

**Riders explore** Theodore Roosevelt National Memorial Park, in Badlands of the Little Missouri. Park honors the President who ranched here as a youth, 1883–86.

**Logging camp** near Little Missouri River was used to cut ties for building of the Northern Pacific Railway. Bunkhouse had rifle loopholes to ward off Indian raids.

**Combines in North Dakota wheat field:** State leads all others in production of rye and durum wheat, is second in barley. Most of state is crop and pasture land.

Photos: Greater North Dakota Association; Northwest Orient Airlines

**This marker** notes geographical center of North America, at Rugby, North Dakota.

**Monument** on Missouri River at Sanish honors the French explorer, La Verendrye.

**North Dakota's 19-story State Capitol** overlooks Bismarck and Missouri valley.

**Oil well rig** towers above flat prairie of Beaver Lodge Field, south of Tioga.

**17 inches of water** spill over gates of Baldhill Dam and its irrigation reservoir.

**Fort McKeen blockhouse** stands in Fort Abraham Lincoln State Park, at Mandan.

# North Dakota

**These columnar cedars,** known as "upside-down trees," are the only known growth of this species in the world. Nearby is North Dakota's famous Burning Coal Mine.

**This cairn** marks boundary between Canada, U.S. in International Peace Garden.

**Lake** adds loveliness to Peace Garden, shared by Manitoba and North Dakota.

Photos: Greater North Dakota Association

# SOUTH DAKOTA IS SCENE OF FAMOUS BLACK HILLS AND MOUNT RUSHMORE

**The Dakota Indians** named this colorful and deeply eroded country *makosica,* or "bad land." Now a National Monument, the Badlands is labyrinth of odd shapes.

Photo: Alfred E. Reichenberger

South Dakota

**The Badlands** has 640,000 acres of jagged peaks, deep canyons. Once an ocean bed, then a swamp and now a desert, this area contains many land and marine fossils.

**Harney Peak,** 7,242 feet, is highest in the Black Hills and highest in state.

**Sylvan Lake,** called by Indians "Tear in Mountains," is 6,300 feet above sea level.

Photos: Publicity Department, South Dakota State Highway Commission

**The herd of buffalo** at pasture in Custer State Park numbers close to a thousand.

Calvin Coolidge used Game Lodge in the park as his Summer White House in 1927.

**Mount Rushmore National Memorial** has giant heads of Washington, Jefferson,

Theodore Roosevelt, Lincoln, sculptured by Gutzon Borglum and his son, Lincoln.

# South Dakota

**Highway through Custer Park** takes you past these impressive "Cathedral Spires."

**South Dakota State Capitol** is at Pierre, where the Bad and Missouri rivers join.

**Soldiers' & Sailors' World War Memorial** is another point of interest in Pierre.

**Homestake,** in town of Lead, is largest gold mine in U.S., discovered in 1876.

**Wind Cave** has formations quite unlike those in any other National Park cave.

**Dinosaur Park** is museum of prehistoric creatures at the state School of Mines.

Photos: Publicity Department, South Dakota State Highway Commission

# "CORNHUSKER STATE" OF NEBRASKA MERGES MIDDLE WEST WITH WEST

**Nebraska** is one of the country's highest-ranking states in growing wheat, corn, rye, hay. The sand hills areas raise much livestock. Most of land is farmed.

# Nebraska

**Mitchell Pass,** near Scottsbluff, is one of the landmarks of the old Oregon Trail.

Ruts worn by covered wagons of the pioneers moving westward can still be seen.

**Nebraska's State House,** Lincoln, towers 400 feet, is topped by symbolic "Sower."

**Graduates of the University of Nebraska** parade on the orderly campus at Lincoln.

**Beef cattle judging at Nebraska State Fair:** The huge 287-acre Fairgrounds at Lincoln attract thousands of visitors to Fair held each September since 1900.

**Union Stockyards, Omaha:** Largest city in state, Omaha is a leading meat-packing and stockyard center, and it leads all the world's cities in butter production.

**Kingsley Dam** forms Lake McConaughy, with storage capacity of two million acre-feet of water for irrigation. It is one of largest earth-filled dams in U.S.

Photos: Division of
Nebraska Resources

# Nebraska

The Burlington "Hump" on the western outskirts of Lincoln is considered one of nation's finest freight assembly yards. It is a marvel of modern traffic control.

J. Sterling Morton, who instituted Arbor Day, lived in this Nebraska City mansion.

Joslyn Memorial Art Museum, Omaha has Early Renaissance, other exhibits.

Soldier Creek winds through the 36,000-acre Fort Robinson Military Reservation.

Homestead National Monument is site of first land claimed under Homestead Law.

# KANSAS, GRASS PRAIRIE AND HIGH PLAINS, IS GEOGRAPHICAL CENTER OF U.S.A.

**Kansas** produces most hard winter wheat, about 20% of nation's supply. 48 million acres are in farm and range land. State slopes from 4,000 feet in west to 750.

**Monument Rocks,** sometimes known as "the Kansas pyramids," rise abruptly from the High Plains, in valley of Smoky Hill River. At north end is "Kansas sphinx."

**This house at Abilene** was the boyhood home of President Dwight D. Eisenhower.

At right is Eisenhower Memorial which houses President's souvenirs, mementos.

**William Allen White** made little *Emporia Gazette* a nationally respected newspaper.

**State Capitol at Topeka** contains striking John Brown mural by John Steuart Curry

**Kansas State College,** originally Bluemont College, has its campus at Manhattan.

**Design of the Kansas Capitol** is based on that of the Capitol at Washington.

**Scott County Lake** is typical of meager natural bodies of water in the state.

**World's largest** municipal free swimming pool, 337 x 218 feet, is at Garden City.

**Patton Hall, Fort Riley:** This is only cavalry school maintained by U. S. Army.

**Salt mining, Lyons:** Minerals are second in importance to agriculture in Kansas.

# Kansas

**Three Kansas landmarks:** Campanile at the University of Kansas, in Lawrence. Cowboy statue in Boothill Park, Dodge City. Madonna of Trail, Council Grove.

**Wyandotte County Lake and Park** are in outskirts of industrial Kansas City.

**Indian burial pit** is point of interest near the flour-milling city of Salina.

**Dodge City** is keen for sporting events, motorcycle races, dog and horse races.

**At right** is cairn near Lebanon marking geographic center of the United States.

622

# THE ROCKY MOUNTAINS

## by MARSHALL SPRAGUE

I regained my health a dozen years ago in the Rockies and perhaps that is why I can't imagine enjoying life unless I'm a mile or so up in the air with my pulse clipping along at 90 or 100 to the minute. I am nuts about the Rockies and about the altitude which gives a special quality to this whole vast beautiful region from Colorado to the Sierras, from New Mexico to Montana.

Life is simpler, for one thing. The mountains are majestic, simple forms, easy on the eye and mind. It rarely rains so we have no dank vegetation to worry about or many bugs or varieties of birds. We don't have to garden or go swimming or build gutters around our houses if we don't want to. The river systems are so few that my own town of Colorado Springs names its principal streets after them and my children can name every river and most of the creeks between here and Spokane. Though our cities are growing to beat the band, they are not crowded in the eastern sense and we don't ever think they will be unless someone invents a machine to manufacture water.

The scarcity of people makes mountain society more relaxed than sea-level society or middle west society. I don't think Rocky Mountain dwellers are kinder or more generous or more hospitable or more honest than New Yorkers. But they are easier to know on brief acquaintance, less suspicious of motives, less reserved, less jumpy. I am told that bear and buffalo never fled from the first hunters out here because it did not occur to them that anyone would want to harm them. Mountaineers are a bit like that today. I notice often how Broadway plays depicting big-city tension—like "Season in the Sun" or "Light Up the Sky" bewilder audiences in Denver or Colorado Springs. Such tension is unfamiliar to them.

We tend to take things easy. Nobody runs for a bus because if he does, he'll have to spend the rest of the day catching his breath. Sports are on the reflective side. We fish for trout in the clear, blue, cold, rippling rivers, some of which we can jump across. We ride horses in the vast clean parks, liking the smell of horses and sage and the look of the sky bluing deeply at the edges. We explore old mining roads in jeeps and we climb mountains which sounds hard but isn't —not the slow way we do it. We picnic a lot. Many towns out this way own pleasant picnic grounds in the hills.

I'll tell you frankly, though, I'd stay East for eating. In season our lettuce, celery, cantaloupe and peas are superb, but beef is seldom first rate because this is where cattle are grown, not fattened. Chickens and pork are so-so, fresh eggs a gamble. Naturally under these conditions good chefs are rare. They just won't stay around and be unhappy working with inferior materials.

People seem to get fresh ideas in the mountains. Every summer a remarkable industrialist named Walter Paepke finances a kind of think center called The Institute for Humanistic Studies in the mining town of Aspen, Colorado, beneath the Elk Mountains. Other industrialists come out for weeks to sit around and talk to each other and to professional thinkers and to hear good music in a big orange tent. They claim the process lets them see their particular industry in relation to what it can do for all humanity. When they return home, everyone in their industry is apt to be better off because of what Aspen did to them.

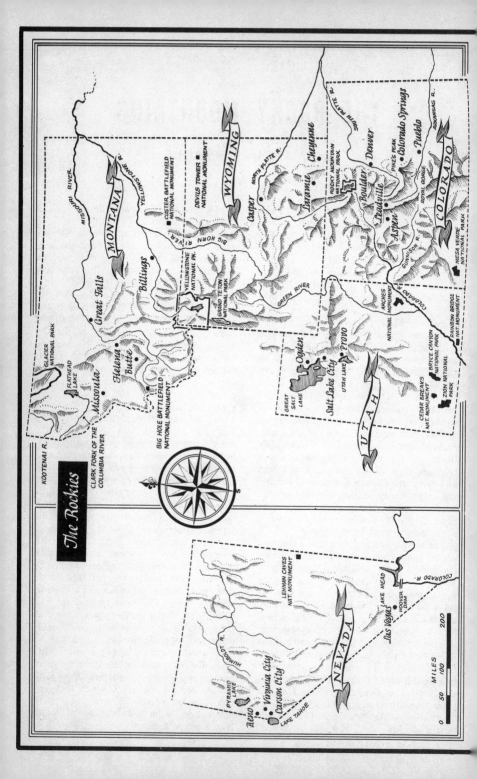

The Rockies

MONTANA

WYOMING

UTAH

COLORADO

NEVADA

KOOTENAI R.

CLARK FORK OF THE
COLUMBIA RIVER

GLACIER
NATIONAL PARK

FLATHEAD
LAKE

MISSOURI RIVER

Great Falls

Helena

Butte

Missoula

Billings

YELLOWSTONE R.

CUSTER BATTLEFIELD
NATIONAL MONUMENT

DEVILS TOWER
NATIONAL MONUMENT

BIG HORN RIVER

YELLOWSTONE
NATIONAL PK.

GRAND TETON
NATIONAL PARK

BIG HOLE BATTLEFIELD
NATIONAL MONUMENT

Casper

NORTH PLATTE R.

Cheyenne

Laramie

PLATTE R.

ROCKY MOUNTAIN
NATIONAL PARK

Denver

Boulder

Leadville

Aspen

Colorado Springs

Pikes Peak

Pueblo

ARKANSAS R.

ROYAL GORGE

MESA VERDE
NATIONAL PARK

GREEN RIVER

COLORADO R.

GUNNISON R.

ARCHES
NATIONAL
MONUMENT

RAINBOW BRIDGE
NAT. MONUMENT

BRYCE CANYON
NATIONAL PARK

ZION NATIONAL
PARK

CEDAR BREAKS
NAT. MONUMENT

GREAT
SALT
LAKE

Ogden

Salt Lake City

Provo

UTAH LAKE

LEHMAN CAVES
NAT. MONUMENT

Reno

Virginia City

Carson City

PYRAMID
LAKE

HUMBOLDT R.

LAKE TAHOE

Las Vegas

LAKE MEAD

HOOVER
DAM

COLORADO R.

N

S

MILES

0  50  100  200

# GLACIER NATIONAL PARK IS ONE OF MONTANA'S MANY WONDERS

**Glacier National Park** is magnificent glacier-carved region astride Continental Divide. Two Medicine Lake is one of 200 lakes, set against the spectacular peaks.

# Montana GLACIER NATIONAL PARK

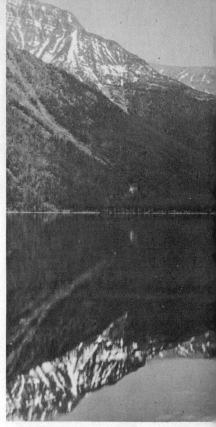

**St. Mary Lake's dark blue waters** mirror great peaks, some over 9,500 feet high.

**Lake McDonald,** largest lake in Glacier National Park, is 10 miles long and over

**Glacier Park Hotel** adjoins the Great Northern Railway station at easterly entrance to the park. There are four hotels and three chalets for visitors.

a mile wide. Because of its depth, up to 437 feet, it is frequently ice-free all winter, though the banks may be deep with snow. Fly-fishing is good here.

**Trails in Glacier National Park** total some 900 miles, and trail tours are very popular. Others prefer hiking, climbing, auto tours, fishing, or just plain looking.

Photos: Top, Glacier National Park, by Hileman; bottom, Great Northern Railway

**Montana's Capitol,** at Helena, is viewed from "Last Chancer," popular tour train named after Last Chance Gulch where discovery of gold was made in 1864.

**Algeria Shrine Temple** and nearby Hill Park are two points of interest in Helena.

**St. Helena Roman Catholic Cathedral** is modeled after one at Cologne, Germany.

Photos: Dorothy Helton, Independent Record Staff, Helena

**Lewis and Clark National Forest,** named for the leaders of the epic expedition, is one of 11 national forests in Montana. Four trail riders follow the Chinese Wall.

**Prospectors still pan for gold,** convinced that sooner or later they'll strike it rich.

**Midland Empire Fair,** at Billings, features rodeo in which ranking riders compete.

**Hungry Horse Dam** forms a 30-mile-long reservoir south of Glacier National Park.

**Visitors to Lewis and Clark Cavern** are awed by the 26-foot Empire State Column.

# Montana

**Winter scene near Billings:** Montana has every advantage for winter sports— plenty of snow and clear, cold weather; hilly country; people with skiing traditions.

**Sheep grazing:** Montana ranks high in production of wool from flocks like this.

**Cowboys separate calves from cows.** Chief livestock markets are Miles City, Billings.

Photos: Burlington Route; top, Northwest Orient Airlines

**Butte,** second largest city in state, is known as "richest hill on earth," pro- ducing almost a third of copper mined in the U.S., zinc, silver and manganese.

**Rare albino buffalo** is one of herd of 300 bison on the National Bison Range.

**University Hall** is center of campus at Montana State University, at Missoula.

**Custer Battlefield National Monument** marks "Last Stand" made by Col. George Armstrong Custer and his 263 soldiers before massacre by Sioux and Cheyennes.

# Montana

**Cowboy** gets light from red-hot branding iron, on one of state's many dude ranches.

**Native blackspot trout** and Dolly Varden abound in larger streams, northwest lakes.

**In Virginia City,** rejuvenated gold camp town, actors re-enact stage-coach robbery.

**Indian pow-wow** on Flathead Reservation features performance of old ceremonies.

**Dark soils** of north and east prairies make state a major producer of wheat.

**John Lewis Clark,** Indian sculptor, carves miniature wild animals of native woods.

Photos: top, Northwest Orient Airlines; center, Montana Highway Commission, E. N. Harrison; bottom, Ray J. Manley, Charles W. Herbert (Western Ways)

# YELLOWSTONE PARK HEADS WYOMING'S LIST OF NATURE'S MARVELS

**Yellowstone National Park** is largest and oldest of our national parks, established 1872. Best-known geyser is Old Faithful which spouts 140 feet every 65 minutes.

Photo: Willard Luce

**Muddy "paint pots"** boil and hiss on the shore of Yellowstone Lake, largest lake in North America above 7,500 feet elevation. It spreads over 138 square miles.

**Upper Falls of the Yellowstone** may be seen from two platforms, one at the head and one halfway down the side of this 112-foot cataract in its 50-foot channel.

Photos: Bill Sears (Western Ways); bottom, Northern Pacific Railway

**Great columns of steam** rise from 18 or more geysers in Norris Geyser Basin, named after Philetus W. Norris, one of the early superintendents of the park.

**Lower Falls of the Yellowstone,** plunging over 300 feet, is park's most spectacular sight. Below the falls is Grand Canyon of the Yellowstone in 1,000-foot gorge.

**The Church of the Transfiguration,** built of logs, has only one room. It nestles against the Grand Teton Mountains, not far from Jackson Hole and Jackson Lake.

**Picture window** behind the altar in Church of the Transfiguration frames magnificent view of the sharp, ragged peaks of the Teton Range, 22 of them over 10,000 feet.

Photos: Grant M. Haist;
bottom, Willard Luce

**Menor's Flatboat Ferry** crosses Snake River at Moose, in shadow of the Grand Tetons. It started operation in 1892, and was authentically restored in 1949.

**Jenny Lake** reflects the blue-green woods and cathedral spires of Teton Mountains.

**This twisted aspen tree** is favorite of camera fans in Grand Teton National Park.

Photos: Willard Luce; bottom left, Grant M. Haist

**Below Jackson,** the Snake River flows through forested hills, in its twisting, winding course. The channel is known as the Grand Canyon of the Snake River.

**Rugged mountain scenery** greets visitors along the Cody Road to Yellowstone Park.

**Devils Tower** was first National Monument, named by Theodore Roosevelt, 1906.

Photos: Willard Luce; Burlington Route; Wyoming Travel Commission

With 3½ million sheep and lambs, Wyoming ranks next to Texas in the production of mutton, wool. State's 33 million acres of farmland are mostly for sheep, cattle.

Speed demons of the West: This unusual camera shot of a group of fast-scurrying antelope was made from low-flying plane. They make long migrations, seeking food.

There are more than 30,000 elk in the state, divided into several herds. Over 10,000 are fed hay each winter in Teton Forest Game Sanctuary, Jackson Hole.

Photos: Charles J. Belden

# Wyoming

**Black and brown bears** enjoy Yellowstone Park almost as much as human visitors do.

**Teton Mountains** edging Jackson Lake give it a setting of Alpine loveliness.

**This sign marks Continental Divide,** the 7,178-foot-high "backbone of the nation."

**Climax of most Wyoming rodeos** is "wild" race, with horses never before ridden.

**Mount Moran:** Wyoming's great ranges include Bighorn Mountains, Absaroka

Range in the east, peaks of Yellowstone Park in northwest, and Tetons in west.

Photos: Grant M. Haist; top right, center left, Alfred E. Reichenberger; center right, Union Pacific Railroad Co.

# COLORADO'S RUGGED BEAUTY BOASTS
# 51 PEAKS OVER 14,000 FEET HIGH

**Colorado has highest average altitude** of any state, 6,800 feet, with Continental Divide of the Rocky Mountains running across the state from north to south.

# Colorado

**Colorado National Monument** is 18,000-acre wonderland. These are "coke ovens."

**Rocky Mountain National Park** has 405 square miles of mountains and lakes.

**Mesa Verde National Park** preserves the remarkable homes of the Cliff Dwellers.

**Black Canyon of the Gunnison National Monument** includes 10 miles of gorge.

Photos: D. L. Hopwood; Burlington Route; Willard Luce; Colorado Advertising & Publicity Department

**Pikes Peak,** 14,110 feet, may be climbed by car, or by cog railroad from Manitou Springs. Auto race to the top is held annually on winding Pikes Peak Highway.

Photo: Colorado Advertising & Publicity Department

# Colorado

**Statue of Broncho Buster** in Denver's Civic Center typifies life of cowboys.

**Red Rocks Amphitheater,** Denver Mountain Parks, has a capacity of 10,000.

**View from Civic Center** shows how near Denver, the "Mile High City," is to the Rockies. City and County Building, above, faces the State Capitol across the Center.

**Balanced Rock** is one of natural marvels in Garden of the Gods, Manitou Springs.

**Mushroom Park** is another of many weird rock formations in Garden of the Gods.

Photos: D. L. Hopwood; top left, G. A. Reims; center, Burlington Route

**There are plenty of thrills and spills** at Colorado rodeos throughout the summer.

**In winter,** skiing is favorite sport at Aspen, Winter Park, Berthoud Pass, etc.

**Royal Gorge,** or Grand Canyon of the Arkansas, has sheer 1,000-foot walls.

Royal Gorge Suspension Bridge, carrying highway across, is highest in the world.

# Colorado

**About 7 million acres** of the state's Great Plains area is devoted to wheat raising.

**Some 800 descendants** of Colorado's once numerous Indians live on one reservation.

**Great Sand Dunes,** named as a National Monument, 1932, cover 80 square miles.

The mounds, constantly changing, often rise to heights of more than 1,500 feet.

**Red Rock Lake,** with Indian Peaks in the background, is in the Roosevelt National

Forest. State has 20 million acres of forest and many fine trails for hiking.

**Turkey ranch:** Raising of poultry, cattle, hogs and horses is important activity.

**Quarries** yield granite, marble, limestone, sandstone, lava, other building stones.

**Dinosaur National Monument** has skeletal remains of dinosaurs, prehistoric reptiles.

**Wheeler National Monument** has striking varicolored configurations of sandstone.

Photos: top left, Konstantin Kostich; Colorado Advertising & Publicity Department; bottom right, D. L. Hopwood.

**Estes Park** is mountain playground and resort on eastern side of Rocky Mountain National Park. It is in lovely valley near Longs Peak, other lofty mountains.

**Grand Lake** is extremely deep; in places the lake bottom has never been sounded.

**Crater Lake** mirrors Lone Eagle Peak. State has 1,500 peaks over 10,000 feet.

# UTAH OUTRANKS ALL STATES IN WONDERS OF NATURE

**This natural bridge** is one of best known landmarks of Bryce Canyon National Park. Over 70% of Utah's beautiful land is in U.S. ownership, as parks and forests.

Photo: Willard Luce

**Bryce Canyon National Park** has 100,000 visitors a year to view amazing area the Piaute Indians called "red rocks standing like men in a bowl shaped canyon."

**Bryce** is entered at rim of the canyon, with trails leading down to the floor.

**Almost every conceivable shape** is found in Bryce, and some sixty different tints.

**Zion National Park** is noted for scenic grandeur. This is First Patriarch Peak.

**Grand Arch Lookout** views Mt. Carmel highway, climbing 800 feet in 3 miles.

**The Great White Throne** is best-known of the monoliths in Zion National Park.

**Checkerboard Mesa** shows unusual result of nature's action on porous sandstone.

Photos: Willard Luce

**Landscape Arch,** 292 feet, is considered longest natural span in the world. It is located in Devils Garden section of Arches National Monument, near Moab.

**The Double Arch,** sometimes called the "jughandles," is in The Windows section.

**Delicate Arch,** alone and sharp against sky, is one of most popular with visitors.

Photos: Willard Luce

**If Millet had been American,** says Henri Cartier-Bresson, he would have painted this instead of the Angelus. Scene is at beginning of Rockies, beyond Salt Lake.

**Hackberry Canyon Ruins** show beautiful stone work of Hovenweep Monument.

**Point Supreme** overlooks Cedar Breaks National Monument, surpassing Bryce.

# Utah SALT LAKE CITY

**Sailing** is one of principal recreational activities on Great Salt Lake, largest inland body of salt water in the Western Hemisphere, 75 miles long and 40 wide.

**Impressive monument** marks spot where Brigham Young said, "This is the place."

**State Capitol building,** Salt Lake City, is seen from gardens of the Hotel Utah.

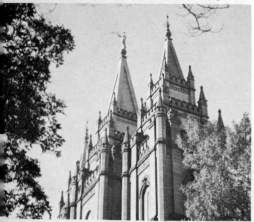

**Mormon Temple** took 40 years to build, with granite hauled 28 miles by oxen.

**City and County building,** Salt Lake City, served as the capitol from 1894 to 1915.

**Newly-completed Pioneer Memorial Museum** is near Capitol, in Wasatch foothills.

**Guide** tells tourists, at Seagull Monument, how gulls saved starving pioneers.

**The Lion House** was home of Brigham Young, Mormon leader, and many wives.

**This little cabin,** preserved on Temple Square, was one of first built by settlers.

Photos: Willard Luce

**Rainbow Bridge National Monument** was established by President Taft in 1910. It includes 160 acres around the great arch, 308 feet high and 275 feet across.

**The Narrows** is 18-foot cleft in Capitol Gorge, Capitol Reef National Monument.

**Utah Copper Mine,** near Bingham Canyon is world's largest open pit copper mine.

Photos: Willard Luce; top, Ray Manley (Western Ways)

**Remnant of old movie set** stands beneath impressive butte in Professor Valley a few miles up the Colorado River from Moab, in southeastern part of the state.

**These mountain meadows** are below timberline of 12,008-foot Mount Timpanogos.

**Mile-long zigzag trail** leads to entrance of Timpanogos Cave National Monument.

**Scenic panorama** is enjoyed by visitors to Dixie National Forest as they stand on Strawberry Point and look across Virgin River country to Zion National Park.

**Sipapu Natural Bridge** is the largest and most impressive of the three water-carved bridges comprising Natural Bridges National Monument, in southeastern Utah.

Photos: U. S. Forest Service; Willard Luce

# NEVADA MATCHES 24-HOUR GAMBLING AND GREAT SCENIC BEAUTY

**Fremont Street, Las Vegas,** glories in dancing dice, spinning wheels of fortune.

**Pyramid Lake,** just 30 miles from Reno, is beautiful blue gem set in the desert.

**Famous Reno arch** across Virginia Street displays slogan that the city tries hard to live up to. Beyond arch are principal hotels, clubs, places of entertainment.

**Spectacular sign** identifies Harolds Club, nationally known gaming establishment.

**Tax on gambling** helped build this new, modern $3 million high school in Reno.

**In this pastoral Reno park,** you wouldn't think you were in Nevada's largest city.

**University of Nevada** has outstanding school of mines and school of journalism.

Photos: Reno Chamber of Commerce

**Roulette** is one popular form of gambling in Reno and Las Vegas, but there are also slot machines, poker games, many others. Players—win or lose—are seldom gay.

Photo: Henri Cartier-Bresson (Magnum)

# Nevada

**Virginia City,** "richest hill on earth" in 1800's, is perched high on slopes of Sun Mountain. It is now having boom of tourists re-living the old bonanza days.

**Double chair lift** at new Reno Ski Bowl carries skiers to height of 9,600 feet.

**The Parachutes** are interesting formations in Lehman Caves National Monument.

Photos: Henri Cartier-Bresson (Magnum); Reno Chamber of Commerce; Willard Luce

**Horseback riding** is enjoyed at many guest ranches near Reno and Las Vegas.

**Lake Tahoe,** 40 minutes drive from Reno, is beautiful vacation setting in mountains.

**Cathedral Gorge,** state park in eastern Nevada, has spectacular stone steeples.

About 87% of Nevada's land is Federally owned, highest percentage of any state.

**State Capitol** is at Carson City, named for Kit Carson, 24 miles south of Reno.

**Among the Indian tribes** in Nevada were the Paiutes, Washoes and Shoshoneans.

Photos: Reno Chamber of Commerce;
center, Willard Luce; bottom left,
Nevada State Highway Department

**Hoover Dam,** on Colorado River, is used for flood control, irrigation and hydro- electric power. It forms 115-mile Lake Mead, the largest reservoir in the world.

**Elephant Rock** is formation in the Valley of Fire, Lake Mead Recreational Area.

**Humboldt National Forest** is part of five million acres of forest reserves in state.

Photos: Belnap Photo Services, National Highway 66 Association; Willard Luce; U. S. Forest Service

# THE SOUTHWEST

## by GLADWIN HILL

A motorist driving across the plateau of northern Arizona recently halted to secure a rattling trunk-latch. As he turned to climb back in the car, he was stopped in his tracks by a strange feeling. It took him several seconds to realize that he was experiencing, for the first time in months and perhaps years, absolute, uninterrupted silence.

Not only were there no people jabbering, automobiles honking, radios blaring, sirens screeching, trains roaring, or airplanes droning. There was not, with the low-lying vegetation, even the sounding harp for random breezes that punctuate the remotest forests of the world. There was only silence.

Yet it was an eloquent silence. It went a long way toward explaining the impassiveness, the contentment even in privation, of the Navajo, systematically living a mile or more from his neighbor on that plateau. It explained generations of cowboys, with their cheerfully lonesome ballads. It explained why a half million people have vied with the rigors of nature to achieve the peace of the Arizona desert; why thousands of others choose to dwell on the isolated farms and ranches of New Mexico and west Texas.

"The great open spaces" are what the Southwest is celebrated for. But it's the quiet and serenity that give the distances meaning for humankind.

The wail of a midnight juke box at a crossroads filling station in New Mexico, the hearty greeting of a prospector or rancher as he clumps into the solitary eat-joint of a sagebrush town, seem to reverberate more through the cosmos than the clangor of millions in the world's cities.

Time moves at a different pace.

Through the clear night air of the desert, the stars speak silently of their incomprehensible antiquity. Down the mile-deep gorge of Grand Canyon lie, layer upon layer, the ashes of a billion years. The seasons roll, some wet, some dry. In the highlands, the winter snows swirl in. On the plains, the tumbleweeds race erratically before the winds. Year in and year out, the sun bakes down, on scattered cottonwoods and live-oaks, on pueblos, shacks, hamlets and towns.

Here the apposition between nature and men, and between men and other men, is plainest. The Indians, with their varied visages and customs, bespeak the mingling of migrations yet untraced, from as far away as Asia. In little towns along the Rio Grande are relics of the Spanish explorers who trod these selfsame routes long before the Pilgrims landed. For every modern, busy city like Phoenix, Albuquerque, and Amarillo, dozens of places like Tombstone and Cimarron provide living links with the cattle-trail and mining-boom days of the 19th century.

The visitor here is not taken for granted as he would be in Cincinnati or Dallas. He gets the same incisive once-over that met passengers alighting from the stagecoaches. Is he a city slicker, a card-sharp, a gold-brick salesman—or someone adaptable to the Southwest community? The wise guy is quickly cut down to size; the condescending remark boomerangs.

The spirit of the region—its great open spaces, its solitude, its individuality—is poignantly reflected in one of its commonest mannerisms: greetings are effusive, farewells laconic—in the tacit wish that the absence will be short.

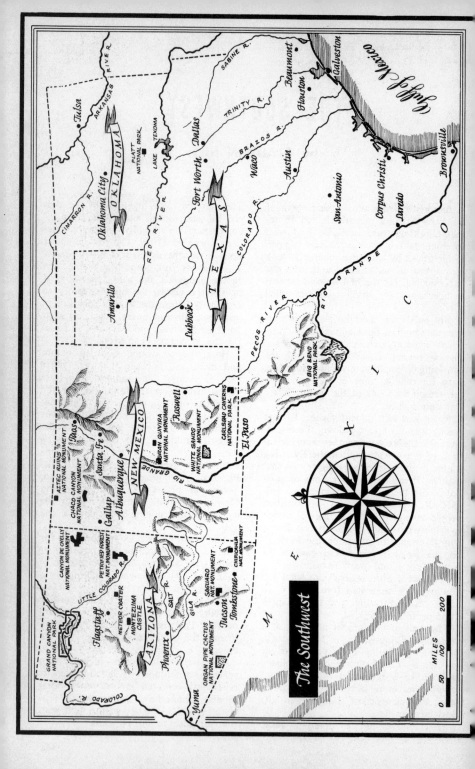

The Southwest

# GRAND CANYON IS TOP SCENIC LURE
## OF ARIZONA'S SUNLAND

**Grand Canyon of the Colorado** is by all odds the greatest single spectacle in America. It cuts a 217-mile gash across Northern Arizona, 4 to 18 miles in width.

Photo: Union Pacific Railroad

# Arizona

**In Monument Valley,** giant rock buttes stick up 1200 feet from the valley floor, near the border between Arizona and Utah. Valley also has many sand dunes.

**Saguaro National Monument** preserves the giant cactus that serves as a natural storage tank for meager desert rainfall. Largest specimens grow to 50-foot height.

**Organ Pipe Cactus National Monument** has 20-foot organ-pipe cacti, other species.

**Chiricahua National Monument** outdoes all others in grotesqueness of its rocks.

Photos: Ray Manley, bottom left, Charles W. Herbert (Western Ways); bottom right, Willard Luce

**Mount Lemmon Highway** has mantle of snow, found only on the higher mountain slopes. Arizona is noted for its many days of sunshine, about 80% of the year.

**Montezuma Castle National Monument** has remarkable Indian cliff dwellings.

**White House,** niched into towering walls of Canyon de Chelly, is 900 years old.

Photos: top, Bill Sears, bottom right, Ray Manley (Western Ways); bottom left, TWA Trans World Airlines

**Vast areas of semi-arid land,** suitable only for grazing, make stock-raising an important industry. State has more than a million head of cattle, even more sheep.

**One of a cowboy's duties** is to locate a stray calf, bring it home to the ranch.

**Cow hand** demonstrates roping of calf so it can be branded with Empire mark.

670

Photos: Balestrero bottom left, Ray Manley (Western Ways)

**At Desert Willow Ranch,** dudes on winter vacation are given a lesson on proper way to saddle a horse for trail riding. Visitors find crisp desert air invigorating.

**Coffee tastes extra special** when it is made from sparkling mountain stream water.

**Note rubber tires** on this modern chuck wagon, vital equipment on working ranch.

**Chuck wagon** keeps ahead of moving herd, provides warm chow at mealtime.

**Dudes from Flying V Ranch** enjoy evening chow in Santa Catalina Mountains.

Photos: Ray Manley (Western Ways)

**Arizona's capital, Phoenix,** is lively, friendly city, protected on the north by the Phoenix Mountains. At top right is odd silhouette of Camelback Mountain.

**Camelback Inn** is one of elegant Phoenix resorts where life centers around pool.

**Phoenix South Mountain Park** has ancient writings on stone, and a small gold mine.

Photos: Phoenix Chamber of Commerce

**Tucson** ranks next to Phoenix in size, and shares its mild, warm dry climate. Both have much business and industry, but are best known as tourist, health resorts.

**Fiesta and rodeo** take place at Tucson in February, at height of winter season.

**Ted DeGrazia,** one of Southwest's leading artists, teaches at his school in Tucson.

# Arizona

**San Xavier del Bac Mission,** consecrated 1797, is considered finest mission archi-tecture in Southwest. This is the mission's famous Arizona Boys Chorus at practice.

**Hopi corn-grinding dance:** The Indians of Arizona are divided into more than 30 tribes, the Navajo, Apache, Hopi, Pima-Papago, Mojave, Yuma and many others.

**Tony Whitecloud** performs hoop dance at the annual Indian Powwow at Flagstaff.

**Navajo woman** demonstrates first step in preparing to weave intricate rug design.

Photos: Ray Manley (Western Ways); center, Phoenix Chamber of Commerce

**Apache Indians** take part in Flagstaff Powwow Parade. Indian reservations are near this city which is sheltered by San Francisco Peaks and Elden Mountain.

**Tombstone** is old mining town which was big boom city of 7,000 in the 1880's, when some of biggest gold mines in state were active. Helldorado Days enact past.

**Hoover Dam,** shown in different view on page 664, is shared by Northwest Arizona and Southeast Nevada. Called Boulder Dam, 1933–47, it was re-named Hoover.

**Baldwins Crossing** has beautiful red rock in the background. This is popular spot with movie makers who find Arizona fine for shooting with 80% sunny days.

**Meteor Crater** is 600-foot-deep depression believed caused by meteor striking earth.

**Painted Desert** is large arid area noted for the great variety of its color effects.

Photos: Valdis Avots; bottom, Frashers Inc., Petrified Forest National Park, and National Highway 66 Association

# CARLSBAD CAVERNS IS TOP ATTRACTION IN NEW MEXICO

**Gargantuan stalagmites** and bewildering variety of other formations are seen in Hall of the Giants in Carlsbad Caverns National Park, an underground fairyland.

**White Sands National Monument** has some 176,000 acres of vast, shifting dunes, stretching to the skyline. The dunes are not true sand, but nearly pure gypsum.

**El Morro National Monument** preserves rock with 17th century Spanish writings.

**Pueblo Bonito** is largest of old ruins in Chaco Canyon National Monument.

**Inter-tribal Indian Ceremonial,** held each year at Gallup, draws Indians from 31 tribes in the Southwest. They parade in covered wagons, dance and powwow.

**Navajo rugs** are woven on a crude loom that rests on side of the Indian dwelling.

**Beautifully costumed Indian women** parade with burdens carried on their heads.

Photos: New Mexico
State Tourist Bureau

# New Mexico

**Organ Mountains,** northeast of Las Cruces: New Mexico varies from 2,876 above sea level to 13,306 feet, a variation caused by great shiftings of earth's crust.

**Library at the University of New Mexico,** Albuquerque, is constructed in pueblo style architecture and is one of most beautiful buildings on 315-acre campus.

**State Capitol in Santa Fe:** Distinctive new building was completed in 1953.

With Palace of Governors, below, state has nation's newest and oldest capitols.

**Cathedral of St. Francis** was built in 1869 to serve needs of Spanish residents.

**Fiesta in Santa Fe** is held annually over the three-day Labor Day weekend.

**This is America's oldest public building,** Palace of the Governors, Santa Fe. It was constructed of adobe, in 1610, and served as State Capitol nearly 300 years.

# New Mexico

**Mission Church at Pecos Pueblo,** now in ruins, was one of largest in the state.

**Mission Ranchos de Taos** has twin bell towers and crosses, beautiful entry door.

**Taos Pueblo** is spectacular Indian village, with primitive cubist skyscrapers. It is at foot of the majestic Sangre de Cristo mountain range, in northern part of state.

**Replica of cliff house** is seen in Frijoles Canyon, Bandelier National Monument.

**Acoma Mission** is unique church in Sky City, Indian pueblo 400 feet above plain.

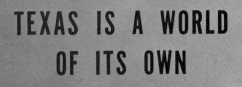

# TEXAS IS A WORLD OF ITS OWN

**One of the world's largest drilling rigs,** this typifies the bigness of Texas, great in size (267,339 square miles), first in oil production and in many farm products.

Photo: Shell Oil Company

**Houston** is the largest city in the Lone Star State, big manufacturing center and one of greatest U.S. ports, with 50-mile canal to Gulf. Shamrock Hotel is at left.

**Shamrock,** in Eastern Panhandle section, is home of the annual St. Patrick's Day celebration, and of the Eastern Panhandle Livestock Show fourth week in February.

Photos: Braniff International Airways; National Highway 66 Association

**Texas State Capitol,** at Austin, has 18 acres of floor space and some 500 rooms. Built of native red granite, it is 308 ft. high, topping most other state capitols.

**State Fair of Texas,** held at Dallas in October, is largest of its kind in the nation, drawing over 2½ million attendance. In background is Hall of State Building.

Photos: Texas Highway Department;
Braniff International Airways

**Corpus Christi Bay and skyline of city:** Sheltered from Gulf of Mexico by Mus- tang Island, Corpus Christi is shipping center and all-year-round playground.

**Alabama-Cooshatti Indians,** only remaining tribe in Texas, live near Livingston.

**Arthur's,** in Dallas, is one of the state's distinguished places for excellent food.

**Galveston's long beach** for surf bathing, good climate, facilities for fishing and boating, attractive subtropical plants, all combine to make it tourist playground.

**San Antonio River** flows through lovely park in downtown San Antonio. One of oldest Texas cities, and third largest, it has interesting past, colorful present.

**The Alamo,** where heroic defenders died, is one of best-known U.S. historic shrines.

**Spanish Governors' Palace,** San Antonio, was used during Spanish rule of Texas.

Photos: Texas Highway Department

**McDonald Observatory,** located in Davis Mountains, is third largest in the world.

**570-foot San Jacinto Monument** commemorates battle for Texas freedom.

**Indian Lodge** is tourist resort in Davis Mountains, towering to 7,000-foot peaks.

**Spring roundup** is like a three ring circus —you have to be quick to see everything.

This typical scene is near Vernon, which has one livestock pasture of 200,000 acres.

**Mission San José** is the most complete of the four Spanish missions standing in San Antonio. Established 1720, it was most beautiful, prosperous in New Spain.

**Church of Our Lady of Mount Carmel** is reproduction of mission founded in 1681.

**At Mission Espiritu Santo,** in Goliad, excavators found ancient Indian homes.

**Purchasing** colorful and serviceable boots is vital shopping-day task for cowboys.

**Christo Rey:** This monument to Prince of Peace is on summit in northwest El Paso.

**Historic field piece** stands near first of the Hilton Hotels, in downtown El Paso.

**International bridge** crosses Rio Grande from Juarez, Mexico, to El Paso, the city that stands at westernmost tip of Texas. Name means "the Pass" through hills.

Photos: Ray Manley, top right, C. W. Herbert (Western Ways)

# OKLAHOMA POSSESSES GREAT RICHES, GREAT CAPACITY TO ENJOY THEM

**Oklahoma City,** capital of the state, has symbols of its wealth—a row of oil wells —right on the State House grounds. City was settled in one day, by homesteaders.

Photo: Oklahoma City Chamber of Commerce and National Highway 66 Association

**Turner Falls,** in the Arbuckle Mountains near Davis, is one of the scenic spots of Oklahoma. The state has four mountain ranges, and 10 million acres of forest.

**Platt National Park,** near Sulphur, in the southern part of state, has streams, springs, waterfalls, swimming holes. It was once part of old Indian Territory.

Photos: Charles J. Belden; National Park Service; Oklahoma Planning & Resources Board

**Oklahoma Agricultural and Mechanical College,** at Stillwater, was founded 1890. It has $50 million in buildings, equipment, 4,976 acres of land, 8,800 students.

**University of Oklahoma,** at Norman, has enrollment of 8,000, and 2,471 acres of land. University of Oklahoma Press is noted for success of regional publishing.

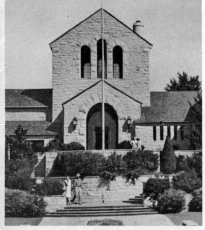

**Will Rogers Memorial** at Claremore honors the Oklahoma humorist-philosopher.

**Indian population** is largest of any state, comprising members of some thirty tribes.

Photos: Oklahoma Planning & Resources Board; bottom, Claremore Chamber of Commerce; El Reno Chamber of Commerce, and National Highway 66 Association

# Oklahoma

**Lake Texoma,** shared by Oklahoma, Texas, is one of our biggest playgrounds.

**Cimarron** and many other rivers in the state provide abundant fishing streams.

**Devils Den** is quiet spot created by some angry upheaval of the earth's crust centuries ago. Now it's ideal for rock-clambering and just plain contemplation.

**Lake o' the Cherokees** is formed by huge multiple-arch Grand River Dam, built in 1938–41, and also called the Pensacola Dam. The lake covers 85 square miles.


694

# CALIFORNIA—THE GOLDEN GATE

## by LAWRENCE E. DAVIES

**WORLD'S GREATEST BRIDGE SPANS GOLDEN GATE AT SAN FRANCISCO.**

A visitor stood in a crowd of 10,000 in the "Wall Street of the West" not long ago watching a ceremony. The financial district of San Francisco had been driven to distraction for four months by the steady, nerve-fraying pounding of a pile driver while it sank supports for a new skyscraper. Now the job was done, the huge hammer silenced, and San Francisco, true to form, brought out pall-bearers, wreaths and eulogists and even put the symbolic remains of Alfred the pile driver on a trans-Pacific liner for burial at sea. The visitor thought he had captured the spirit of this metropolis built on a dozen hills. This spirit is an elusive thing, but fun-loving tolerance surely is an ingredient.

The town shows a maturity greater than that of many older ones. It has stability, based on the knowledge that neither earthquake nor seven disastrous fires could down its spirit. Withal, it has never been afraid to be exuberant.

Fog may account for some of San Francisco's character. The relentless billowing of the fog inward through the mile-wide Golden Gate, sometimes leaving the tips of the Golden Gate Bridge towers hanging like ghostly spires, is a fascinating sight almost every afternoon from mid-June through August.

Lake Tahoe, nestling 7,000 feet high in the Sierras, vineyards and wine cellars, natural wonders like Yosemite, all contribute to the character and spirit of the region. But nothing, in the opinion of this adopted Far Westerner, is more awe-inspiring, more majestic, more likely to instill a sense of humility, than a cathedral-like grove of giant redwoods, "nature's oldest living things."

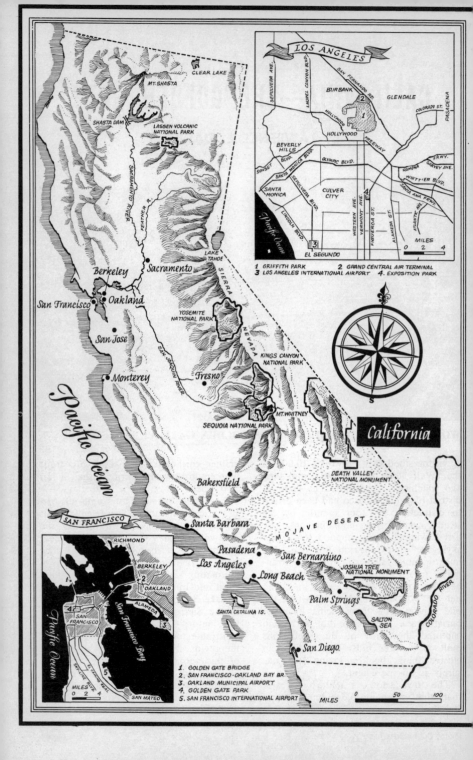

LOS ANGELES

SEPULVEDA AVE.
LAUREL CANYON BLVD.
SAN FERNANDO RD.
BURBANK
GLENDALE
PASADENA
COLORADO ST.
HOLLYWOOD FREEWAY
HOLLYWOOD
BEVERLY HILLS
SUNSET BLVD.
SANTA MONICA BLVD.
OLYMPIC BLVD.
SANTA MONICA
SAN MONICA BLVD.
CULVER CITY
WESTERN AVE.
VERMONT ST.
FIGUEROA ST.
ALAMEDA ST.
RAMONA FRWY.
GARVEY AVE.
WHITTIER BLVD.
SANTA ANA FRWY.
ATLANTIC AVE.
LINCOLN BLVD.
Pacific Ocean
EL SEGUNDO
MILES
0  2  4

1  GRIFFITH PARK                    2  GRAND CENTRAL AIR TERMINAL
3  LOS ANGELES INTERNATIONAL AIRPORT    4  EXPOSITION PARK

MT. SHASTA
CLEAR LAKE
SHASTA DAM
LASSEN VOLCANIC NATIONAL PARK
SACRAMENTO RIVER
FEATHER R.
Berkeley
Sacramento
Oakland
San Francisco
LAKE TAHOE
San Jose
SIERRA
YOSEMITE NATIONAL PARK
Monterey
NEVADA
SAN JOAQUIN RIVER
KINGS CANYON NATIONAL PARK
Fresno
Pacific Ocean
MT. WHITNEY
SEQUOIA NATIONAL PARK
California
Bakersfield
DEATH VALLEY NATIONAL MONUMENT
SAN FRANCISCO
Santa Barbara
MOJAVE DESERT
Pasadena
San Bernardino
Los Angeles
JOSHUA TREE NATIONAL MONUMENT
Long Beach
RICHMOND
BERKELEY
OAKLAND
ALAMEDA
Palm Springs
SAN FRANCISCO
San Francisco Bay
SANTA CATALINA IS.
COLORADO RIVER
Pacific Ocean
SALTON SEA
EL CAMINO REAL
BAYSHORE RTE.
SAN MATEO
MILES
0  2  4
San Diego

1.  GOLDEN GATE BRIDGE
2.  SAN FRANCISCO-OAKLAND BAY BR.
3.  OAKLAND MUNICIPAL AIRPORT
4.  GOLDEN GATE PARK
5.  SAN FRANCISCO INTERNATIONAL AIRPORT

MILES
0        50        100

# YOSEMITE PARK HEADS THE NATURAL
# WONDERS OF NORTHERN CALIFORNIA

**Yosemite National Park** is a peaceful empire of 1,189 square miles, with giant sequoias, tumbling waterfalls, and lakes which reflect the spectacular mountains.

Photo: Konstantin Kostich

**Yosemite Valley** is in the heart of the great national park's scenic marvels, with Half Dome looming ahead. Park lies on western slope of the Sierra Nevada.

**Ski-tow at Yosemite** is sort of uphill sled. National parks and many other places provide Californians with tobogganing, snowshoeing, skiing, sleighing, ice-skating.

Photos: Southern Pacific
Lines; Konstantin Kostich

**Yosemite Fall** first leaps a sheer 1,430 feet and then, after a series of cascades, plunges another 320. Park has five great falls, one 10 times height of Niagara.

Photo: United Air Lines

**San Francisco,** with its roller-coaster streets, ranks with Paris and Rome as one of world's greatly loved cities. Cable cars have won fight to keep clanging

Photo: Henri Cartier-Bresson (Magnum

**"Top of the Mark"** is the many-windowed vantage point where San Franciscans and visitors meet for cocktails while they watch the great city spread out below.

**Mark Hopkins Hotel** is built on Nob Hill, where railroad-builder's mansion stood.

**Ferry Building,** foot of Market Street, is less active because of Bay Bridge.

Photos: Henri Cartier-Bresson (Magnum); bottom left, Moulin Studios; right, Redwood Empire Association

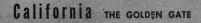

**Golden Gate Bridge,** connecting San Francisco with communities to the north, was completed in 1937 at cost of $35½ million. Main central span, 4,200 fee

**Fisherman's Wharf** is landing point for San Francisco's many Italian fishermen.

Visitors love brightly painted fishin boats, and many fine seafood restaurants

702

in length, is the longest single span in the world. The bridge carries 6 lanes for auto traffic, has 2 sidewalks. Clearance above San Francisco Bay is 220 feet.

**Sidewalk stands on Wharf** cook freshly caught crabs in steaming iron cauldrons.

**San Francisco's Chinatown** is an exotic city-within-a-city of more than 20,000.

**San Francisco-Oakland Bay Bridge** was opened to traffic in 1936. It is double-decked, with six traffic lanes for auto on the upper level, and three truck lanes

**Mission Dolores,** in downtown San Francisco, was founded on June 29, 1776.

**Trader Vic's,** with main restaurant i San Francisco and one in Oakland, i

and two interurban tracks on the lower. The bridge is illuminated at night with yellow sodium vapor lights, the rays of which can penetrate the frequent fogs.

one of bay area's many notable eating places. Vic's has South Seas atmosphere.

**Unique cable cars** were doomed to oblivion, but aroused public saved many.

Photos: Strohmeyer Photographs; bottom left, Californians Inc.; center, Trader Vic's; San Francisco Chamber of Commerce

# California THE GOLDEN GATE

**Union Square, San Francisco:** At left is St. Francis Hotel, one of best known.

Beneath square is four-level garage with capacity for more than 1,700 automobiles.

**San Francisco meets the Pacific** on long white beach extending over 3½ miles.

**Outdoor flower stands are to Union Square** what cafés are to Champs-Elysées.

Photos: Californians Inc.; bottom right, Redwood Empire Association

**Sather Gate** is famed entrance to the University of California at Berkeley.

Campanile's high lookout gives splendid view of San Francisco and whole bay area.

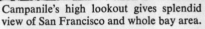

**Trader Vic's** in Oakland is even more South Seas than San Francisco version.

**Hoover Tower,** at Stanford University, houses library on war, revolution, peace.

**Lake Tahoe,** shared by Nevada, California, is of glacial origin and covers nearly 200 square miles. Mark Twain called it "fairest picture the whole earth affords."

**Sutter's Fort,** in California's capital city of Sacramento, contains authentic exhibits showing life in the early days and during the hectic Gold Rush period.

Photos: Southern Pacific Lines; Sacramento Chamber of Commerce

**Lassen Peak** is the only recently active volcano in the United States. Violent eruptions occurred in 1914 and 1915, after sixty-five years of inactivity.

Photo: National Park Service

**This is the rugged coast** along Del Norte County, near boundary of Oregon. Area from San Francisco north to the Oregon border is known as the Redwood Empire.

**In Eldorado National Forest,** a "shovel" loader places huge logs on truck. Except for its valuable redwoods, California must import much of the lumber it needs.

**These Giant Sequoias in Mariposa Grove,** Yosemite National Park, are probably the oldest living things in the world. Ring counts show some to be 4,000 years old.

Photo: Ralph H. Anderson, National Park Service

711

**The Napa, Livermore and Sonoma valleys** produce grapes for table use, raisins and wine. California farms are outstanding in use of irrigation, modern methods.

**California wineries** make about 90% of the country's domestic wines, brandies.

**Blossomtime in Santa Clara Valley:** It's called "Valley of the heart's delight."

Photos: Redwood Empire Association; bottom right, San Jose Chamber of Commerce

# SOUTHERN CALIFORNIA

## by GLADWIN HILL

There is an exotic Oriental dish with some name like mooey-mooey composed of so many ingredients it is said that no two people have ever agreed on what it tasted like.

The same quality is shared, for similar reasons, by Southern California. The "S" in Southern California, incidentally, is always capitalized—in Southern California. It is climatically and culturally quite different from northern California (spelled with a small "n"), which bears it approximately the same relationship as Albany does to New York City: the legislature meets there.

At first blush, Southern California is a bewildering melange: a land of forested mountains, barren deserts, shimmering seashore . . . of Indians and atomic scientists . . . and the Mexican "wetbacks." People from every state in the union, who annually hold Iowa picnics and New England picnics . . . but who concur that they never had it so good.

Southern California is a melting pot which has not yet come to heat. The population is stratified not economically or socially, but chronologically. There are the Spanish-named Old Families. There are the descendants of the 19th-century pioneers. There are the folks from the big influx of the 1920's, living in an increasingly imaginary world of orange-groves and annuities in 100-cent dollars. There are the Okies of the 1930's—many now prospering entrepreneurs. There are the industrial immigrants of World War II, who hurtled from Alabama's cotton patches to suede shoes in half a decade. And there are the "vets"—the nation's biggest concentration of them—who formed the nucleus of the continuing post-war migration.

The keynote, the strand running through all these diverse elements, is "living." "California living" has become a tag associated with everything from clothes to condiments. It derives primarily from *Southern* California and its bland climate, which encourages people in a thousand pastimes, from skiing to skin-diving, from sun-bathing to salad-making.

The swimming pool is Southern California's trade-mark, not as a badge of affluence (they cost less than a car), but as a symbol of people's defiant devotion, in the frenetic atomic era, to something more than the humdrum business of Making Ends Meet. An even more universal symbol, no longer exclusive to the region but indigenous to it, is the patio. You may stage barbecues in it, or just sit in it, or just have it. The point is that you're proclaiming that there's more to life than four walls and a roof.

"California living" takes many forms, some of them ridiculous. It connotes Pasadena's palm-shaded New England-style houses, their roofs determinedly peaked (by transplanted New Englanders) to shed completely non-existent snows.

It connotes the paradox of the Cadillac, the badge of "arrival" on the one hand in the Hollywood movie colony, and on the other along Central Avenue, Los Angeles' Harlem . . . and in many cases the pickup truck of the large-scale cotton grower, who counts his holdings in square miles.

It isn't the people who are crazy. It's the pattern. The common trait of Southern Californians is that they're all converts. "You may not like it at first," they advise visitors. "But after you've been here a while—" Once the visitor finds some kind of niche in the pattern, he's set. And pretty soon, he's saying: "You may not like it at first, but—"

# SOUTHERN CALIFORNIA MEANS HOLLYWOOD, ORANGE GROVES, COAST AND DESERT RESORTS

**Palm Springs,** in the desert 70 miles southeast of Los Angeles, is an opulent resort that is said to have the world's highest per capita count of swimming pools.

**Hollywood** is center of world's movie industry. Hollywood Boulevard becomes "Santa Claus Lane" at Christmas and is gaily festooned, brilliantly floodlighted.

**Grauman's Chinese Theater** is noted for glamorous movie premieres and for the concrete slabs bearing hand and foot prints and messages from celebrities.

Photos: Hollywood Citizen-News;
Hollywood Chamber of Commerce

**Wilshire Boulevard,** famous Los Angeles thoroughfare, sweeps through MacArthur Park and on to the Miracle Mile section with spectacular shops, hotels, offices.

**New Chinatown** is Los Angeles center for curio shops and Oriental restaurants.

**Union Station,** in modified mission architecture, has 135-foot clock tower.

Photos: TWA Trans World Airlines; Konstantin Kostich; All Year Club of Southern California

**Biltmore Hotel** is on edge of Pershing Square in heart of downtown Los Angeles.

A multi-level garage has recently been constructed beneath the palm-lined park.

**Guests at Beverly Wilshire** enjoy lunch beside the big "Copa Club" swimming pool.

Fashion shows, fencing exhibitions are among events attracting crowds to hotel.

**The famous Rose Bowl,** at Pasadena, is packed with nearly 100,000 fans on each New Year's Day to see the keen rivalry of the annual Rose Bowl football game.

**Santa Anita Race Track,** with mountains as backdrop, is one of handsomest. Mid-winter racing events attract throngs to $1 million plant with stands for 30,000.

Photos: Pasadena Tournament of Roses Association; All Year Club of Southern California

**Redlands,** named for red soil of region, is packing and distributing center for wide citrus growing area. It is protected on the north by San Bernardino Mountains.

**Lake Arrowhead,** a mile high in the San Bernardino Mountains, is reached by scenic Rim of the World Drive, a 100-mile loop from San Bernardino and return.

Photos: Redlands Chamber of Commerce; TWA Trans World Airlines

**Walt Disney's Magic Kingdom of Disneyland,** at Anaheim, California, is newest amusement park for young and old. This is the "Turn of the Century" Main Street.

A "real" pirates' galleon sits at anchor in Disneyland courtyard, sails a-billow.

Lifelike alligators "threaten" the sightseeing boat on the river at Disneyland.

**Disneyland from the air:** On left are Adventureland and Frontierland, at top center is Fantasyland and on the right, Tomorrowland. Entrance is at bottom.

**Frontierland** revives America's past in a busy transportation center of early days.

**"Mark Twain"** is authentically re-created paddle wheeler that carries 300 people.

Photos: Disneyland, Inc.

**San Diego** has one of the finest natural harbors in the U.S., attracting naval, commercial and pleasure craft. Growing industries have given population big boost.

**Serra Museum,** of Spanish mission design, honors days of Father Junípero Serra.

**Tower of California Building,** in Balboa Park, is outstanding San Diego landmark.

**La Jolla,** just north of San Diego, has lovely homes on cliffs overlooking the sea.

**Alligator Head,** secluded sandy cove, is La Jolla's most popular spot for bathing.

**The coves,** headlands and flower-covered paths of Laguna Beach have served as in-spiration for many landscape painters. The town has many rustic homes and shops.

**Rodeo Parade** at Palm Springs attracts gay-costumed riders from ranches for many miles around. Other events include golf and tennis tournaments, circus week.

**Youthful rider** shows her skill in parade that passes along Palm Springs main street.

**Young horse,** too, puts on his best manners for event sponsored by Mounted Police.

Photos: A. Milton Runyor

**Palm Springs Tennis Club** is a beautiful oasis in the desert Its swimming pool is one of well over 1,000 in Palm Springs, probably world's highest per-person count.

Photo: Charles W. Herbert (Western Ways)

**Palisade Glaciers,** near Big Pine, are the southernmost of the Northern Hemi- sphere. The gleaming "living ice" is two miles long, a mile wide, deeply crevassed.

Photo: American Airlines

**General Sherman Tree,** Sequoia-King's Canyon National Park, is *Sequoia gigantea.*

**Sierra Nevada Mountains** form eastern boundary of King's Canyon National Park.

**Close-up** of comely lass in Giant Joshua Tree: These desert lilies often grow 30 feet high and 3 feet thick. A forest of them covers desert area near Palmdale.

**Santa Barbara,** founded 1786, is called "Queen of the Missions." It is the only California mission whose altar light has never been extinguished since founding.

**Mission San Gabriel** was founded in 1771 by the pioneer missionary, Junípero Serra.

**Mission St. Charles Borromeo** overlooks Carmel Bay. It has grave of Father Serra.

**Mission Santa Ynez** prospered in 1820, at which time it owned 12,000 head of cattle.

**Mission San Diego de Alcalá** was first of the 21 missions built by the Franciscans.

Photos: Southern Pacific; TWA Trans World Airlines;
All Year Club of Southern California; United Air Lines

**California** ranks next to Texas in crude petroleum production. This is the valley where most of the rigs of the Ventura field stand, pumping black gold night and day.

**Typical pumping unit** in the oil fields is this conventional rocker-arm type of pump.

**Oilmen** tackling a new field have to slice mountains, bulldoze roads, haul in rigs.

Photos: Shell Oil Company

**Date clusters** are covered with burlap or paper cones while the fruit is ripening.

**Orange growing** in California is world's most intensively-developed crop culture.

**Abundance of water** from melting snows of the Sierra Nevada, together with long hot summers, helps make the San Joaquin Valley vineyards a vast green garden.

**Wine is stored** in these huge barrels. Man on ladder uses "thief" to draw sample.

**Cotton production** centers on Alcalá, a quality variety that is in great demand.

Photos: All Year Club of Southern California; Wine Institute; Kern County Board of Trade

**Cabrillo Boulevard,** Santa Barbara: To the right is the municipal swimming pool and the Santa Barbara channel. To the left is the city and Santa Ynez Mountains.

**Santa Barbara's** white stucco courthouse resembles palace of a Spanish prelate.

**Pigeons and swallows** make their home in ruins of old Mission San Juan Capistrano.

**Santa Catalina Island** is 24 miles south-west of Los Angeles harbor. Avalon is the main center of this glamorous sport and resort showplace. Casino is at right.

Photos: Santa Barbara Chamber of Commerce; All Year Club of Southern California; Southern Pacific

# THE NORTHWEST

## by RICHARD L. NEUBERGER

Abundance is the dominant impression one gets of the Northwest. Everything is in profusion—trees, wildlife, water, flowered orchards, leaping salmon in the rivers. Even the vast interior desert of sagebrush is split by the mighty Columbia, champing in a deep lava gorge. Irrigation canals have wrested alfalfa fields and symmetrical panels of row crops from the choking grip of cactus and tumbleweed. At no other place in the land does so much annual rainfall descend from the skies as along the Northwest's timbered seacoast. This has produced majestic "rain forests" where Douglas fir giants scrape the heavens.

Seattle, Portland and Spokane are teeming cities, but essentially the realm seems untrammeled. On the Lolo Trail, sheer above Idaho's crystalline Lochsa River, stand rock cairns that helped to guide Lewis and Clark to Oregon, unchanged since the great explorers saw them 150 years ago. The Northwest is that much linked to its frontier beginnings. I have walked along the Lolo, knowing that my shoes were fitting into the bygone moccasin prints of the first of all westbound Americans.

Northwesterners are conscious of the region's hurtling rivers, which claw at granite cliffs with white-capped talons. In this one sprawling region lurks 42 per cent of all the undeveloped hydroelectric power in the United States. The Northwest has no other industrial fuel—no coal, no petroleum, no natural gas. If manufacturing payrolls are to ease the economic pressure on the forests of Oregon and Washington, this will come about only because of the generation of more low-cost water power. Already the rivers that tumble over concrete spillways are re-

**Mount Rainier is framed by cave of snow.**

sponsible for the major factories that dot the region.

The traveler, looking from his bus seat or Pullman berth, knows clearly when he has come to the Northwest. The trees are thicker, taller and more numerous. The peaks may not be intrinsically as high as those in the Rockies, but their cushion of snow is deeper, their glaciers more active. James Bryce said that nowhere else on the planet were sea and forest and upland so united in a single vernal panorama, and this is the Northwest's ultimate glory.

The Northwest's favorite legend is that of Paul Bunyan, the mighty lumberjack, who used a fir tree for a toothpick and measured the stuffing for his Christmas goose in metric tons. This tells a good deal about the region and its people. Northwesterners were radiant when Hell's Canyon on the Snake River turned out to be a few feet deeper than Grand Canyon on the Colorado River.

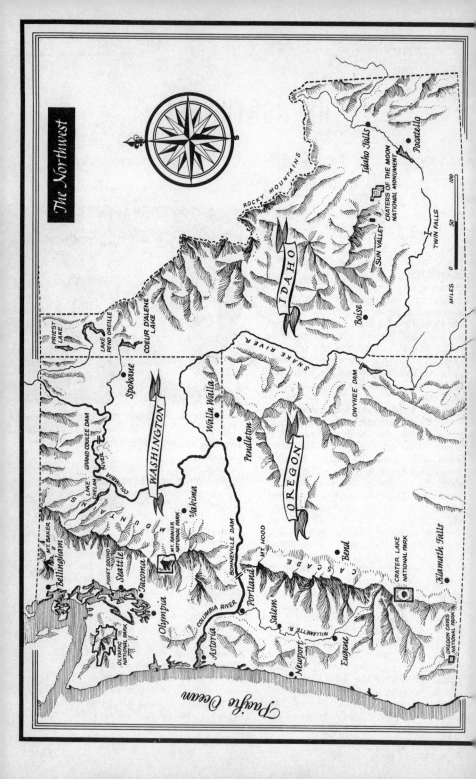

# SUN VALLEY IS GLAMOR RESORT
# OF MAGNIFICENTLY RUGGED IDAHO

**At Sun Valley,** snow falls deep and powdery from early autumn on, the sun shines brilliantly, and the Sawtooth Mountains give protection from cold northern gales.

Photo: Sun Valley News Bureau

**Sun Valley Lodge** offers ice skating, the thrilling ski runs of Mount Baldy, milder slopes of Dollar and Half Dollar Mountains, even swimming in heated pools.

Photo: Sun Valley News Bureau

**Sun Valley** is year-round resort. Fishing for rainbow trout is favorite summer sport.

**Boise** is Idaho's capital and largest city, with its monumentally classic capitol.

**Craters of the Moon National Monument:** The splatter cones, terraces and weird piles of stone, caves and natural bridges resemble the moon seen through a telescope.

**Indians say** a dip before sunrise at Bathtub Rock will restore youth to the aged.

**Thousand Springs** gush forth from the lava edges and plunge down into Snake River.

**Trail Riders** explore the wilderness in Idaho's Primitive Area, a million-acre land of mountains and streams, plateaus and ridges, meadows, four National Forests.

**Shoshone Falls** is largest of the Snake River waterfalls, a thousand feet across its horseshoe curve and 212 feet deep. Irrigation dams make the flow irregular.

Photos: Ross Madden (Western Ways); Willard Luce

# CRATER LAKE AND CASCADE RANGE FEATURE OREGON'S RUGGED GRANDEUR

**Mt. Hood loop,** a wide, paved highway, encircles Oregon's highest peak, 11,245-ft. Mt. Hood is in the imposing Cascade Range. Rhododendrons grow on slopes.

# Oregon

**Portland** is Oregon's largest city with more than a half million in the urban area.

This view is from Washington Park, with Mt. Hood in the distance, 50 miles away.

**Known as "City of Roses,"** Portland has Rose Festival in June, with Floral Parade.

**International rose test gardens** cover a large acreage in city's Washington Park.

740

**"Joaquin Miller Chapel"** is seen on the guided tour through famous Oregon Caves.

**Pioneer figure** atop Capitol at Salem symbolizes westward march of settlers.

**Bachelor Butte** is the predominant peak seen from Todd Lake and meadows, west of Bend. The lake is a favorite trout fishing spot in the central Oregon area.

**Gladioli** are an important flower crop in Grants Pass region, Josephine County.

**Indian maiden** displays her costume at the Pendleton Round-Up in eastern Oregon.

**At Crater Lake National Park,** visitors are looking toward Wizard Island, a small lava cone that rises 700 feet high out of the water of this mysterious blue lake.

**Astoria's fishing fleet** waits for run of salmon to hit Columbia River or the coast.

**Ancient Indian writings** are found on rock cliffs of Picture Gorge, near Dayville.

Photos: Oregon State Highway Commission

**Vista House lookout,** atop Crown Point, gives this view of Columbia River Gorge and the scenic path the mighty river has swept out through the Cascade Mountains.

**Bonneville Dam,** built 1933–43, is one of the Northwest's hydroelectric giants.

**Fish ladders** enable salmon to circumvent dam and swim upriver to spawning grounds.

**Norwegian freighter** docks at Coos Bay, one of coast's great lumber shipping ports.

**Old fort at The Dalles** displays many items pioneers brought in covered wagons.

# Oregon

Winter brings a snowy white mantle to Mt. Hood and the trees at timberline.

When you come to Timberline Lodge for skiing, you feel you're scraping the sky.

Oregon Caves Chateau is near entrance to the spectacular underground Marble Halls.

Baker's First National Bank displays a multimillion dollar collection of gold.

Seal Rock State Park, south of Newport, is good place to view wild and color-ful Oregon coast. Seals may frequently be seen on rocks beyond the breakers.

744

# WASHINGTON'S BOLD FEATURES OFFER SOME OF WORLD'S LOVELIEST SCENES

**Majestic Mount Rainier** is the 14,408-ft. peak that the Indians called God. Clear water of Reflection Lake mirrors snow-crowned top of state's highest mountain.

**Hikers** tackle the slopes of Mt. Rainier close to timberline. On a clear day you can see the Cascades billowing north to British Columbia, south toward California.

**Olympic National Park** includes nearly 850,000 acres, with most of the major peaks of the Olympic Mountains. This is Mt. Olympus, from Hurricane Ridge Road.

Photos: top, Northwest Orient Airlines; Washington State Advertising Commission

**Seattle's crowded skyline** testifies to its importance as Washington's largest city (620,000 in the urban area) and as world port, transcontinental rail terminus.

**Floating bridge** is unique feature of Lake Washington, within Seattle city limits.

**Government locks** connect Puget Sound with Seattle's inland lakes and canals.

**A young visitor to Washington** studies the variety of boats docked at Westport, on sheltered Grays Harbor. Evergreen State has lakes, rivers, ocean, and inland sea.

**Spokane** is hub of the Inland Empire, the vast northwest area that produces wheat, apples, lumber. A pioneer trading post in 1872, it's now second city in the state.

**Mt. Spokane** is center of 3,000-acre state park. This view shows Mt. Kit Carson.

**Lookout** on top of 5,878-ft. Mt. Spokane gives splendid view of eastern Washington.

**Gold Creek** in Chelan National Forest shows the rugged nature of this region.

**Olympia,** state capital of Washington, is the southernmost port of Puget Sound.

Photos: Washington State Advertising Commission; center left, Northwest Orient Airlines; bottom left, U. S. Forest Service

**Grand Coulee Dam,** finished 1942, is the largest concrete dam in the world. Water from reservoir flows to farms through a 4,000-mile system of irrigation ditches.

**Toppenish** is headquarters of the Yakima Indian Agency. This is July 4th pow-wow.

**Fishing at Long Beach:** This is claimed to be the longest in the world—28 miles.

**Tacoma's Fort Nisqually,** built by Hudson's Bay Company, was a trading post.

**Apples** from Yakima and Wenatchee, "Apple Capital of the World," are famous.

# Washington

**Spirit Lake,** at foot of Mount St. Helens, is 44 miles from Castle Rock over a new highway. It has a Forest Service camping ground, excellent trout fishing, hunting.

**Truck-trailers,** trains and rivers bring Douglas fir and other woods to the mills.

**Sheep graze** in Gifford Pinchot National Forest, with Mount Adams in background.

**This combine** is working on pea harvest which now exceeds the value of wheat in many Washington counties. The state also raises barley, oats, potatoes, corn, hops.

# 49TH AND 50TH STATES

## by A. MILTON RUNYON

The creation of two new states so far away from their nearest neighbor states is an appropriate miracle for the jet age. Hawaii is in mid-Pacific, some two thousand miles from the American mainland. Alaska is in the land of the midnight sun, and even its southernmost city, Ketchikan, is about 550 miles north of Seattle. But thanks to modern jets, the senators and representatives from our newest states can get to Washington faster and more comfortably than many of the law-makers from the original thirteen states!

The two new states present a great contrast. Hawaii is a community of eight main islands and a dozen smaller ones, about equal in area to Connecticut and Rhode Island. But the 50th state is just a little more than *one per cent* of the area of her newest sister state. Alaska is more than twice as large as the tremendous state of Texas, and six times as large as Great Britain. The Aleutian Islands, like giant steppingstones, stretch far out into the Pacific Ocean, and the Panhandle runs nearly 400 miles down the coast of the continent to the southeast.

As to the population, the contrast runs somewhat the other way. Alaska has only a little over 200,000 inhabitants, about as many as Salt Lake City. Hawaii has three times as many people—some 600,000. Alaska's residents include many thousands of Eskimos and American Indians. Hawaii can boast of probably 12,000 citizens of pure Hawaiian stock. The others are of a dozen or more principal nationalities; they come from China, Japan, the mainland of Portugal and the Cape Verde Islands in the Atlantic, the Philippines, Korea, Puerto Rico, the American mainland.

**Leis greet new arrivals in Hawaii.**

Sugar is Hawaii's number one crop, with the pineapple industry occupying about one third as much land as the sugar plantations. There are nine pineapple canneries.

The newest big business of the "Aloha State" is tourism, with new hotels and faster transportation attracting new visitors all the time—for the lovely scenery, the tropical island color, and a climate where it's always spring.

The Klondike gold rush first brought world attention to Alaska. Mining has continued to be an important activity and Alaska has produced over 700 times its purchase price in gold alone. Fishing, largely salmon, ranks as the number one industry today. Fur trapping still provides a million and half dollars in revenue. And there is expanding use of forests and of hydroelectric power.

Alaska, with its comparatively warm summers, has a great deal to offer the tourist and the sportsman in search of dramatic scenery, unspoiled wilderness.

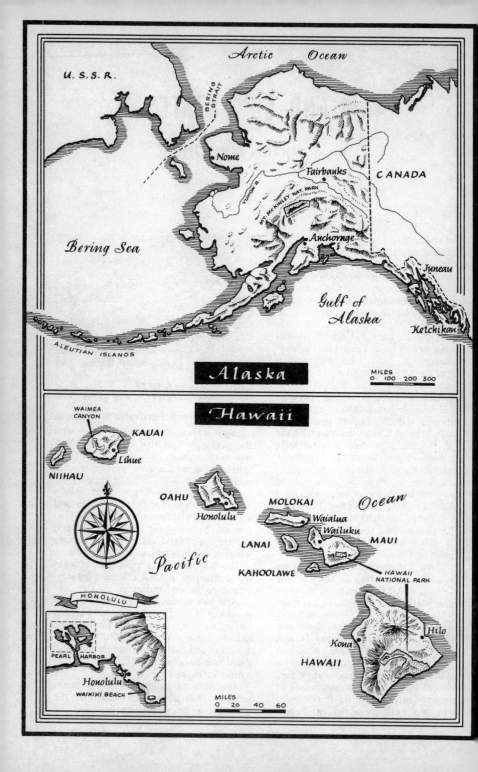

Arctic Ocean

U.S.S.R.

BERING STRAIT

• Nome

Bering Sea

Fairbanks •

YUKON R.

MT McKINLEY NAT. PARK

CANADA

Anchorage •

Juneau •

Gulf of
Alaska

Ketchikan

ALEUTIAN ISLANDS

Alaska

MILES
0  100  200  300

Hawaii

WAIMEA
CANYON

KAUAI

Lihue

NIIHAU

OAHU

Honolulu

MOLOKAI

Ocean

Waialua

Wailuku

MAUI

LANAI

KAHOOLAWE

HAWAII
NATIONAL PARK

Pacific

HONOLULU

PEARL HARBOR

Honolulu

WAIKIKI BEACH

Kona

Hilo

HAWAII

MILES
0  20  40  60

**MILD CLIMATE, LOVELY BEACHES MAKE HAWAII TRUE GARDEN SPOT.**

# HAWAII IS OUR TROPICAL PARADISE

Ever since Captain Cook discovered the Hawaiian Islands in 1778, their magic has been known to the world—a land of mild climate the year round (the mean annual temperature is about 75°), of fine white sand beaches, of subtropical ocean waters, and of smiling, friendly citizens. It's wonderful to have as our 50th state!

Photo: Hawaii Visitors Bureau

# Hawaii

**The bi-annual transpacific yacht races** are alternated with the local invitation series.

**Fishing with thrownet** is real art; needs sharp eye, quick coördination.

**At famous Waikiki Beach,** Honolulu, vacationists may go for exciting rides in outrigger canoes and double-hulled catamarans. Diamond Head is at the left.

Photos: Hawaii Visitors Bureau

**Luxurious Royal Hawaiian Hotel** is right at the edge of Waikiki beach, and so is the friendly Moana. At right is the Outrigger Club, for surf boards and canoes.

**Little island youngster,** clad in bright Aloha shirt, makes friends with visitor.

**During Aloha festival,** Hawaiian enacts old ways, pounding poi in the old style.

**A half-hour's drive** from Honolulu's center, across famous Nuuanu Pali, brings you to beach area on windward side of Oahu, a splendid place for surf fishing.

**Waimea Canyon,** on the island of Kauai, is the "Grand Canyon" of Hawaii, cutting through the verdure of the lush, green island with gorges similar to Colorado's.

Photos: Hawaii Visitors Bureau

756

**You won't be able to match** the skill of these surfboard riders at first try, but the simpler styles are not hard to learn. First successful ride is a great thrill.

**The Blow Hole,** on Koko Head, is a salt water geyser, caused by rush of the tide.

**Ala Moana yacht harbor,** at entrance to Ala Wai canal, has boats from afar.

Photos: Hawaii Visitors Bureau

# Hawaii

**S.S. Lurline** passes Diamond Head. Voyage from California is a delightful one.

**Girls with bare brown shoulders,** flower leis, perform the symbolic Hawaiian hula.

**At Kauai island,** natives gather round the shores of Nawiliwili bay for a "hukilau" during which they pull in huge nets from the indigo-colored sea, loaded with fish.

Photos: Hawaii Visitors Bureau; top left, Matson Lines

**Pineapple fields** are colorful part of the Hawaiian landscape, with the green of the leaves contrasting with the brilliant blue of the sky, the reddish brown of the soil.

**Pearl Harbor's** huge navy base may be seen by boat trip, leaving from Kewalo Basin.

**Flower leis,** made of colorful and fragrant blossoms, say "aloha" to Hawaii's visitors.

# ALASKA IS LAST FRONTIER OF U.S.

Alaska is easily reached by plane, or by Inside Passage as far north as Juneau, and from there across the Gulf of Alaska to Prince William Sound. This beautiful trip visits the main industrial cities. Within Alaska, planes are used for long distance runs, dog teams for short ones. The Alaska Railroad serves the gold mines, coal fields, Mt. McKinley National Park.

**ALASKA'S FIRST GOLD RUSH RESULTED IN FOUNDING OF JUNEAU.**

**Mendenhall Glacier** is one of the few that can be reached by automobile road.

**Salmon fishing areas** are not far from Juneau; fresh water fish are abundant.

Photos: Pan American World Airways

**Fairbanks** is center for tourists who arrive by Yukon River from Whitehorse.

**Eskimo family** at Nome keeps busy making shoes from walrus hide, carving ivory.

**Started as a supply point** for miners in 1890's rush, Ketchikan is usually first Alaska community visited by tourists. Hundreds of fishing vessels use good port.

**Busy Fairbanks,** metropolis of interior Alaska, combines pioneer frontier and civilization. The town still has log cabins, but its business district has modern shops.

**Many of the caribou** migrated to Canada when the Eskimos began shooting them with the white man's rifle. Recently the caribou has begun to return to the tundra.

**Salmon fishing** and canning has been one of Alaska's principal sources of employment.

**New apartment building** in Anchorage shows cosmopolitan nature of the city.

Photos: Shostal Press, bottom left, Photo Researchers, Inc.

**Indian Meeting House** and totem poles are seen at Totem Village, near Ketchikan.

**Cruise steamer,** bound north, passes through Lynn Canal in sight of glaciers.

**Mt. McKinley National Park** is second in size only to Yellowstone. This wilderness is topped by Mt. McKinley, 20,270 feet, the highest point in all North America.

**Gold dust and nuggets** in the Miners and Merchants Bank are melted into ingots.

**This bus** is on Alaska Highway, 1527 miles long, Dawson Creek, B.C., to Fairbanks.

Photos: Pan American World Airways; top right and bottom right, Canadian Pacific Railway